HOOPLA

HOOPLA

INSIDE THE TORONTO RAPTORS' FIRST SEASON

JACK BATTEN

M&S

Canadian Cataloguing in Publication Data

Batten, Jack, date.
   Hoopla!: inside the Toronto Raptors' first season

ISBN 0-7710-1067-2

1. Toronto Raptors (Basketball team).   2. Basketball – Canada.   I. Title.

GV885.52.T67B37 1996   796.323'64'09713541   C96-931532-5

The publishers acknowledge the support of the Canada Council and the Ontario Arts Council for their publishing program.

Typesetting by M & S, Toronto

Printed and bound in Canada

McClelland & Stewart Inc.
The Canadian Publishers
481 University Avenue
Toronto, Ontario
M5G 2E9

1 2 3 4 5   00 99 98 97 96

To D. Cobb and T. Frayne,
power forwards

CONTENTS

INTRODUCTION

In the winter of 1954-55, I was the student manager of the University of Toronto Law School basketball team. Don't scoff. This team managed an amazing accomplishment. That winter, the players from the law school, which was a tiny place in those days, numbering fewer than one hundred students, fought their way past teams from much bigger colleges and faculties to the university's intramural final, where they lost a closely contested two-game, total-points series to feared St. Michael's College – feared in athletic terms – which could draw its team from a student body of two thousand people. It was David and Goliath all over again in the final, except the little guy came out second best.

My duties as student manager were minimal. I was to post notices of games on the law-school bulletin board, swipe a couple of towels from the Hart House locker room for guys to dry off during timeouts. But the job got me a seat on the players' bench for games, and, for the first time, I had an up-close view of the marvels of basketball.

I watched Lionel Schipper, our star guard, put up his gorgeous outside shot. Of course, in those years, it was called a set shot, and Lionel delivered it with both hands on the ball and his feet fixed to the floor. Now, the good outside shooter gets off his shot, which is called a jumper, with one hand, while his feet propel him high into the air towards the basket. I watched Jack Iwanicki, the law-school centre, fight for rebounds under the basket, with guile, tenacity, and courage. Those are the same qualities that fine centres display now; the difference is that today's centres are a foot taller than Jack's six-foot-one and have absorbed a lot more in the guile department. And I learned a great deal about basketball intensity from Alan Eagleson.

Yes, *that* Alan Eagleson, the one who became famous as the head of the NHL Hockey Players' Association. Al was a sub on the law-school team, and he burned furiously with basketball competitiveness. In the second game of the final series against St. Michael's, the coach sent Al into the game during the third quarter; within a few seconds, taking umbrage at the rough way a St. Mike's player was treating Jack Iwanicki, Al clocked the guy with a right-hand punch. The referee tossed Al out of the game, but from Eagleson that day I learned that basketball, the prettiest of team sports, had to make room for the same intensity accommodated by other team sports.

Ten years earlier, long before law-school basketball, I had watched the Toronto Huskies at Maple Leaf Gardens. It was the first year of operation for the Basketball Association of America, the forerunner of the present National Basketball Association, and the Huskies were a member of the new league. In fact, by stretching a point, you could say that the very first NBA game ever was played at the Gardens in Toronto. That came on November 1, 1946, when the Huskies opened the BAA season with a home loss, 68–66, to the New York Knicks.

I wasn't at the first historic game, but I went to three other Huskies games. Tickets in the blues cost two dollars, and transportation from my house to the Gardens – well, to within two blocks of the Gardens – set me back ten cents on the old Bay Street trolley. A guy named Ed Sadowski was the Huskies' big attraction. He was six-foot-five, 240 pounds, the team's centre and coach, and a formidable presence on the court. He was the first basketball player who generated the kind of thrills in me that, until then, only Maple Leaf hockey players and Joe Louis had stirred.

Sadowski was bigger than anyone I'd ever seen, and yet he moved with what passed in those days for finesse. The only trouble was that Sadowski didn't stick around Toronto for long. He was gone from the city by Christmastime, traded to Cleveland, where he finished fourth in the league in scoring. The Huskies didn't last much longer than Sadowski, just to the end of the season. Then, with a record of 22–38, out of the playoffs and not drawing much at the Gardens, the franchise folded. Basketball was gone.

Buffalo filled the gap. On Saturday nights, I used to drive with a couple of other acne-faced, basketball-mad adolescents to Buffalo's War Memorial Auditorium for the college doubleheaders. This was big time. The schools in the Buffalo area – Canisius, Niagara, St. Bonaventure – rated with the basketball powers of the day, with Duquesne and Notre Dame and CCNY, and each Saturday, twelve thousand fans, including me and my Toronto pals, packed into the Aud for two games between top college teams. Five hours of basketball, and afterwards, Buffalo being racy beyond the imaginings of kids from Toronto, there was time to take in the last burlesque show at the Palace and hurry back to the hotel for one illicit beer each.

Later, Buffalo again came to the rescue of basketball fans. This was in the 1970s, when the city got an NBA franchise, the Buffalo Braves. For two seasons, the Braves played eight of their home games at Maple Leaf Gardens. I bought two season tickets on the floor right behind the visiting-team bench, eight bucks per ticket per game. The basketball was worth the cash outlay. The Braves featured one authentic star, Bob McAdoo, and one almost star, Ernie DiGregorio, who made up in general adorableness what he sometimes lacked in good play selection.

McAdoo was a scorer. He was a rangy guy, six-foot-ten, who put the ball up every time it was passed to him. "Two for Mc-A-*dooo!*" the announcer would bellow after each basket. McAdoo led the league in scoring for three consecutive years in the mid-1970s.

Ernie DiGregorio was a cute little guy from Providence. He played point guard and had a lot of moves. Sometimes too many moves; his spectacular forays into the other team's end often ended with him throwing the ball away. Still, Ernie Di was a popular player. The Braves as a team, however, weren't popular enough in Buffalo, and in 1978 the franchise was moved to San Diego, then to Los Angeles, where it survives today as the L.A. Clippers.

In the 1980s, taking my basketball mostly by television, I developed a fondness for the Boston Celtics' Larry Bird. A fondness? Well, okay, a crush. As I sit at my computer writing this, I am wearing a slightly tattered Larry Bird T-shirt. I own a Larry Bird windbreaker, a Larry Bird coffee mug, the June 9, 1986, issue of *Sports Illustrated*, which has a cover of Bird putting up a left-handed hook shot against Houston as the Celtics rolled to victory in the NBA finals, and – rarest of all items in my Birdiana collection – a paper placemat from the Larry Bird Restaurant in Terre Haute, Indiana. Bird grew up just down the road from Terre Haute in French Lick, Indiana, where he still has a home.

What was it that made me so nuts about Larry Bird? I mean, who else *cares* that a six-foot-nine guy with a sort of hick face and a penchant for hitting left-handed hook shots in the clutch happened to live in a place with the odd name of French Lick? And, more generally, what is it that continues to draw me to the sport Bird once played? What in particular do I like about basketball?

I like the sound of basketball. The squeak of the shoes on the floor. The thump of the ball when the point guard dribbles it up the floor. The sound of a shot that passes cleanly through the rim of the basket and catches the bottom of the netting. That sound is often a pure *swish*, but sometimes it's more complicated, closer to a *pffft*. And the voices. I like the sound of the voices, especially the voices of the coaches when they call to the players. "See the ball!" Coaches always holler that line. They mean that, when their players are on the defensive, guarding the opposing offensive guys, they should keep track of where the ball is. Don't lose sight of the ball. Somebody might pass it to an offensive player who's loose in the paint, and you'll miss it. "See the ball!"

I like the language of basketball. "In the paint," for example. It's a nice expression. It refers to the free-throw lane, an area in front of the basket, twelve feet wide by eighteen feet, ten inches deep. It's called the paint because it's painted a different colour from the rest of the floor, generally something darker, and it has meaning in the rules. An offensive player can't hang around in the paint without the ball, waiting for a pass, for longer than three seconds. If he does, and a referee catches him, it's a three-second violation, and his team must turn the ball over to the opposing team. That's what "in the paint" is all about.

In many ways, the language of basketball reminds me of the ways of speaking that come out of jazz. The expressions seem hip and spontaneous, and they definitely owe something to black culture. "Dunk" is a typical word of that sort. A dunk is a shot that a player makes when he jumps up high enough to drop the ball down into the basket. The *down* is the important part. A dunk is also referred to as a "jam," and a player never "scores" a dunk or "shoots" a dunk. He "throws down" a dunk. Usually it's a thunderous, backboard-rattling dunk. Or jam. Or "spike."

Basketball plays have distinctive names, too. "Pick and roll." That happens when a player without the ball, usually a big guy, takes up a position in the offensive zone in between a teammate with the ball, usually the point guard, and a defender. The big guy is setting a pick. Then he rolls around the defender and heads for the basket. Pick and roll. The guy with the ball, the point guard, can either take a shot, if he's open, or pass the ball to the guy rolling towards the basket, if *he's* open. It's a common play in basketball, beautiful to watch if it's executed properly. And the sound of the play's name – pick and roll – is so beguiling.

Even the names of the players' positions have a hip ring to them. The "point guard" is the player who brings the ball up court and initiates the offensive play. His duties are comparable to a quarterback's in football. The other guard is the "shooting guard," or the "off guard," and he's expected to be a good outside shooter, a guy who can put up the "trey," the three-point shot. Of the two forwards, one is the "small forward," usually a guy who's gifted at scoring and passing, and the other is the "power forward," whose principal duties are in the rebounding department. The "centre" – the one name that offers nothing fresh – takes care of rebounding *and* scoring.

To simplify the names, some basketball people refer to the positions by number. It may make for anonymity – the way the crooks in Quentin Tarantino's movie *Reservoir Dogs* were called Mr. Pink, Mr. Green, Mr. Blue, and so on – but it's useful. Thus, the point guard is the 1, the off guard the 2, the small forward the 3, the power forward the 4, and the centre the 5. And coaches will say, "I got a guy who can play the 2 or the 3, either one."

I like all of that, the language, and I like, in basketball, the offensive movement, the flow, the plays, the shooting. Teams need a strong defence to win, but it's the offence that provides the awesome stuff. And the NBA has been clever over the years about shaping rules that encourage offensive play. The twenty-four-second clock does that; the team with the ball has to get off a shot within twenty-four seconds or surrender possession of the ball. The rule against zone defences does the same job. Defensive players aren't permitted to cover an area of the floor, a zone; they must cover a man, and that makes it less difficult for the offence to set up a play. And the three-point shot makes for more scoring; any shot taken from outside an arc twenty-two feet from the basket counts for three points. That seems tough, shooting a ball through a hoop eighteen inches in diameter and ten feet off the floor from a distance of twenty-two feet or more. But some players, over the course of a season, hit an amazing 50 per cent of their three-point shots.

Which is part of the point: basketball players *are* amazing. In terms of athleticism, the things they do on the court, the physical feats they routinely pull, they are probably the most remarkable of all players in all sports. It isn't just the shooting, putting the ball in the air and making it come down in the basket, though that's breathtaking enough. It's the many other things: the high, vertical leaps to grab rebounds, the swift passes that move the ball as if it were on a string, the drives to the basket, during which players alter the direction of their bodies in mid-air. And these are big bodies. These are guys six-foot-six, soaring through the air. Even guys bigger – some seven-foot centres can soar. Now that *is* amazing.

And it's yet another reason why I like basketball.

All of which explains why my head snapped around in the fall of 1992 when David Stern, the commissioner of the National Basketball Association, announced that the league was open to extending a franchise to Toronto. The NBA was coming to Toronto. Michael Jordan and Charles Barkley, John Stockton and Karl Malone, Scottie Pippen, Patrick Ewing, David Robinson, Hakeem Olajuwon – all the great players were coming to Toronto. Of course we didn't know then that, in the time between the announcement and the first season of the new Toronto team, Michael Jordan, the greatest player of them all, would retire from the game, launch a failed baseball career, give that up, and return to the NBA. All we knew was that basketball would have a team in Toronto, and I, like all other fans of the sport, was delirious with anticipation.

But not quite so delirious that I couldn't make a rational, business-like decision. I would write a book about the new team, whatever it was going to be called and whoever turned out to own it. In fact, that's where I would begin the book, with the contest between the ownership groups that bid on the franchise. Then I would trace the team through its formative stages – the putting together of the squad that would take to the court – and through its first year of play in the NBA.

That was the plan, and this book is the result. It's about the team that came to be called the Raptors. It's about the man who put together the Raptors' ownership group, John Bitove, Jr.; about the man who selected the players, Isiah Thomas; about the man who coached the players, Brendan Malone; about the players themselves, those who started with the team and got traded away, those who started and stayed, those who joined the team during the season; about them, the Raptors, and about the players they played against, Michael Jordan and Magic Johnson and the others; about the people who reported on the Raptors, the media; about *all* the people who, in one way or another, put on the basketball shows at the SkyDome. And it's about how these different people some-times came into collision and sometimes gloried in triumphs.

But mostly it's a book about basketball, that terrific game.

1

THE FANS GET IT

John Bitove, Jr., loved the Seattle game.

This was the National Basketball Association game at the SkyDome on Tuesday night, November 21, 1995, the Seattle SuperSonics versus the Toronto Raptors, and Bitove, the Raptors' president, a boyish, exuberant man of thirty-five, had a specific reason for adoring the game. It wasn't that the Raptors unexpectedly won, though that was part of it. It was something that was even more satisfying to Bitove than victory.

"What made me so proud," Bitove said not long after the Seattle game ended, "was what happened with the crowd in the last five minutes of the fourth quarter. The whole stadium was up on their feet, cheering and clapping and yelling *dee*-fence. They were into it. They were *willing* us to win. In the earlier games, the fans either treated what was happening as a sort of strange event or they didn't react at all to the play on the floor. But with Seattle, it was a *game*. It was when basketball really arrived in Toronto for the first time, when the twenty-one thousand people in the place were absolutely tied to the game's outcome. That's the beauty of the sport, that link between the crowd and the players on the floor, and it first happened, the whole beautiful thing, at the Seattle game."

The win over the SuperSonics was the seventh home game, the eleventh game overall, for the brand-new Raptors. The team had begun the 1995-96 regular season on November 3 in terrific style by beating the New Jersey Nets at the SkyDome. Then things got less terrific, at least in terms of winning, because the Raptors lost the next four home games and three more on the road, bringing them, as of November 17, to an unimpressive – actually miserable – 1–7 record.

As an expansion team, made up mostly of players who'd been cast off by other teams, rejects, older guys, the Raptors weren't expected to do much winning. But the Toronto bunch, even in losing, didn't disgrace themselves. One of the four early losses at home was to the very seasoned, very together Utah Jazz – by a mere three points. And Houston, the reigning NBA champions, in another early game at the SkyDome, had beaten the Raptors only when Robert Horry, the Rockets' small forward, hit a three-pointer at the final buzzer to make the score 96–93.

The qualities that the Raptors most often displayed in these home games, to single out the two most obvious, were toughness and discipline. The toughness came from the kind of players the team had signed. These were guys who played hard, never seemed to quit, and hung in the games until the end.

The discipline was Coach Brendan Malone's doing. Malone had never held an NBA head coaching job until Executive Vice-President Isiah Thomas hired him for the Raptors. But he was experienced, fifty-three years old, and had invested more than a quarter-century in coaching at every level. He'd been a head coach in high school and university, and an assistant coach in the NBA, first with the New York Knicks and, from 1988 to 1995, with the Detroit Pistons, where he handled, among other players, his future boss, Isiah Thomas. Malone's long suits as a coach were organization and game preparation. He got his teams ready to play and geared to a plan. And that's the way the Raptors looked from the start, schooled and determined.

As for the players, the principal responsibilities in the early games fell to a half-dozen of them, the five starters and the sixth man.

Damon Stoudamire was the one who ran the show on the floor. He was the kid of the roster, the twenty-two-year-old point guard from the University of Arizona, taken by the Raptors as their first pick in the college draft the previous summer. Stoudamire had a blunt, muscular body, and he was short – not as shrimpy as the mouse he had tattooed on his left biceps, Mighty Mouse, but probably an inch or two under the five-foot-ten he was listed at by the Raptors. Despite his lack of size, however, he appeared to be the real goods, quick, durable, sharp at moving the ball briskly up the floor, smart about distributing it among his teammates. He was also the team's most consistent scorer, about equally skilled at shooting from outside and at driving to the basket.

Alvin Robertson supplied much of the Raptors' spirit and fire. He played the off guard, an intense guy, close to fanatical in his competitive fervour, wearing a perpetual scowl during games. He'd been around the league since 1984 and had earned a reputation for fiendish defensive play. In 1985-86, basketball writers had named him the NBA Defensive Player of the Year.

Another veteran, eleven years in the league, Ed Pinckney, the power forward, took care of much of the Raptors' rebounding. He was an intelligent man, both off and on the floor, and he had a good instinct for where missed shots were going to come off the rim and a gutsy attitude about pursuing the ball in the heavy traffic of players battling under the basket.

Pinckney got help on the boards from fourth-year man Oliver Miller, who started at centre. Miller's rotund body suggested another Ollie, the one who was Stan Laurel's partner. But Oliver Miller was amazingly athletic and had a delicacy to his touch with the ball in scoring and passing that, given his round shape, seemed paradoxical.

Willie Anderson played small forward. He was in his eighth NBA season, a quiet, soft-spoken man, a gent off the floor. On the floor, he possessed a reliable outside shot and was swift at going to the basket, even though he had a history of stress fractures in both legs.

And Tracy Murray was the team's sixth man, first off the bench to relieve at shooting guard or small forward, four years in the league, a guy who loved to take the three-point shot, something he did with a sweet, effortless stroke.

Friday night, November 17, the Raptors, with that dismal 1–7 record, took on the Minnesota Timberwolves at the SkyDome. Here was a game that might end Toronto's losses. For one thing, Minnesota itself had only a single victory in the early season, and, for another, the Timberwolves were an outfit habitually identified with lousy luck and inept management.

Minnesota had entered the league in the NBA's previous round of expansion (just before the arrival of the Raptors and the Vancouver Grizzlies in 1995), joining in 1989, along with Orlando and a year after Miami and Charlotte. And while the other three teams had already qualified for the playoffs at least once in their short histories, Orlando going all the way to the final in 1994-95, the Timberwolves hadn't experienced a tiny taste of post-season play. They'd never won more than twenty-nine games in a single season (out of eighty-two games played per year) and had become a constant at the bottom of the standings.

The current edition of the Timberwolves, the one at the SkyDome on November 17, boasted a couple of proven stars. They were the tall, fairly agile centre Christian Laettner and the slick guard Isaiah Rider, but both had grown grumpy over the years of losses; melancholy stars are a hazard with expansion teams. Laettner, a garrulous sort, kept begging to be traded to a winning organization, while Rider, a cantankerous type, regularly missed practices and team flights, as if to say, Please, let me out of here, too. They weren't happy campers, Laettner and Rider, and to make matters worse – with Minnesota, it never rained but it poured – Laettner was out of commission for the SkyDome game with a sprained ankle.

As it developed, Laettner's presence in the lineup probably wouldn't have made much difference. Well, maybe a little. The Raptors scored 54 of their 114 points in the 114–96 win from in close, off layups, dunks, and other shots taken in the paint, and Laettner's size and experience might have prevented some of that. But maybe not. This was the Raptors' night to dominate.

And the domination started early. In the first quarter, the Raptors went on a 14–0 run that all but put the game away. Toronto's tough defence refused to let Minnesota score; Isaiah Rider, who revealed himself to be an active, feverish player, got his points, thirty of them on the night, but no other Timberwolf scored more than ten. And everyone on the Raptors got into the offensive act. Stoudamire was ingenious at finding the open man – he would end the game with thirteen assists – and Miller and Anderson showed particular finesse at finishing off plays.

But it was Tracy Murray who supplied the spectacular stuff. Murray came into the game late in the first quarter, and over the following few minutes he put up five consecutive three-point shots. He hit all five.

On the first, he was moving to his left, dribbling the ball, on the right side of the court. He stopped, squared up, jumped, released the ball in a medium-high arc, all very smooth. Swish. Three points.

On the second, Murray took up position in his favourite shooting spot, in the corner, the right-hand corner in this case, and Stoudamire found him with a pass. Murray shot as soon as the ball nestled in his hands. Same smooth motion, same medium arc, same result.

The third was a replica of the second, except Murray's shooting spot was in the left corner.

The fourth came off a series of rapid-fire Raptor passes that ended with Murray firing from outside the key directly in front of the basket.

And for the fifth, shooting from the right side, Murray showed impeccable form: body squared to the basket, staying compact as he jumped, ball released at the optimum point at the end of his extended arm, just the way it's shown in the instruction manuals. And the ball found its unwavering way into the basket.

Five shots, five buckets, fifteen points.

It was that kind of night for Murray and the Raptors. The players, as a team, shot a very respectable 56 per cent from the floor. Stoudamire had twenty points, nineteen for Murray, Miller eighteen, Anderson seventeen. And the Raptors beat Minnesota for their second win of the season.

Right after the Timberwolves game, the Raptors flew to Landover, Maryland, for a game the next night, Saturday, against the Washington Bullets. Washington was, in recent years, another bottom dweller, a team that had finished in last place in the Atlantic Division of the Eastern Conference (the Raptors were in the Central Division of the same conference) for the previous three years. Though they appeared to have improved themselves vastly for the new season, nobody was yet predicting wonderful things for the Bullets.

The game, Toronto versus Washington, turned out to be close all the way, and with time running out in the fourth quarter, the Bullets up by a point, the ball was in Damon Stoudamire's hands. That was by design. Stoudamire had already emerged as the Raptors' go-to guy, the player most likely to produce a basket at crunch time. Which is what he did against the Bullets. With the time clock showing 2.5 seconds left in the game, Stoudamire put up a ten-foot jumper. It was good, and the Raptors had their first win on the road, 103–102, their second win in two nights.

Now the Raptors were heading back to Toronto for the November 21 game against Seattle, a team to which descriptives like "inept" and "bottom dweller" didn't apply. Over the preceding three seasons, the SuperSonics had won fifty-five, sixty-three, and fifty-seven games. None of this gaudy winning had yet produced a championship, since Seattle had faltered in the playoffs each year, but the SuperSonics remained formidable, one of the four or five teams that figured to be right in it for the NBA title in 1995-96, the kind of team that ate expansion franchises for breakfast.

John and Randi Bitove's guests at the Seattle game were a couple whom Randi had never met. Randi is John's wife. She's a slim woman, with a willowy figure, dark, glossy hair, great cheekbones. Her best colour is black. Black pantsuits, perfect little black dresses, though she's been known, as she did for the Seattle game, to add accessories – scarves, pins – in shades that approximate the other Raptor colours, silver and red and purple. Randi grew up in Chicago, the daughter of Howard and Lois Zenner; Howard is an executive with the clothier Hart, Schaffner & Marx. She met John at the University of Indiana where both were studying business. Randi went back to her home town to take an MBA at the University of Chicago, and married John a year later, in 1985. They have three kids, two boys and a girl, JJ, Brett, and Blair. Basketball? Randi learned the game early as a cheerleader at her Chicago high school.

Usually Bitove invited representatives of Raptors sponsors to join him at games, executives from firms like Ford, Air Canada, and Nike that had put advertising money into the team. But his guests for this night's game against the SuperSonics, Graham Savage and his wife, Elise Orenstein, made it more of a social occasion. Savage was a vice-president at Rogers Communications, and had been a big help to Bitove in thinking through the Raptors' approach to game telecasts. In fact, Bitove had made Savage a member of the Raptors board of directors for a brief period, but, when the board decided to go with inside directors, people with a financial stake in the organization, Savage stepped down.

In a sense, Savage and Orenstein – she's a lawyer – represented one part of the audience that Bitove was seeking for the Raptors. They were reasonably affluent, had young kids who'd be drawn to the Raptors and Raptor products, and they appreciated the game's artistry. Savage was a basketball fan from way back, a guy who could whip off Michael Jordan's relevant statistics from memory, and Orenstein had the sort of philosophy about basketball that warmed Bitove's heart.

"I come from the arts side of things, music, dance," Orenstein says. "These are people that have a hard time getting financing, and it peeves me that athletes are paid such huge salaries. But basketball players, I don't mind the money they get, because they deliver on the dollar. With basketball, the game never feels violent, and it's great family entertainment."

After an early dinner at the Founders Club, an exclusive little dining room on the 300 level at the SkyDome, the two couples – Randi hit it off splendidly with Graham and Elise – made their way towards the basketball court for the game against the SuperSonics, and that's when Savage–Orenstein got a small surprise. So *this* is where the president of the Raptors has his seats?

The owners of many NBA teams have an ego thing when it comes to where they sit for home games.

"It's all about being close to the players," Bitove says. "Some owners sit in the corner seats at an angle to the team bench. Some sit in the seats at the end of the bench. Some sit right *on* the bench, down at the end beside the twelfth guy on the roster."

Larry Miller, the Utah Jazz owner, not only sits on the bench – he stands in the team huddles, slaps the players on the bum when they're introduced at the beginning of games, does everything to get into it except wear a uniform.

None of this is for John Bitove.

"We didn't buy the team for a toy," he says. "It's a business to be respected, and you can't get that if an owner's sitting among his employees – the players."

Thus, Bitove chose his seats in the SkyDome with discretion.

"I thought it was important, as the front man of the organization, to sit in average seats," he explains, "because there are more average seats than there are super seats. It's also probably good for staff morale when all the Raptors people see me sitting up where I am."

Up where Bitove is, is in row J of the S level, S for Silver, in the temporary stands on the east side of the SkyDome, the side opposite the players' bench. That works out to be somewhere in the shallow outfield when the

Blue Jays are in town. Bitove's seats, numbers one through four – he sits in number one, on the aisle – place them just about even with the hoop at the south end and give him a view north up the court. The tickets for these seats cost $91 each. That may not sound "average," but the figure is almost half the price of the prime seats down at courtside. But price and view aren't what it's all about for Bitove. It's about image and symbolism.

And, as Bitove told Graham Savage on the night of the Seattle game, he had one more motivation in choosing the position of his seats.

"See where the TV cameras are?" Bitove said to Savage.

The cameras are mounted on a platform at the top of the temporary stands. They're behind and above the Bitove seats.

"They can't find me here," Bitove said, nodding at the cameras. "Sitting here, I don't get on TV, which is the way it should be. No owners on the tube."

Oliver Miller was the Raptor who captivated the crowd in the first quarter of the Seattle game. The round man with the delicate touch. He kept the Raptors in contention. This wasn't surprising. Centre was the only weak spot in the SuperSonics' otherwise-powerful lineup. Seattle used Ervin Johnson at the pivot (good blocker but vulnerable to smooth moves), Sam Perkins (clever but getting along in years), and Frank Brickowski (journeyman). And Miller had his way with anyone he faced in the first quarter. He did it with nicely timed layups and short jumpers. He took six shots, hit on five, and when the opposing centre resorted to pushes and shoves to deter Miller, the refs sent him to the free-throw line, where he went three for three. One quarter, thirteen points.

"Oliver Miller! The Big O!" Herbie Kuhn, the public-address announcer, trumpeted in extraordinary glee, and the crowd picked up on Herbie's enthusiasm. Oliver Miller, a guy who looked like the fat kid in the schoolyard, last choice in the pickup games. But he could *play*.

Miller waved a towel at the seats as he came off at the end of the quarter, and the people in the seats roared back their pleasure.

Thanks to Miller – and to Willie Anderson, who scored nine points mostly on daring slashes to the basket – Toronto trailed Seattle by only four points at the quarter, 31–27.

The larger game, as the second quarter opened, was developing into intriguing games within games. For example, Damon Stoudamire versus Gary Payton. Point guard against point guard. Payton had a big edge here. He was the comparative veteran, five years in the league, at least four inches taller than Stoudamire, a cocky guy who never seemed to shut his mouth on the court. "Not comin' this way, man," he'd say to Stoudamire as Damon would take a step in the direction of the basket. "Not past me, man." And Payton had it correct. He was the defensive master among NBA point guards, a hound on the trail of his opponents, and on almost every penetrating move that Stoudamire took, Payton skittered into his path. First quick step against first quick step, anticipation against anticipation, and Payton was stepping right and guessing right almost every time. Stoudamire put up only seven shots in the first half, not always good shots, and scored a lowly six points. Payton, apart from his demon defensive work, added sixteen points on offence.

Another game within the game: Ed Pinckney versus Shawn Kemp.

Kemp was a remarkable case. A head case, some might say. He was the acknowledged Seattle superstar, the man-child. He was twenty-six years old but had played in the NBA for seven years. That was because he had entered the league – only four or five other players had ever managed this – almost directly from high school, just a kid, physically Herculean but emotionally an adolescent. He was famous – infamous, maybe – for his crashing dunks and, at least in his early career, for his post-dunk celebrations, which included grabbing his crotch.

Pinckney was dealing with Kemp, muscling him, keeping Kemp off the boards, holding him to just five points in the first quarter. But late in the second quarter, perhaps significantly after John Salley, the Raptors' backup power forward, relieved Pinckney, Kemp struck.

The sequence began when Willie Anderson took a pass under the Seattle basket, found himself all alone, and rose up to put down a strong-but-elegant one-handed jam. The crowd loved it. They got into a sustained cheer. Seattle, Payton with the ball, hustled out of its end on a fast break. The pass went to Kemp on the right wing. He flew at the basket, the ball clutched in his right hand, the right arm coming around in a windmill motion. Kemp's path put him above the hoop, still elevating, when he slammed the ball through the basket. The rim quivered and the backboard shook. Kemp landed behind the baseline, feet wide apart, knees bent, shoulders hunched forward, an expression of unrelieved ferocity on his face.

Seconds before, the SkyDome had thundered with noise. Now, if a pin had dropped, it would have been heard.

At the half, Seattle led by a point, 58–57.

Early in the third quarter, Detlef Schrempf went to work for Seattle. Schrempf, from Germany, ten years in the league, was Mr. Versatility, a small forward who could drive the basket, make the pass, hit the jumper. In this quarter, in the space of nineteen seconds, he put in two driving layups at the end of SuperSonic fast breaks, got fouled on each, and sank the free throws.

Brendan Malone called a twenty-second timeout. Time to settle down the troops. Time to call a play. Time to remind Damon Stoudamire that he was the guy who was supposed to be leading the way out on the floor.

So, three seconds after time was back in, Stoudamire took the toss-in from Oliver Miller and, with a barely perceptible pause, put up a twenty-four-foot three-pointer. A minute later, Stoudamire, on a pass from Alvin Robertson, drove around Gary Payton for a layup. For practically the first time all night, Payton had nothing to say.

The game went like that over the rest of the third quarter, back and forth, fast breaks, a game of speed. Stoudamire making two delicious steals that produced Raptors points. Ed Pinckney pulling down six rebounds. The Raptors actually staying with this very good Seattle team, playing them straight up, and pulling to a most surprising three-point lead at the end of the quarter.

The Toronto lead climbed to nine points by the 8:16 mark of the fourth quarter. (The time clock in NBA games measures the number of minutes and seconds *left* in a quarter, which is twelve minutes long; 8:16 meant the fourth quarter had eight minutes and sixteen seconds left to play.) A couple of substitutes had scored the points that pushed the Raptors so far in front, small forward Carlos Rogers with two buckets and John Salley with one. But it was Stoudamire who was making the difference. He was out-working and out-smarting Gary Payton. He was driving past Payton to the basket, and then either shooting or dishing off the ball to an open Raptor. Stoudamire's play had an obstinate, defiant feel to it. He made brilliant moves, but they were without flash or ostentation. Going to the basket, where Willie Anderson floated, Damon Stoudamire spurted.

From the beginning of the fourth quarter, there'd been a rumble in the crowd, an underground churning of excitement. As the Raptors built their lead, the rumble broke through in bursts of explosive cheering. A roar for Oliver Miller when he leaped to block Frank Brickowski's layup. Another roar when Stoudamire rebounded the block. Then, in a switch of noisy emotions, a disappointed *nooo* when Payton stole the rebounded block from Stoudamire. A louder *nooo* when Payton drove for a layup. The lead was dropping, and the crowd was nervous and aghast.

Dee-fence! *Dee*-fence!

The fans went into the chant every time Seattle had the ball. But it wasn't working. The SuperSonics were coming back. Detlef Schrempf sank two free throws at 5:25, and the Raptors were in front by only four points.

Brendan Malone made two changes of personnel. Ed Pinckney back in for John Salley; Willie Anderson in for Tracy Murray. Anderson's appearance was a surprise and a relief. At 7:10 of the third, he had limped off the court. The injury looked like a sprained ankle. Now he was back, not moving like a gazelle, but not limping either.

Payton hit a ten-foot jumper, and the lead was two for the Raptors.

Dee-fence! The crowd had grown seriously agitated.

At 3:39, Stoudamire stepped in front of a Seattle pass in the Toronto zone and stole the ball. He broke down court, jammed on the brakes twenty-six feet in front of the SuperSonics' basket, and put up a three-pointer. It was good. Five-point lead.

A Payton layup cut it to three. An Anderson three-pointer raised it to six. And the SuperSonics called time out. They walked back on the floor with a set play, which resolved itself into a Payton pass to Schrempf twenty-four feet from the Toronto basket on the right side of the court. Schrempf hit the shot. Stoudamire missed a three-pointer, and Hersey Hawkins, the Seattle off guard, raced down court to bang in a nineteen-foot jumper. It was a one-point lead for the Raptors, the clock showing 1:12, and the crowd, everyone standing, everyone shouting, had passed from agitated to frantic.

Stoudamire once more ran past Payton. Payton reached in and

smacked Stoudamire's left arm. That, Stoudamire being a left-hander, happened to be his dribbling arm. A ref called a foul on Payton for the contact, and Stoudamire went to the line. This was big pressure on the rookie, two free throws with the game winding towards its end. Stoudamire hit both. Raptors by three.

Dee-fence!

Seattle worked the ball around the Toronto zone. Who was open? Shawn Kemp was usually the first choice in these crunch situations. Payton whipped the ball to Kemp, who had a medium-length jumper, from about ten feet out. Kemp put the ball in the air. It hit the rim, bounced to the left side, and, among the grabbing hands, Ed Pinckney came down with the rebound.

Stoudamire brought the ball up court. The clock showed 39.3 seconds left. Stoudamire passed the ball to Anderson. The Raptors were moving in a busy rotation, trying to shake one man free. Alvin Robertson had the ball. The time clock was ticking towards 19 seconds, and the shot clock was down to .03 seconds. Somebody had to take a shot or the Raptors would give up the ball on a shot-clock violation, for holding the ball longer than twenty-four seconds. Willie Anderson had it. He was twenty feet from the basket on the left side. Anderson released his shot. The time clock showed :16.9, and the shot clock showed .01. The ball dropped through the basket, and the crowd went nuts.

Toronto was in front by five points, the crowd screamed *dee*-fence, Seattle took one more shot, a three-point try by Hersey Hawkins, which missed, and when Stoudamire grabbed the rebound, it was all over. The third win in a row for the Raptors, a victory against a quality team, and an amazing night of basketball.

In the Raptors' dressing room, swarming with media, players' kids, and various visiting firemen, puckish Oliver Miller explained his outbreak of twenty-three points. "It was my wife's birthday tonight, and I could hear her shouting, 'Shoot the ball, honey!'"

Damon Stoudamire acknowledged that Gary Payton had taken his measure in the first half, but that he'd turned things around in the second. "I attacked the basket in the second half," he said in his low-voiced, distracted way. "That's my game, attacking."

Brendan Malone gave much credit to the crowd. "They got behind us and didn't quit until we won."

The buzz from the victory lingered in the emptying SkyDome.

"You know what that reminded me of?" Graham Savage, basketball historian, said to John Bitove. "It was like a Lakers game in the 1980s. Magic Johnson, James Worthy, all those guys, the way they used to run and run all night. That's what it was like tonight, both teams running. I never thought the Raptors could run with Seattle. Never would have thought it, but they did."

Elise Orenstein, the artistic one, had her own take on all the running. "The two teams got into a rhythm. It was as if there was a musical phrase coursing through the game."

John Bitove wanted to share in the analysis and the celebration, but he had work to take care of. Homework.

The Bitoves live in a choice part of posh Forest Hill, a couple of blocks north of Upper Canada College. The house is a tear-down. They bought an older home, knocked it down, and put up something more modern and efficient.

"We built the house in 1993," Randi says. "What an unbelievable year that was. We built the house. Got the Raptors. And had our daughter Blair. All in 1993. I remember going to the hospital to have Blair, carrying an NBA bag as an overnight case. John videotaped the scene with me pointing very obviously at the bag."

The front door of the new house opens on a marble-floored hallway looking down to a large, airy kitchen. As you proceed along the hall, a formal dining room is on the left, and on the right, the living room and John's study. An imposing oak desk dominates the study, and the shelves are busy with items that mark Raptor milestones. Pride of place goes to an enormous encased scrapbook. Randi assembled it for John's thirty-fourth birthday. Pasted into it are all the clippings from all the newspapers that touched on the Raptors. The positive stories are there. So are the ones that put the knock on the whole silly notion of a Toronto team in the NBA. There were plenty of the latter.

Late on the night after the Seattle game, Bitove sat at the desk in his study and wrote a critique of the evening. He wasn't writing about the basketball, about what the Raptor players had done that evening. Basketball was Isiah Thomas's department. Bitove wrote about everything else that happened at the SkyDome over the two and a half hours.

The NBA prides itself on offering the fans a "total entertainment package." No moment during a game is left empty or silent. When the players aren't performing on the court, somebody else – dancers, a mascot, contest participants – is. It's part of the NBA "experience," and the Raptors had adopted the policy, then upped the ante a couple of notches.

Thus, during timeouts, at intermissions, in any break whatsoever from the basketball action, the Raptors' Events and Operations staff do their numbers. The floor show features virtually non-stop snippets of taped music, all up-tempo; video clips, played for laughs, shown on the scoreboard over the floor; hustling routines from the Raptor Dance Pack, a team of a dozen or more young women – and a couple of men – skilled in the sizzling branches of the Terpsichorean arts; hijinks by the team mascot, an acrobatic guy dressed in a furry red costume that approximates the prehistoric Raptor; and one-minute party games that involve patrons pulled out of the stands – adults, teenagers, little kids – games built on the premise that everybody is a good sport. The Nike Full Court Challenge is one example. Two kids, seven or eight years old, dash onto the court at one end and climb into over-sized Nike shoes and shorts; egged on by Herbie Kuhn, the announcer, they dribble small-scaled basketballs to the other end, and the winner is the kid, if any, who sinks a basket. The contest lasts sixty seconds. The crowd eats it up. And John Bitove takes it very seriously.

"In one way, I can't completely enjoy the basketball," Bitove says. "Not like the average person who's there to watch and be entertained. I sit and examine everything that's happening on the floor. If something's wrong, I don't make notes. I store it in my head and keep running over it and over it until I get home and write out a memo to the staff."

At his desk that night, he made notes on the performance during the Seattle game. First number by Dance Pack: dancers came out five or six seconds too late and dance ran past the end of the timeout. Herbie waited too long to get the crowd into the noise in the third quarter. Maybe more variety in the music for the second half? Bitove wrote on, compiling the memo that would land on the desks of a dozen people in Events and Operations next morning.

"Know what I feel like?" Bitove says. "I feel like the producer of a Broadway show. A big musical comedy. We're trying to be the best in the league with our entertainment. Set new benchmarks for the NBA. And my job is to look at the overall product, how it works with the basketball, check the details, all that. It's the way I imagine the producer of a Broadway show must operate."

A Broadway producer? There's something in that, but in this case, the show that John Bitove is producing is one that, as we shall see, was inspired by his own basketball dream.

2

JOHN'S DREAM

Right off the opening tip, the tall forward with the good build and the masses of brown hair stole the ball for York Mills and drove on George S. Henry's basket. This was in the spring of 1976, the game for the North York high-school championship was being played in front of a thousand fans in the gym at York University, and the kid with the steal, going in for the first layup of the game, was John Bitove, Jr.

"I was *so* nervous," he remembers. "I'd never played in a game where there were a thousand screaming fans. I was running down the floor and the ball almost fell out of my hands."

So what happened?

"I scored."

That small incident in a 1976 high-school basketball game – the steal, the nervous moments, the drive, the score – is a pretty good analogy to the deal Bitove pulled off seventeen years later. In October 1992, NBA Commissioner David Stern announced that the league was open to a one-city-only expansion to Toronto. The first group into the bidding was headed by the construction magnate Larry Tanenbaum. His group, Palestra, was perceived from the start as the odds-on favourite, even though two more groups entered the contest, one led by Michael Cohl and Bill Ballard of concert-promotion fame, and the other by thirty-two-year-old John Bitove, Jr. Bitove's group was rated far off the pace, but, when Stern revealed the winner of the Toronto franchise on September 30, 1993, the unanimous choice of the league's expansion committee was the Bitove group. The kid had stolen the bid and slam-dunked the franchise.

It's not a bad analogy, the high-school basketball game and the franchise victory, except for one small but crucial detail. In the high-school championship game, Bitove's team lost by one point. In the expansion deal, he didn't lose a thing.

In the very beginning, in early 1991, Larry Tanenbaum didn't go looking for an NBA team. One came looking for him. The owners of the Denver Nuggets, anxious to move out of money-losing Colorado, hit on Toronto as a likely destination and on Tanenbaum as both a wealthy fan who would buy a large piece of the new team and a contractor who would build its new stadium. Tanenbaum threw himself into the project; he came up with a design for a combined basketball-hockey facility and negotiated a site for the building on the Canadian National Exhibition grounds. But the plan collapsed when the City of Denver, owners of McNichols Arena, where the Nuggets played their home games, refused to allow the team to escape from a lucrative long-term lease.

"Out of that disappointing experience," Tanenbaum says, "I got the bug for basketball. I was determined to get a team for Toronto."

David Stern steered Tanenbaum to the New Jersey Nets. The team seemed prime for a move, but the trouble was that there were too many Nets owners – eight of them – and they tended to bicker. "One day, the vote on whether to move would be four-four," Tanenbaum says. "The day after, it'd be up to five-three. It never reached eight-zero."

Next, Tanenbaum was approached by a New York group. It had a signed offer to buy the San Antonio Spurs, and for a fee it would assign the offer to Tanenbaum and Toronto. It was Stern who torpedoed that scheme.

"David was beside himself, he was so upset," Tanenbaum says. "The Spurs were the only major sports team San Antonio had, and Stern didn't want the NBA to be the bad guys who took it away from the city."

But Tanenbaum's persistence seemed to strike a chord with Stern. He assured Tanenbaum that if he, Tanenbaum, could persuade the NBA owners to agree to a one-city-only expansion, then he, Stern, would favour Toronto. There were twenty-seven NBA teams, with twenty-seven owners or ownership groups, and through much of 1992 Tanenbaum and his cousin, lawyer Joel Rose, flew thousands of miles to lay their message on each and every one of them. Along the way, there was much talk of money.

"One time, Harold Katz phoned Stern in a very excited state," Tanenbaum says. "Harold owns the Philadelphia 76ers, and he told Stern he had a guy, meaning me, who was willing to pay eighty million for a franchise. Stern called Harold a schmuck. Stern said, 'We can get a *hundred!* Why're you selling for *eighty?*'"

However much money was at stake – a final figure wouldn't be arrived at until after the franchise decision – the NBA owners warmed to Tanenbaum's persuasions and voted in principle for a one-time expansion to Toronto. On October 21, 1992, Tanenbaum put the matter on an official footing by giving the league a non-refundable $100,000 (U.S.) down payment on Palestra's bid for the franchise. (Palestra was the company Tanenbaum had formed to handle the bid.)

"Stern asked me if I minded competition," Tanenbaum says, "if I minded other groups bringing in their bids. I said I didn't mind as long as the ground rules were the same for everyone, as long as it was a level playing field."

Through the late fall and early winter of 1992-93, Tanenbaum shaped Palestra into a seemingly irresistible package. He brought in Labatt and the CIBC as equal partners, a third all-round. He persuaded Richard Peddie, chief executive officer of the SkyDome, to take a leave of absence and lend to Palestra his proven sports-marketing skills. And he stocked his board of directors with men who pulled their weight in various pertinent fields: Paul Godfrey, publisher of the *Toronto Sun*, in the media; Jack Donohue, former coach of Canada's National Team, in basketball; and Sam Pollock, former Montreal Canadiens general manager and at that time John Labatt chairman, in back-room finesse with athletes and beer.

"I was totally confident of our position," Tanenbaum says. "We *started* the whole expansion movement, and we had made friends throughout the NBA. Or I thought we had."

John Bitove, Jr.'s, mother, Dotsa, from the Lazoff side of the family, grew up in Fort Wayne, Indiana, and for the last two weeks of most of young

John's summers he visited his American cousins in this Hoosier basket-ball hotbed. He caught the fever for the game. Actually, it was love at first sight for Bitove and almost any sport. At York Mills, he quarterbacked the football team, competed in the high jump in track, played basketball and soccer, and was a member of the school's Ontario Championship rugby team. But, of all the games, it was basketball that had the power to fascinate him.

"I remember having a conversation on our front porch with a friend of the family when I was fifteen," he says. "I told him I didn't understand why there wasn't an NBA team in Toronto, and, if there wasn't one here soon, I was going to bring it in myself. Of course I was just a kid dream-ing dreams."

Bitove took a business degree from Indiana University in 1983 and a law degree from the University of Windsor the very next year. He managed this feat of academic speed by studying business at one school in the summers and law at the other in the winters. "I've always been in a hurry," he says. He spent two years in Ottawa holding down junior posi-tions in the Conservative government, then plugged into the Bitove Corporation back in Toronto. His father, John Senior, launched the busi-ness in 1949 with the Java Shoppe, a twelve-seat restaurant in north Toronto, and had built it into a food-services colossus. Bitove Corp., with twelve hundred employees, provides the food outlets at Pearson International Airport and the SkyDome and runs such hangouts for the sports-and-rock crowd as Wayne Gretzky's and the Hard Rock Café. It was the family company that provided the initial financial backing for John junior's adventures in making a kid's basketball dreams come true.

Bitove had introduced himself to the NBA initially in 1990 by pitching an international basketball tournament in Toronto. He would organize it if the NBA would allow one of its teams to take part. Russ Granik, the league's chief operating officer, gave him a thumbs down; the pre-season McDonald's Open, a European event established in the late 1980s, was the only occasion for which the NBA let any of its teams off the leash. Still, the notion of a Toronto tournament got Bitove's name circulating in international basketball circles as a young man of promise.

That became significant in the summer of 1992, when Borislav Stankovic went scrambling for a site to stage the 1994 World Champion-ship of Basketball. Stankovic was the head of FIBA, the international basketball governing body, and he had lost the original host city, Belgrade, to the civil war in the former Yugoslavia. He began to ask about this Bitove. Could he put on the Worlds in Toronto? Or was it so much hot air? Bitove responded by assembling a strong local committee that eventually raised $13 million, all in private money. That impressed Stankovic. What also impressed him was Toronto's proximity to the United States, virtually guaranteeing that the NBA would send a team – Dream Team II, which would be by far the Worlds' major attraction – without fear of foreign disturbances. On October 18, 1992, after a meeting in Munich where Toronto was favoured in a 4–3 vote over Athens, FIBA gave Bitove the shot he wanted.

In the long run, the staging of the Worlds got Bitove valuable NBA connections. These weren't primarily at the top level, not with Stern and Granik (though both were properly grateful to Bitove for providing Dream Team II with a worldwide platform – a TV audience of 1.5 billion would tune into the final game between Russia and the Dreamers). Bitove's major connections in the course of organizing the Worlds were with middle-level NBA officials. They became Bitove fans, admirers of his determined style. They slipped him favours in the contest for the Toronto franchise. And on the day in the fall of 1993 when he stepped into the NBA offices in New York as the president of the new Toronto team, they greeted him in a flurry of high fives.

But in the short run, Bitove was worried. Just three days after the awarding of the Worlds to Toronto, the NBA opened the bidding for the Toronto franchise.

"For a day or so, I felt paralysed," he says. "The timing couldn't have been worse for us, two massive projects at once. But it was *my* dream. *I* was the one who wanted an NBA team. So I just set out to plan how I was going to win the bidding."

One of the jokes around Bitove's office was that he brought David Peterson into his NBA group because Peterson had silver hair. There was truth to the joke. In 1993, Bitove didn't look a whole lot different from the kid who scored off the steal in that game in 1976. He needed a slightly more craggy presence to get the attention of the NBA's middle-aged owners, and Peterson – former premier of Ontario, Bay Street lawyer, deft with the media, silver-haired – filled the bill. There was just one catch.

"Basketball?" Peterson said at his first meeting with Bitove. "I don't know a thing about basketball."

"Ask your kids," Bitove said.

Peterson's two sons were eleven and fifteen at the time, and, as he later told everyone, especially the NBA owners, "I did my own due-diligence study. I mentioned basketball to my boys, the NBA coming to Toronto, and they were more excited about me getting into that than about me being premier."

Unwittingly, Peterson and his sons acted out a principle that later entered into the Bitove group's marketing strategy. To quote from the relevant section on advertising: "Leverage for Kids to Capture the Interest of Their More Affluent Parents."

So Peterson came on board as the group's front man. Now Bitove needed money men.

One evening late in February 1993, Gary Slaight threw a surprise fortieth birthday party for his wife, Donna, at the chic midtown Toronto restaurant Bistro 990. Slaight is the president and CEO of Standard Radio – CFRB and Mix 99.9 – and son of Allan Slaight, who owns Standard Broadcasting. Gary, the genial host, worked the room, greeting, hugging, schmoozing. A couple of hours into the party, he got to chatting with John Bitove, Jr. Bitove hadn't been invited on his own hook; Randi was a close friend of the birthday girl, and the two women had recently worked together on a fund-raising drive for the Art Gallery of Ontario. But Slaight knew enough about Bitove to make a suggestion. If you're looking for a partner to put money into the basketball bid, he said, you ought to talk to my dad.

Bitove's first reaction was that this was party talk. Slaight had probably had a couple of drinks and was just blue-skying.

"I was completely serious," Slaight said later. "Around Standard, we'd always discussed buying a sports franchise."

The day following the party, Bitove mulled over Standard as a partner. It made instructive mulling: it was the largest privately owned communications group in the country, with more than $300 million in annual sales, heavily into outdoor advertising, video, and radio stations. Bitove had been approached by other investors keen to throw money at him, but none made as much sense as Standard. It combined money plus communications skills. Bitove phoned Allan Slaight.

The elder Slaight, like David Peterson, had never seen an NBA game. But he wasn't one to let gaps in life experience stop him from backing winners; it was Slaight, whose taste in music is reflected in his extensive collection of jazz and country CDs, who launched the wildly successful Toronto rock station Q107. At a meeting with Peterson and Bitove in Standard's offices a few days after Bitove's phone call, Slaight looked over some figures that Bitove's people had assembled. Percentage of adult audience very likely to attend at least one Toronto NBA game: 29. Projected TV revenue for Toronto's first year of play: $5 million (U.S.). Among the mass of figures, the most important was missing: how much would the NBA charge for the franchise? The most recent expansion fee, in 1987, had been $32.5 million (U.S.). The new price would likely triple that. But Slaight wasn't going to make his decision on numbers alone. Instinct entered into the equation.

"It didn't take a lot of analysis," he says, "to know that the NBA would be successful in Toronto."

Two days after the meeting, Allan Slaight declared himself a member of Bitove's group.

Now Bitove needed a bank. "NBA owners don't take you seriously if there isn't a banker in your corner," he says. His first choice was the Bitove family bank, CIBC. In fact, his first choice as partners in the franchise bid were the SkyDome group, notably CIBC and Labatt. But Larry Tanenbaum had scooped them before Bitove realized the game was afoot. He looked elsewhere.

David Peterson lined up a meeting with the Bank of Nova Scotia, Canada's fourth-largest bank with assets of $107.6 billion. It was an inspired choice on two counts. For one, Scotia loved Allan Slaight; in 1985, the bank had funded his acquisition of Standard Broadcasting to the tune of $165 million, and, within eight years, Slaight had retired the entire loan. For another thing, Scotia had undergone a change at the top, CEO Cedric Ritchie stepping down in favour of the more adventurous Peter Godsoe. In the 1980s, under Ritchie, Scotia had concentrated on corporate lending. In the nineties, the shift was to the retail market, and Godsoe liked the fit with pro basketball.

"We see an NBA team as a wonderful retailing opportunity," he says.

"The bank has over 230 branches in greater Toronto, and basketball will appeal to a lot of those customers."

When it came time to divvy up the shares, Bitove took 44 per cent, Allan Slaight and Standard another 44, with 10 for Scotia, and 1 for David Peterson. On the suggestion of Ralph Lean, a savvy Peterson law partner at Cassels Brock & Blackwell, a fifth investor was cut in for an additional 1 per cent. He was Phil Granovsky, chairman of Atlantic Packaging, and he brought to the group intimate and painful experience in the franchise-bidding wars. A small, charming man in his early seventies, he had come second to CIBC–Labatt in the contest for the baseball franchise that became the Toronto Blue Jays. At one of the early meetings of the Bitove partners, Granovsky displayed his original baseball brochures. Bitove studied them closely, looking for clues about how to avoid finishing in second place.

Michael Cohl of the third bidding group was no johnny-come-lately to pro basketball. He had lobbied for a Toronto team as early as 1985. But now, for the 1993 bid, he recognized that he needed a point man. Someone who was presentable in the businessman mode, since Cohl absolutely never wore a suit and tie, and his rumpled, casual style would be a problem for the straight-arrow NBA owners. And he needed someone who knew the capital markets; though Cohl and his partner Bill Ballard exuded youth and vigour and rock'n'roll creativity, they lacked the financial backing of banks and large corporations. After interviewing many candidates, Cohl tapped Bob Foster for the point-man job.

Foster, a natty Bay Street merchant banker, had worked on the original financial structuring of the SkyDome – and on its later restructuring as well. He had sat on the SkyDome's board, and these various activities had brought him into regular contact with Richard Peddie, Labatt, and the Bitoves. He also knew Larry Tanenbaum and considered Allan Slaight a friend. "The sports-entertainment area in Toronto has its own small group of players on the financial side," Foster says. "You *know* all the other guys, and that sometimes makes for an odd game."

Nevertheless, Foster picked his way past old business associates and around present pals to help assemble a Cohl–Ballard slate of investors.

They included Jim Fifield, CEO of EMI Music; Mark Routtenberg, who brought sports experience as a minority owner of the Montreal Expos; Eph Diamond, former chairman of Cadillac–Fairview, now president of Whitecastle Investments; Liberty Media Corporation, a division of TCI Telecommunications, the largest cable operator in the United States; and the U.S.-based international bank, Citibank, whose role was to handle the long-term debt financing.

And then there was Magic Johnson.

"At the time," Foster says, "there was a lot of criticism that no blacks were being brought into NBA front offices."

But was Johnson to be a latter-day Joe Louis, a Las Vegas-style greeter who made fans and owners feel warm all over?

"We thought, no question, he'd be a great ambassador for the game," Foster says. "And we also planned to appoint him general manager. But, number one, he bought into the group. Magic Johnson was a contributing equity owner. We thought that would show something positive in our favour."

Foster was satisfied that the entire Cohl–Ballard group spelled winner. "You looked at those names," he says, "and you had to think, My gracious, this is *most* impressive."

But that could be said of the others, of the Tanenbaum and Bitove groups. Each of the bidding groups boasted people of established, even dazzling, credentials. Palestra still seemed to hold the inside track, but the contest was a long way from won. Each of the groups was looking for an edge, and one might find it, perhaps, from an unexpected source.

3

THE CONTEST

When Himal Mathew was born in Darjeeling, his parents formed his given name by dropping the last one and a half syllables from the name of the mountain range that towered over the town. Three years later, the Mathew family left the lower Himalayas and made their way to Nigeria (where they got caught in a civil war), Angola (where a Portuguese mercenary had dumped them), and Quebec (where they eventually put down roots in the Eastern Townships). Himal studied political science at Queen's University and went into the advertising business. That placed him, on a morning in early April 1993, in the position of client-services director at Cossette Communication-Marketing in Toronto and leafing through the newspapers in search of new clients. It struck him, "thinking laterally," as he says, that this Bitove group, the people that the newspapers said were trailing in the race for the basketball franchise, could benefit from some creative strategy. Mathew picked up his phone and invited John Bitove, David Peterson, and Allan Slaight to come by the agency's offices.

On the morning of the meeting, Bitove and company were greeted by basketball players – huge cardboard blowups of players from early George Mikan to later Michael Jordan. They lined the walls of Cossette's first floor, in the elevator, along the corridor of the second floor. Larry Bird, Kareem, and Dr. J. The Cossette art department had clipped photographs from *The Encyclopedia of Basketball*, enlarged them to grander-than-life-size, and mounted them for display. Message: at Cossette, we're into basketball.

Around the board table, the Cossette gang – Mathew, copy writer Jim Garbutt, art director Brian Hickling – introduced themselves and their work. But they came at the subject of basketball in a way that at first struck the Bitove people as amusingly oblique.

"The basketball teams I played on at Leaside High were completely terrible," Garbutt began. "We never won. This one game, when I was in Grade 13, Runnymede was just destroying us. All of a sudden, I called a timeout. The other players looked at me, like, *What?* But I told them I had this feeling I'd got a hot hand and they should feed me the ball. I didn't know what had come over me, but I meant what I said. The game started again, and the guys fed me, and I took this shot from way beyond my normal range. And the ball swished in. *Unbelievable!* I hardly hit another basket, but that shot from downtown was my biggest moment in high-school basketball."

The point about Garbutt's story – the Cossette people had thought this through – was that they would present themselves to the Bitove group in the same way they'd present the Bitove group to the NBA: as regular guys, sincere, straight-up people who cared about basketball. The NBA owners were roll-up-their-sleeves-and-get-to-work men. Cossette would get across the image of Slaight, Granovsky, *et al.*, not as members of the corporate élite, but as self-made guys who took care of their own money and would do the same with the NBA's.

At the end of the meeting, the Bitove partners said they would think over Cossette's provocative ideas and stepped out of the boardroom into what Slaight remembers as "a corridor of human flesh, all applauding." These were the rest of the Cossette employees, crushed into the hall, clapping, cheering, chanting. "Get the franchise!" "Bring the team to Toronto!" Slaight, Bitove, and Peterson rode the elevator to the first floor and emerged into another swarm of chanters. "Go get the team!"

"Allan phoned us that very afternoon to say we had the account," Mathew says. "Two days later, we were shooting videos of the partners, and, before the week was over, we sent out the first package to the NBA owners."

Enclosed in a small black case, the package served as an introduction of the Bitove group in its new Cossetted image. Across the front of the case, in words that Garbutt had written, was a sentence in white letters: "The NBA is all about sweat, pain, fouling, elbowing, shoving, and brutal aggression." Inside, another sentence completed the thought: "And that's just to get a franchise."

The black case contained biographies of each Bitove partner, on paper and on video. For the video, the partners, looking candid and down-to-earth, spoke the thoughts that Garbutt helped them shape.

Bitove's segment began with his familiar and heartfelt ambition. "Since I was fifteen," he said to the camera, "I've had a dream of bringing the NBA to Toronto." He worked through an evocation of his dad's humble beginnings and the building of the Bitove empire and wound up with his personal notion of family values. "When our name is attached to something, that sometimes means more than money."

Peterson, statesmanlike but relaxed, said, "When I was premier of Ontario, I had to make the decision whether to go ahead with the SkyDome or not. I chose to go ahead, and today we have one of the most outstanding facilities in the world of sports. We'll build a basketball stadium that the entire league will be proud of."

Even the banker, Peter Godsoe, who did his segment in one take, came across as a heck of a standup guy, though properly money-conscious and four-square behind the project. "The Bank of Nova Scotia has the financial expertise and the staying power to see the team come to fruition."

Cossette had thought further about the Bitove approach to the bidding. They'd make the NBA owners see the Bitove partners, especially John, as viscerally reactive to basketball, as guys who had more than a dash of Horatio Alger, respectable and trustworthy with a buck. And as people who liked a little creative wit. Garbutt took care of that in the second package that went out to the NBA owners, the one that documented the partners' financial histories. The line across the front read: "To be a player in the NBA, you need to consistently put up some great numbers." Inside: "And that's before you get the ball."

On a Thursday in mid-June 1993, Bitove met up in Phoenix, Arizona, with Peterson, Slaight, and Borden Osmak, a senior Bank of Nova Scotia v-p assigned to the basketball project. Bitove was coming off a lobbying expedition to Seattle and Portland, where he had had chats with the presidents of two NBA teams, the SuperSonics and the Trail Blazers. The others had flown in from Toronto, and at a game that evening all were the guests of Jerry Colangelo, the CEO of the Phoenix Suns.

This was a crucial event from at least three standpoints. For one thing, Colangelo was a man whom the Toronto guys needed to impress, since he was chairman of the NBA expansion committee, one of the five league executives who would choose the holder of the Toronto franchise. For another thing, the game that Colangelo had invited the Torontonians to attend at the America West Arena was of huge significance: it was the second meeting between the Suns and the Chicago Bulls in the NBA championship final. And finally, this would be the first NBA game that the trio of Peterson, Slaight, and Osmak, three potential team owners, had ever seen in their whole lives.

Slaight stood in Colangelo's box that night – actually it was late afternoon in Phoenix since the game was set for a five o'clock tipoff, local time, to meet the prime-time TV schedule in the East – and he felt the pre-game throb of the crowd, the fans pumped to a roar that shook the arena.

"My God," Slaight shouted at Colangelo, "the people in here really turn it up for the playoffs."

Colangelo gave Slaight a funny look.

"Oh no," Colangelo said, "it's like this from the first whistle of the first game in the pre-season."

The playoff game was a thriller. Chicago finally won it, 111–108, and the Bulls would go on to take the championship in six games, their third title in a row.

Outside the arena after the game, the Phoenix night was baking in 109 degrees Fahrenheit. The four Toronto guys hardly noticed. They were too excited.

"If that's what pro basketball is all about," Slaight said, his face radiant, "when Toronto gets a slice of it, they're gonna eat it right up."

The four rode a cab to Bitove's suite at the Hyatt Hotel. Bitove ordered drinks, and the men took turns raving about the thrill of the game, the atmosphere in the arena, the constant tumult of the crowd, the tremendous sense of event in the place.

"You know something?" Bitove said when a gap opened up in the conversation. "This is a hell of a group in this room, and we're having *fun*."

The other three drank to that.

"It was kind of a watershed moment," Bitove remembers. "Allan, David, and Borden had really got a taste of basketball for the first time. They loved it. There was real chemistry among us. Himal Mathew and his people were on the job back in Toronto. And I just felt that, from there on in, we were on a roll."

The margins of pages 127, 128, and the top of 129 in Allan Slaight's autographed copy of *Playing Hardball* by David Whitford are heavily scored in blue ballpoint ink. The book, published in April 1993, traces the adventures of a Denver business consortium in luring a National Baseball League franchise to its city. And the marked pages in Slaight's copy describe one episode in the process, an occasion in March 1991 when an eight-man National League delegation descended on Denver to size up the prospective ownership group and to check on the city's baseball facility.

The delegation had warned the Denver group in advance that the visit was to be kept strictly low-key. No public displays, no fuss. But the group ignored the warning and put on a spectacle that included red carpets, cheering fans, and fawning dignitaries. The baseball delegates might have been furious at this blatant flouting of their instructions. Instead, they revelled in the attention, and in the end the gamble paid off when the league awarded the group the franchise. Slaight had taken his ballpoint pen to the incident, because he and his partners were planning to steal those pages from Denver's book.

On July 29, 1993, a mission of three NBA officials – expansion-committee chairman Jerry Colangelo, NBA chief operating officer Russ Granik, and league counsel Joel Litvin – arrived in Toronto to assess the three competing bidders on their home turf. Granik, a shy man, had sent word that the groups were to treat the visit as a virtual secret, without displays of an embarrassingly showy nature. This was the rule that the Bitove group, in a performance orchestrated by Cossette, now set out to ignore.

First, the helicopter. It was waiting, a Bitove treat, on the tarmac at

Pearson International when the three visiting Americans arrived on their flight from the United States. It whisked them south over the city, and on the way they got the definitive guided tour from a man who had once governed what they were gazing upon, David Peterson. There was one small problem: vicious winds gave the helicopter a rough shaking, something Granik, feeling a little green, really didn't care for. "I was sweating like crazy over that one," Bitove recalls. But the helicopter landed safely at the Island Airport, and a limo shot the delegation to city hall for an encouraging word from Mayor June Rowlands.

Next stop, the top floor of the Scotia Plaza at 60 King Street West. The vast room gloried in wall-to-wall broadloom, floor-to-ceiling windows, a lavish buffet courtesy of Bitove Corp., and, revived for a second run, Cossette's collection of basketball blowups. Murray Beynon assumed centre stage. He was the architect of the Bitove group's proposed stadium, and, performing a show-and-tell with large mounted cards, he walked the guests through his design: 22,500 seats; forty private lounges at courtside, each accommodating twelve fans; 125 smaller loges along the arena's west wall, good for six to eight people apiece; a giant Jumbotron; a state-of-the-art sound system capable of picking up every squeak of the players' sneakers.

At the grand finale of his exposition, Beynon directed the three visitors to the north windows for the view up Bay Street to the southeast corner of Dundas. There, on a spacious piece of vacant property, an enormous banner fluttered in the light breeze. "Centre Court," the banner announced in capital letters. This was to be the name of the new stadium, and the piece of prime land at Bay and Dundas was to be its site. Cadillac–Fairview owned the property, and the Bitove group was in negotiation for its purchase.

An express elevator dropped Bitove, Slaight, Peterson, and the three Americans to Scotia Plaza's ground floor. The six men stepped off the elevator and – revival time again – into a corridor lined with three hundred bank employees. All wore T-shirts emblazoned with the slogan WE WANT THE BALL! And all were chanting the same plea: "*We Want the Ball!*"

A video film caught Colangelo, Granik, and Litvin at the instant they confronted the horde. The film reveals that the first, startled reaction of each man was to turn back into the elevator, to seek refuge from all that naked enthusiasm. But, almost immediately, another emotion took over. The three men faced the crowd and seemed to give themselves up to the noise and people, to the joy of the staged event. They smiled. They were experiencing the fervour, and they *liked* it.

The tour continued north on Yonge Street, through the Eaton Centre (where the employees of Cadillac–Fairview, the centre's owner, sported WE WANT THE BALL! T-shirts) and onto the stadium site. It was alive with pre-arranged hoopla: half-court basketball, kids from the Y shooting from three-point land, hot-dog vendors, NBA banners overhead. As the three visitors would recognize, the banners were authentic, the kind that flew only in league arenas. Bitove's new friends among the employees at NBA headquarters in New York had rushed them to Toronto for the occasion.

That night, Colangelo, Granik, and Litvin took in a Blue Jays game at the SkyDome. They sat with the Bitove crowd in the Bitove box and ate and drank from the kitchens of Bitove Corp. The waiters who served them wore T-shirts. The T-shirts begged WE WANT THE BALL!

The other two Toronto groups, unaware of the Bitove extravaganza, played the committee's visit by the rule. No fuss.

The Cohl–Ballard group entertained their guests to lunch and a presentation at the Queen Elizabeth Building on the CNE grounds. That was where their new stadium was to be erected; it would be a clever, multi-purpose arena with retractable walls that could convert from a twenty-two-thousand-seat basketball facility to a concert amphitheatre for thirty thousand or, downsizing, to intimate auditoriums of three thousand and ten thousand for smaller productions. To demonstrate their pride in the design, Cohl–Ballard gave the three Americans a virtual-reality stroll through the new building. "Our time with the committee was very carefully orchestrated," Bob Foster says. "It gave them a high-tech sense of what we could do in basketball."

For the benefit of the delegation, Larry Tanenbaum revealed Palestra's stadium site on the railway lands east of the SkyDome (a location Palestra kept secret from the media during the entire bidding procedure). The lands belonged to Marathon Realty, which, Tanenbaum happily declared, had thrown in its lot with Palestra. Steve Stavro, owner of the Maple Leafs, was also close to committing to Palestra. Tanenbaum told the delegation that the new stadium would be dual purpose, for basketball and hockey, and that the Leafs would almost certainly supply the hockey. And, at the meal Tanenbaum hosted for Colangelo, Granik, and Litvin at the exclusive Toronto Club, a sober, dignified event, Stavro and Leaf president Cliff Fletcher were conspicuously among the guests. Tanenbaum thought everything was falling into place – the hockey connection, the stadium site in a location that had already proved itself, with the SkyDome, as a draw for the top-ticket Toronto sports audience.

After the Toronto visit, Tanenbaum saw Palestra maintaining its lead in the bidding battle. So did everyone else – except John Bitove.

4

MAKING THE PITCH

Himal Mathew's thoughts drifted to fatherhood. It was late August, and he and Jim Garbutt were sitting in on a pivotal meeting with the Bitove group in David Peterson's office at Cassels Brock & Blackwell. But Mathew's wife was two weeks away from giving birth to the couple's first child, and that prospect kept distracting him from the important matter at hand, which was: how was the Bitove group to present itself at the meeting with the full NBA expansion committee in New York City on September 20?

The thinking among the Bitove partners, Mathew realized, was to go for the glitz approach. The NBA offered the last word in slick, high-tech glamour product, and the Bitove group would prove to the committee that they, too, were up to speed on glitter. They were guys who could produce NBA-style entertainment, and, to prove it, they'd go into the meeting with a full-blown high-tech show.

Mathew roused himself from thoughts of babies in time to join Jim Garbutt in a surprised dissent from the group's idea.

"I told the guys," he says, "that one of our strengths from the start was the captivating way John talked about basketball. A high-tech presentation would mask that. In fact, we were getting away altogether from our original strategy. Our approach was supposed to be about our guys as individuals, as people the NBA owners would be comfortable with. That's what our New York presentation had to be about. It wasn't about technology and Hollywood."

Without argument, Bitove and the others clicked back into line. "After Himal and Jim spoke their minds," Bitove says, "we threw out everything we'd been thinking about and committed again to the more humble approach." Technology was out. There would be no videos at the presentation, no logos, no computerized garnish. Instead, the partners would offer themselves, unadorned, as solid, self-made men. The meeting broke up with everybody on track.

On September 13, Creston Mathew was born, son of Himal and Joanne.

Over the weekend of September 18 and 19, the Bitove partners hunkered down in their war room in one of the three suites that made up the top floor of Manhattan's Omni Berkshire Place Hotel. With Jim Garbutt scripting and Himal Mathew kibitzing, the men rehearsed their routines for Monday's presentation to the expansion committee, which would take place in one of the hotel's spacious meeting rooms. In rehearsal, everybody loved Allan Slaight's opening.

"In Edmonton in the 1950s," he said, "I worked six days a week as a radio news reporter. I had a wife and three children, and my weekly rent was higher than my weekly salary. To make ends meet, on Sundays, my day off, I took a childhood hobby of mine and turned it into a part-time profession. I performed magic shows."

"Good, Allan," Garbutt said. "Now let's try it from the top once more. Don't rush the last line."

The Bitove group anticipated they'd be facing an audience that would be tough, nitpicking, and large. The expansion committee – chairman Colangelo, plus four owners, including Philadelphia's Harold Katz – would be joined by David Stern, Russ Granik, a dozen league lawyers, and almost as many broadcasting consultants. Bitove and the others also knew that a draw had placed them last on the list of presenters, following, in order, Palestra, the Cohl–Ballard group, and Arthur Griffiths of Vancouver. (Vancouver had been added to the agenda when Griffiths, owner of the Canucks hockey team and builder of a projected twenty-thousand-seat sports stadium, petitioned the NBA to consider further expansion to Canada's West Coast.)

"Okay, Allan," Garbutt said. "Then we segue into your TV experience. We should play up the part where you were president of Global. Ready?"

Larry Tanenbaum and his Palestra partners led off on Monday at 10:30 A.M. with a bells-and-whistles presentation. A video. A team name. Team caps and jackets. Visuals in slick array. The video, promoting Palestra, Toronto, and basketball, came from the expert studios of Tudhope Associates. The team name? Toronto Thunder. Goldfarb Consultants had tested it on focus groups and drew a highly favourable response. "Thunder" offered exciting marketing possibilities. Thunder *roll*. Thunder *bolt*. Thunder *clap*. CIBC promised to create a series of Thunder*force* accounts in its eighteen hundred branches across the country. The team logo featured a thunderbird streaking through its centre. Tanenbaum displayed caps and jackets adorned with the logo for the committee members. Roots had run up the clothes under tight security in its Toronto factory and smuggled them into the Omni in unmarked boxes.

"We had an outstanding presentation," Tanenbaum says. "It was professional to the last degree."

Then came the committee's questions and comments.

"If you guys think you're going to promote further than seventy-five miles outside of Toronto," David Stern said to the Palestra people, "you'd better think again."

Stern was speaking of the NBA's strict territorial rules about marketing. That point didn't bother Tanenbaum as much as the hostile tone he thought he heard in Stern's voice.

"Are you prepared to pay $160 million for the franchise?" somebody else asked sharply.

Tanenbaum, who had been thinking of $100 million, gave a measured response. "We're prepared to pay $160 million, if you can show us we'll make money at that figure."

"Well, you'll have to pay more than you're probably thinking."

When Palestra's time was up, Tanenbaum left behind a dozen brand-new Toronto Thunder caps, jackets, and bags as souvenirs for the committee members.

"Now," Tanenbaum says, "knowing what I do, I wish I had that stuff back."

Michael Cohl wore a suit and tie to the Cohl–Ballard presentation. "I've never seen a man so uncomfortable," Bob Foster says. Still, the session went smoothly. The group played a promotional video, emphasized the cutting edge of its arena design, assured the committee of its fiscal strength, and put Magic Johnson on display. "Our one problem was location," Foster says. "We couldn't get around the fact that the committee perceived the CNE grounds as not the right place for a basketball stadium. They thought it was too far out from the downtown core, without direct transportation, and those elements meant we wouldn't attract the fans in the corporate community who were essential. Location killed us."

The Bitove group went on shortly before 6 P.M. Introduced by David Peterson, who served as the group's MC, each partner stood before the committee, unaccompanied by technology, and offered a monologue that mixed autobiography and franchise data. Bitove spoke of money and merchandising. Allan Slaight laid out his long experience in communications. Peterson took care of the community-relations angle. Architect Murray Beynon presented the stadium design. And Borden Osmak from the Bank of Nova Scotia swore the bank's unswerving commitment to the franchise.

"I started in business in 1945, when I bought three old paper-bag machines for $5,000," Phil Granovsky told the committee. "Today, my company's called Atlantic Packaging, and it's got four paper mills, thirteen plants, and twenty-five hundred employees. But, you know, if there's one thing I like as much as making money, it's giving money away. I mean giving it to worthy causes. I'm one of the biggest contributors in Canada to Israel and other Jewish causes. And I'm here to tell you that I'll give as much to basketball as I've given to my business and my charities."

Granovsky's speech was the shortest among the Bitove group, but, as it later turned out, it had a resounding impact on one key man in the room.

"And now if you'll bear with us for a few more minutes," Peterson said near the end of the hour, "we're going to turn down the lights in the room, and we'd like you to use your imaginations and dream the same dream that we've been dreaming the last year."

Peterson's words were the signal for Jim Garbutt to swing into action. Garbutt was stationed in a curtained area at the side of the room, his finger poised over a tape machine that was hooked into four large speakers in the room's corners. "I felt like the Wizard of Oz in the dark behind the curtains," Garbutt says. "I was just hoping I'd land on 'play' and not 'fast forward.'" His finger found "play."

"Good evening, everybody," an authoritative voice burst from the speakers, crowd noises behind the voice. "I'm Jim Gordon, and I'm joined by my colleague and partner, Spencer Ross. We're just minutes away from the tip in this fabulous new basketball arena at the Eaton Centre in downtown Toronto, Canada, for the first regular-season NBA game played by a Toronto team since the Toronto Huskies forty years ago."

Gordon and Ross were basketball announcers who handled NBA games on radio. They were reading from a script that Garbutt had written, a look-ahead to the beginning of NBA basketball in Toronto on a night in November 1995. Garbutt had taped the broadcast with Gordon and Ross at a studio in Hell's Kitchen the previous Saturday. And he had gone for authenticity in everything; the crowd noises came from the recording of a Pink Floyd concert, the same track that the Phoenix Suns played in their arena during team warmups.

"Well, Jim, I've been around a lot of basketball buildings," said Spencer Ross, "but I've never seen anything as intimate as this. It reminds me of an opera house."

Gordon and Ross gushed over the stadium's location ("a three-pointer from City Hall") and the fans' enthusiasm ("It feels like the seventh game of the championship in here").

"Well, Spencer," said Gordon, winding up the three-minute tape, "judging from what we're seeing tonight, the ownership group has hit all the right buttons. This is what the NBA envisioned when it set its sights on international expansion."

The tape ended in a hard crescendo of crowd frenzy.

Harold Katz couldn't restrain himself any longer. He got out of his chair, pushed past his fellow committee members, past the lawyers, past everybody, and made straight for Phil Granovsky, whom he had never met until that day. He wrapped Granovsky in a huge, fumbling embrace. "I *love* a story like the one you told us," he beamed.

Well, well, the others in the Bitove group thought, what's *this?* Going in, they'd heard that Palestra had Katz in its hip pocket. Maybe not. Maybe nothing was as it had once seemed.

"Let's have the questions," Stern said to the committee, and, for the next several seconds, the room remained still and quiet. Katz finally broke the uneasy spell.

"Yes, okay, what exactly is a loge?"

Murray Beynon answered patiently, and another silence fell on the room.

"It was getting embarrassing," Slaight remembers. "We expected the committee to give us rough treatment. But there were only four or five questions, and they were so damned lame I was frankly beginning to feel deflated."

Bitove read the lack of questions as a huge endorsement. "It's like what Bobby Knight has always said, the Indiana coach," Bitove says. "It's not the will to win, it's the will to *prepare* to win that separates winners from losers. We were so prepared that the people in the room couldn't think of anything we *hadn't* covered. So I left the meeting feeling like a winner."

It was after nine o'clock on the night of the presentation before the Bitove group finally sat down to dinner. They ate at an up-scale Italian restaurant in midtown Manhattan called Paper Moon. Lois Zenner, Randi Bitove's mother, had chosen the place. Lois and Howard Zenner, still with Hart, Schaffner & Marx, had transferred to New York the year after Randi married Bitove. By dinnertime, the Bitove party had swelled to about twenty-five people: Bitove's parents, in from Toronto, the Zenners, the Cossette gang, Peterson, Slaight, Osmak, Beynon, Granovsky, and assorted spouses and companions. The mood was mellow.

"I'd spent practically every day since the spring with those men," Himal Mathew says. "We'd developed a very strong sense of camaraderie, but at the restaurant, all of us sitting at a long table against the wall, there was an even better feeling. It was as if the tension was off, and everybody was kind of glowing."

After dinner, many from the party moved on to Dangerfield's, the comedy club. It turned out to be a slow night. "Peterson was funnier than any of the comedians on stage," Jim Garbutt remembers.

The clock reached one in the morning, and the party had dwindled to

four survivors, Mathew, Garbutt, Allan Slaight, and his elegant compan-
ion, Emmanuelle Gattuso. They strolled to the Plaza Hotel and settled at
a table in the Oak Room. Mathew, who has a fondness for single-malt
whisky, chose the drinks, glasses of twenty-five-year-old Macallan. He
and Garbutt asked for cigars and lit up. Then Slaight reached into his
pockets. He brought out coins and cards, and, in the early-morning hours
of September 21, amid the hushed opulence of the New York bar, he
performed sleights of hand that seemed to Mathew and Garbutt, at that
golden moment, to be entrancing in the most gentle and profound way.

The secretary in John Bitove's office had misspelled the name on the telephone message slip. "Russ Granek" had called, and he'd like Bitove to get
right back to him. This was on the Tuesday, the day after the New York
presentations, and Bitove found the message waiting for him early that
afternoon when he arrived at the office after his flight home. Bitove
returned the call. The NBA office, he was told, wanted to check on a few
points about his plans and promises, but the bottom line was that the
expansion committee had voted unanimously in favour of the Bitove
group. Less than twenty-four hours had passed since the presentations at
the Omni Berkshire Place, and Russ Granik was telling Bitove he was the
NBA's man in Toronto.

The official announcement would come on Thursday afternoon, nine
days away, and, until then, Bitove and his partners would have to keep
mum. That proved an excruciating proposition for Allan Slaight and
David Peterson. On the day Bitove broke the winning news to them,
Slaight was throwing the Standard Broadcasting First Annual Golf
Tournament, and Peterson was the guest speaker at the dinner after the
golf. His topic: the process of pitching for an NBA franchise.

"Peterson made a wonderful speech," Slaight says. "But the thing was,
standing up there in front of an audience of communications people,
David and I wanted to jump up and down and shout, *We got it!*"

Larry Tanenbaum was understandably the most stricken basketball
man in Toronto. Palestra, the favourite, had been passed over, and
Tanenbaum was sure he knew why.

"It was really David Stern who made the selection, and he didn't want
us," Tanenbaum says. "It wasn't the will of the owners speaking in the

decision. It was Stern speaking. He neutered the committee. He wanted an organization in Toronto he could control. He knew that wouldn't be Palestra. We'd shown him we were too strong to be told what to do."

Late Thursday afternoon, September 30, John Bitove, Jr., wasn't in his office to hear the official announcement. He was at his son's soccer practice. JJ was five, and his dad had missed the previous week's practice, and he had promised the boy it wouldn't happen two weeks in a row. But he carried a cellular phone, and his secretary relayed the NBA's message. He had his quiet moment of triumph at the side of the soccer field. There were problems ahead that he couldn't know about: the deal for the site of the Stadium at Bay and Dundas would fall through and the NBA would set the franchise fee at a whopping $125 million (U.S.). But for now he felt only relief, satisfaction, and joy. Later in the evening, he would celebrate with Randi and the Bitove family over dinner at Wayne Gretzky's. He'd celebrate the franchise victory, and he'd celebrate another event. September 30 was his birthday. The kid had turned thirty-three.

5

SETTING UP SHOP

Brett Bitove spoke it first.

"Daddy," he said one day in the winter of 1994, "I like raptors. That's what you could call the team."

"Really?" John Bitove answered his four-year-old son absently. "That's nice."

A generation gap was at work in this brief exchange. Raptors, as a name, as an animal, as an entity, as anything, didn't mean much to John Bitove. But Brett was one of millions of little kids who had been entranced by the Steven Spielberg movie *Jurassic Park*. The raptors, or velociraptors, as they were called officially, were the movie's stars. Small compared with other members of the dinosaur family, they were about the size of a leopard, but quick, smart, and vicious. At the beginning of the movie, the palaeontologist played by Sam Neill explained to the chubby ten-year-old boy that raptors attacked in coordinated patterns and ate their prey alive. Kids in the audience felt delicious shivers of excitement at that, and it got even better when the raptors turned out to look adorable as well as scary. John Bitove didn't know about this. All he knew was that he had to find a catchy name for his new basketball team.

A couple of weeks after the conversation with Brett, Bitove heard from the NBA's Creative Services people in New York. Creative Services worked on helping the league's teams develop marketing plans for their merchandise; selling basketball gear around the world was an NBA-wide enterprise, and Creative Services, among its other duties, helped to guide new teams towards names and logos that would attract the kids and families who purchased the merchandise that bore the names and logos.

"In our research," the man from Creative Services told Bitove on the phone, "we're getting a lot of strong reaction to the name Raptors."

"*Raptors!*" Bitove said. "My kid's already mentioned that one."

Other names were tossed into the mix. Beavers. Bobcats. Scorpions. T-Rex. Tarantula. Bitove put them to various tests.

Chris Galt, an executive at Cossette Communications, organized a focus group made up of kids aged ten to twelve, all boys. For $75 each, the boys sat in a room at Cossette for a couple of hours and mulled over five possible names for a basketball team.

"The boys went for Raptors all the way," Galt says.

So did the voters in a nation-wide contest that Bitove set up through outlets in Sears stores and Cineplex–Odeon theatres. Out of approximately 150,000 ballots cast, 24 per cent of the voters chose Raptors. Bobcats and Dragons came next, with 15 and 14 per cent of the vote.

Bitove invited the presidents of the three leading makers of sports apparel in the U.S. to check out the Raptor name and the logo that went with it. These men, from Nutmeg Mills, Starter, and Pro Player, would be manufacturing the caps and windbreakers and other clothing with the Toronto team's name and colours. How did Raptors strike them? What about the colours – red, silver, purple, black?

The three experts had advice on the colours, on which shades were impossible to duplicate on clothing, which colours simply didn't sell to buyers. Bitove absorbed all the words of wisdom.

And then David Beckerman, the head of Starter, dropped in a personal opinion.

"You know," Beckerman said to Bitove, "if you go with Raptors for a name, you people will either be geniuses or the biggest putzes who ever lived."

Bitove shrugged. "It's not me who wants it. It's the kids."

On May 15, 1994, Bitove announced that the new Toronto basketball team would be called, just as Brett Bitove had advised his daddy months earlier, the Raptors.

Somewhere along the line, Isiah Thomas picked up good manners. At a point between his childhood in the Chicago inner city and his mature years as the star point guard of the Detroit Pistons, he learned about courtesy calls. And that was what he was making one night in late April 1994.

Thomas wanted to thank the people who had a say in naming him to Dream Team II, the élite collection of twelve NBA players who would represent the United States at the World Basketball Championships in Toronto that summer. Thomas's selection had now become moot, because, a couple of weeks earlier in a Detroit game against Orlando, he had torn his Achilles tendon. He couldn't play. But he was still dialling around to express his thanks.

One call went to John Bitove. As the organizer of the Worlds, Bitove had been invited to chip in ideas on the makeup of the American team, and he had plumped for Thomas, as well as Thomas's backcourt teammate on the Pistons, Joe Dumars. It was ten o'clock at night when Thomas reached Bitove at his office. The two men had never before met, never talked.

"Well, I'll be blatant about it," Bitove said after Thomas offered his thank-you speech. "We were kind of using you in the Worlds, because the Pistons are the most popular NBA team in Toronto, and, between you and Joe Dumars, we thought it'd help draw crowds. So, I appreciate your call, but I want you to know I had other motives."

Thomas laughed at that, and, after a few minutes of chat, Bitove decided he felt so comfortable with this superstar basketball player on the other end of the line that he would bring up the matter that was keeping him at the office so late into the night.

"The part about this new team that's the scariest for me," he said, "is hiring a general manager. If you were me, if you were hiring a GM, what traits would you be looking for in the guy?"

Thomas didn't hesitate. It was as if Bitove had raised a subject to which he'd already given a lot of thought. "The man you want has got to be more progressive than most teams have today," he began. "The NBA's grown so much on the business side, but, on the basketball side, it's lagging behind. Teams don't go about scouting in the right ways. There aren't enough European players in the league. Teams don't hire assistant coaches with any system. There's too much old-guard attitude in putting together staffs. There have to be new ways of attacking all the different issues."

Thomas and Bitove talked for an hour and a half, and all of the conversation centred on the single subject: what makes a good general manager of a basketball team?

"When we finally hung up," Bitove says, "there was a definite feeling that our minds had connected over the telephone lines."

Isiah Lord Thomas III was the seventh son of a seventh son. Altogether, there were nine children in the family, seven boys and two girls, and Isiah was the youngest. His father left the family home when Isiah was three years old, and he was raised by his mother, Mary. The family lived in a series of houses in a desperate neighbourhood called K-town on Chicago's west side, K-town because the names of its streets started with K – Keeler, Kostner, Kedvale, Kilbourn. Everything for the Thomases was in short supply – money, space, food. For a time, Isiah slept on an ironing board, and a dinnertime staple was the "choke" sandwich, made of stale bread and aged meat. It beat the "wish" sandwich, same bread and nothing in between but you wish there were.

Isiah, the precious baby of the family, found he had positives going for him in these grim surroundings. A remarkably sheltering mother. A prodigious talent for basketball. The urgings of local drug addicts and guys on the street – one of them his own brother – that he not end up in their shoes. And, among other positives, Isiah won a scholarship to a Catholic boys' school called St. Joseph's in the plush suburb of Westchester.

St. Joseph's later won fame of sorts in the 1994 documentary film *Hoop Dreams*. It was the school where the two slightly hapless inner-city innocents, the movie's central characters, tried out their basketball talents. Isiah, not hapless at all, had been there more than fifteen years before the kids in the movie. From K-town to St. Joseph's took a bus ride with two transfers and a mile walk. Isiah travelled the route twice daily on the round trips. He brought the school a basketball championship; it helped him to a basketball scholarship at Indiana University.

John Bitove, Jr., saw Thomas at Indiana – but from a distance, from the stands in the basketball arena. Bitove, the fellow student, watched Thomas, in his sophomore year, lead Indiana to the 1981 NCAA championship.

"I gotta be that guy's agent," Bitove told everyone in the family. "He's going big places."

In later years, John junior never mentioned his earlier epiphany to Thomas. But John senior would give it away. "Agent?" Thomas said. "Partners is better."

Thomas left school early, after his sophomore year (though he later returned to Indiana in the summers and completed his degree in criminal justice) to turn professional with the Detroit Pistons. He found, in the Pistons, an organization in disarray. After the 1986 season, after Atlanta routinely defeated Detroit in the first round of the playoffs, Thomas could stand his team's lack of pride no longer. He went to the owner, a man named William Davidson, who had made his fortune by turning around ailing companies and who had acquired the basketball team in 1974.

"We have no tradition, no heritage, no nothing here," Thomas, the kid guard, told Davidson, the sixtyish tycoon. "For us to be successful, it's got to *mean* something to be a Piston."

Davidson built the team a grand suburban stadium, the Palace in Auburn Hills, and he reinvigorated the front office. To Thomas, this was more like it. He had got himself to the NBA for one purpose, to win the championship, and, whatever it took, he was willing to put himself on the line. Talk to the owner? No problem. Rearrange the team roster? He'd take a shot at that, too, even if he was just a player.

It was Thomas who was widely regarded as the motivator for a February 15, 1989, trade that sent Detroit's high-scoring-but-skittish forward Adrian Dantley to Dallas for Thomas's childhood Chicago buddy Mark Aguirre. The thinking behind the trade was strategic; without Dantley, Dennis Rodman, a much-needed defensive force, became a starter, and Aguirre, a fine clutch shooter, came off the bench to provide the points. It made exquisite sense to everyone except the Dantley family, who called Thomas many unflattering names.

Above all, Thomas was prepared to lay his body down for a championship. That became most strikingly apparent in the NBA final of 1988, the Pistons versus the Los Angeles Lakers. In the third game of the series, Thomas fell on his tail bone. He was in agonizing pain, but he took medication and managed 10 points, 12 assists, and 9 rebounds. After game five, his wife, Lynn, gave birth to the couple's first child, Joshua. No pain there, not for the father, but definitely a distraction. Thomas went into game six with a sprained ankle, a dislocated finger, a sore knee, a cut cheek, and a poked eye. He scored forty-three points in the game, but, with twenty-eight seconds left and the Pistons up by one, 102–101, Thomas, limping and aching, missed an eighteen-foot jumper, and the Lakers came back to win, 103–102. In the seventh and deciding game, Thomas got ten points in the first half, but his ankle stiffened so severely that he could play little and score not at all in the second half. The Lakers won the game by three points and took the championship.

The following year, in the final, Detroit wiped out the Lakers in four straight games. Thomas had his NBA title, and, a year later, with Detroit beating Portland in five games in the final, he had another.

Thomas wasn't the dominant point guard of his era. Magic Johnson of the Lakers wore that crown. Thomas won plenty of honours – *Sporting News* Rookie of the Year, selection to twelve straight All-Star games, MVP in the 1990 NBA final – but it might be argued that he was too often over-looked. All he did was lead the Pistons to a lot of victories. And yet, in the category of individual recognition, he was, for example, passed up as a member of the first Dream Team that went, most famously, to the 1992 Barcelona Olympics. As point guards, the U.S. Olympic basketball selec-tion committee named, as expected, Magic Johnson, and, as not neces-sarily expected, Utah's John Stockton. Did Thomas feel slighted? In a game between Detroit and Utah shortly after the Olympic announce-ment, he burned Stockton for forty-four points.

On January 7, 1994, while Thomas was still a player, the Pistons called a press conference to announce that Isiah would be "a Piston for life." Implied in the arrangement was that Thomas would be permitted to buy a team-ownership slice after his retirement and to assume an unspecified management role.

That seemed appropriate. Thomas had already demonstrated his busi-ness and leadership skills in other areas. For six years, he had served as president of the NBA Players' Association, guiding the way to a meaning-ful pension scheme for former NBA players. And, in the non-basketball sector, among other investments, he got into OmniBanc, a Detroit bank holding company, and American Speedy Printing Centers, a franchisor of six hundred print shops. In such ways, Thomas had made himself a wealthy man, a man of influence, but the deal with the Pistons, as sensible as it seemed, went sour within a few months. All Thomas will say is that "the business of business got in the way."

But what the failed arrangement meant was that, after Thomas ripped his Achilles tendon in April 1994, after he decided that, in any event, he had lost his passion for playing basketball, after he had made up his mind to retire, he was available to John Bitove, Jr., if Bitove had something in mind.

In the two weeks following his telephone conversation with Thomas, Bitove called around the league to canvass other views of the man who had so intrigued him.

"People told me three things about Isiah," Bitove said later. "They told me he's intelligent. They told me he's competitive. And they told me he takes no prisoners. Some people have a problem with that last one. It's not cool with some people to want to win so badly. But it turned me on."

Bitove rang Thomas in Detroit. "Maybe we should talk," he said.

"Yeah," Thomas answered. "Maybe we should."

They arranged a meeting.

"In that conversation on the phone," Bitove says, "neither of us said what it was we should talk *about*. But we both knew."

The two men got together in a Detroit hotel room. Thomas had a few questions, a couple of conditions. He wanted the option of buying a piece of the Raptors' ownership. That wasn't a difficulty. Bitove and Thomas fell into comfortable agreement: Thomas would run the Toronto team's basketball.

And a few days later, on May 24, Isiah Thomas was introduced to the Toronto media as executive vice-president, basketball, of the Toronto Raptors.

Jay Cross's first assignment with the Raptors was a toughie. Bitove hired Cross in late July 1994 as the team's stadium project manager. Cross, who had a career in real-estate management and development with Prudential Insurance and Markborough Properties (and who had been a member of the Canadian Olympic yachting team in 1976, 1980, and

1984), was in charge of putting up the basketball stadium at Bay and Dundas. Except he thought it should go somewhere else. So, for that matter, did John Bitove.

There were three reasons for this view.

One, Cadillac–Fairview, the Raptors' partner in the Bay–Dundas stadium, was experiencing a tough financial period and might make a shaky associate in the deal.

Two, Cross had discovered the availability of the property occupied by the Post Office Building at 40 Bay Street. The building had been designed by Charles Dolphin, the man responsible for the fine old Toronto Stock Exchange, and it was distinguished by its bas-relief limestone sculptures, featuring scenes of communication and travel. It also happened to be vacant and on the market, and, since it occupied six acres of downtown land that was handy to the subway, the GO train, and plenty of parking lots, the property added up to a choice location for the basketball stadium.

And, three, the Bay–Dundas site didn't allow sufficient space to put up a combined basketball–hockey facility.

The last reason reflected a fundamental shift in thinking around the Raptors offices. From the beginning, the idea was that the stadium would be for one sport only – basketball. That idea had been revised. Now Bitove, Cross, and some others looked on hockey – whether it was the Toronto Maple Leafs or a minor pro club – as a welcome partner. In large part, the new approach had its origins in a radical design that architect Murray Beynon had come up with.

"Traditionally," Bitove explains, "stadiums in North America are built for hockey first, and then basketball gets squeezed in. That's even true of brand-new stadiums like the United Center in Chicago. Since a hockey surface is much longer than one for basketball, two hundred feet compared to less than one hundred, it means that, for basketball, you get all sorts of seating compromises. You get especially terrible seats at each end, which is what we were going to avoid with a basketball-only facility. Then Murray showed us his fantastic new concept."

Beynon's design incorporated a system of sliding banks of seats at each end, which would roll back for hockey and forward for basketball. The result would be an engagingly intimate feel for basketball fans, with the worst end seats eliminated altogether and with the least-expensive seats in the entire stadium no more than 170 feet from the court. By contrast, fans in the cheap seats at Chicago's United Center are the length of a football field away from at least one of the two baskets on the floor. At the same time, with Beynon's design, hockey fans would get the good sightlines and proximity to the ice that traditional hockey arenas provide.

"What we're *not* doing," Bitove says, "is relegating hockey to second place the way other arenas have always put basketball in a subordinate position."

At a meeting of the Raptors board of directors on September 20, 1994, Jay Cross made his presentation. Forget Dundas–Bay. Set the sights on the Post Office property. And go for a combined basketball-hockey design. Nobody could find reason to question the rethinking, and the objective became to get the new stadium up and running at 40 Bay Street in time for the 1997-98 NBA season.

In the meantime, for the first couple of seasons, from the Raptors' first game in November 1995 through to the beginning of the 1997-98 season, the Raptors would play their home games at the SkyDome.

"Nobody would ever mistake the SkyDome for a great place to watch basketball," Bitove said. "But it worked for the World Basketball Championships, and it'll work for a couple of NBA seasons."

In late November of 1994, Isiah Thomas had been settled into his job as the Raptors' basketball boss for almost six months. He hadn't exactly settled into Toronto, since his family – wife, Lynn, and children, Joshua and Lauren – stayed behind in the Detroit suburb of Bloomfield Hills, in the home that Thomas had bought in 1987. Thomas planned to build a house in Toronto, on Old Colony Road in the tony north Bayview Road area, and, for the short term, he had set up digs in the Westin Harbour Castle Hotel and was spending long hours at the Raptors offices developing a philosophical approach to building a team.

Thomas is a shade over six feet, in trim physical shape, possessed of a sweet smile, unblinking brown eyes, and an encompassing sense of calm. He's also a man who likes to talk, not dominating the conversation, just making his positions clear. Often, without any particular prompting, he lets thoughts of a semi-aphoristic nature float into his talk, seemingly random comments that usually have nothing to do with basketball.

"Here's what'll help kill racism in the world – cyberspace. You get people communicating on the Internet, they'll only be paying attention to one another's ideas and jokes, what they have to say. They won't be looking at the person and thinking to themselves, 'Oh, this guy is black. I'd better adopt a certain attitude.'"

Or, "I was asked to speak to the black community in Toronto. But they're Caribbean. They're different from me. What advice can I give them? Just because I have the same colour skin, what can I tell them?"

A similar current of analysis, after six months at his Raptors desk, ran through Thomas's ideas about the ways to shape the basketball team. He had done much homework, partly a matter of calling on men who had successfully managed teams in other sports, in hockey and football as well as in basketball, and sorting through their experiences to find the ones that made sense in his own situation. And then he began to move from theoretical to practical.

"Chemistry comes first," he said. "I have to hire people in the office that I'm compatible with from every angle, people I can work with, have fun with, on a daily basis, people I can disagree with, fight with, and can still say to myself afterwards, yeah, I can stomach that person under all conditions. I have to have that kind of chemistry flowing through the office, because it's the same chemistry I'll get on the basketball floor playing every night. One flows into the other."

Commitment, Thomas went on, was next, a commitment to a specific goal. Thomas knew what that goal was.

"Suppose a new team sets an objective that it wants to make the second round of the playoffs. So they build for ten years and make the objective and *lose* in the second round. What good is that? Our focus is to win the NBA championship. Nothing less. Then it comes down to how committed we are to getting the job done. It isn't a matter of who the best players are. It's a process of wearing the other guys down, wearing the other organizations down."

Thomas offered a particular instance of commitment in the NBA: the New York Knicks, the team that had reached the previous spring's final, though they lost in seven games to Houston.

"The Knicks are clearly not the most talented team in the league. Patrick Ewing at centre is their one talented guy. Then they have Charles Oakley at power forward. He has very limited skills in terms of running and athleticism. At small forward, Anthony Mason and Charles Smith, they're okay. The same goes for the different guys at guard, Greg Anthony, Rolando Blackman, John Starks, all okay. Just okay. But what makes the Knicks win is that their coach, Pat Riley, has got twelve guys bonded and committed to winning. In the course of an eighty-two-game season, some teams quit. Their attitude changes during the long season. Guys start to miss free throws, guys you counted on to be there aren't around. They've quit on the floor. Their commitment has disappeared. But the Knicks are an example of a team without great talent that has stayed committed."

Thomas has also decided that, in picking the guys who would eventually play for the Raptors, he would be prepared to accept players who were, in his word, "untraditional." Again, he had a specific example of this type.

"Chris Webber. He's the guy in college who started the thing about the long baggy shorts that everybody wears now. Chris Webber is a forward who doesn't have the fundamentals, doesn't have a good shot, doesn't have the low-post moves. He doesn't fit the traditional system of basketball. But he still goes out and gets you twenty points and fifteen rebounds every night. Now, what happened to Chris Webber is that Golden State got him, after a trade, as the second pick in the college draft. Golden State watched him play for them in the first year, and, even though he was getting his points and rebounds, Golden State said, We don't like Chris because he doesn't fit into the traditional way of playing basketball that we like. So they traded him to Washington for Tom Gugliotta. Okay, Tom's nice. He's got good postup moves, can hit the outside shot, won't cause you any trouble in the community. Very traditional. But Webber is still the guy who goes out and gets twenty points and fifteen rebounds every night. The moral is that a basketball organization has to be flexible enough to incorporate the Webber type of talent into the team, because that's the type that is coming out of the schools today. Untraditional players in long baggy pants."

Isiah Thomas was thinking of hiring Brendan Malone. This was in the summer of 1994, and the job Thomas had in mind for Malone was not head coach of the Raptors. The two men had been associated for six years on the Detroit Pistons, Thomas as player, Malone as assistant coach, and

Thomas respected Malone's eye for basketball talent. He thought Malone might make a good director of scouting for the Raptors, a guy who would get out and assess the college players and, as well, do a little Raptors assistant coaching. Thomas thought about Malone for the job, but ultimately backed away from that idea and hired Bob Zuffelato instead. Zuffelato had been around the NBA for a number of years, with experience both as an assistant coach for three teams and as a front-office guy, a director of player personnel for the Milwaukee Bucks. He got the Raptors' scouting post.

But, in May 1995, Thomas thought about Malone again. On the week-end of May 27 and 28, in the gym at Seneca College, a community college on the northern edges of Metro Toronto, the Raptors were holding a camp for free-agent players. These were players who might be good enough for the NBA but had contracts with no team. Thomas needed someone to run the camp, to put the players through their paces and keep things turning over smoothly while he sat on the sidelines and checked out the camp's participants as possibilities for the Raptors. He called Malone and asked him to handle the task. Malone agreed. He was just getting packed to leave on a family holiday, but he was also a man out of work. The Pistons had cleared house to make way for a new head coach, Doug Collins, and Malone wasn't in a position to turn down a weekend gig that – who knew? – might lead to a permanent job.

Thomas was amazed at how beautifully Malone conducted the two-day free-agent camp.

"He was very organized," Thomas remembers. "He showed presence. He had command with the players. He had their respect, and it opened my eyes."

At the time, Thomas still hadn't hired a head coach for the Raptors. He'd approached a few people. He had spoken to Kevin McHale, the former Boston Celtic who was an old Thomas friend (even if the two men played for teams, Boston and Detroit, that were bitter rivals through the 1980s), but McHale, back in his home state of Minnesota, had a job he was committed to as assistant vice-president of basketball operations with the Timberwolves. Thomas had interviewed Jim Cleamons, assistant coach of the Chicago Bulls, but Cleamons wanted too much money to join the Raptors. Other candidates occurred to

Thomas, but, as of the weekend of May 27 and 28, he had no one nailed down for the job.

That was the background as the training camp finished up late on the Sunday. What happened next, what thought processes Thomas and Malone went through, who said what, who advanced the notion that Malone might fill the bill as head coach, remains slightly murky.

"For some reason," Malone said later, "Isiah said he was thinking of hiring me as coach."

That seems an overly coy remembrance of events. Malone, a blunt Irishman, must have been more aggressive in advancing his own cause than he suggests. Still, Thomas was the boss, the guy who could dangle the coaching job. He was also the man who had considered hiring Malone a year earlier, albeit for another job, and he was the man who was freshly impressed with Malone's leadership talents.

"I knew there'd be a lot of pain in the first years as an expansion team," Thomas says, "and Brendan was someone who was both a good teacher and a person who could get through the tough times and get the players through the tough times."

Thomas told Malone on Sunday that he had one more candidate to talk to and that he would get back to Malone by Wednesday of that week. Malone returned to Detroit. He and his wife, Maureen, still had a holiday to organize.

On Wednesday, Thomas phoned Malone. "Be here on Friday," he said. "We're holding a press conference."

And that was the day, Friday, June 2, 1995, when Brendan Malone was introduced as the first head coach of the Toronto Raptors.

"So," Malone says, "we never really finished our family vacation."

In the matter of stocking up on players, the NBA didn't make it easy on Toronto and Vancouver as the two teams entered the league. For the new clubs, for their first year, the salary cap – the limit on the total amount that teams could pay in a year to all its players – was set at $15.2 million, which was a mere two-thirds of the cap for the existing teams. In the annual draft of college players, Toronto and Vancouver were barred from holding the number-one pick for their first four years of operation. And, in the expansion draft, the process by which the two new teams selected players from the existing clubs, those twenty-seven teams could protect from the draft their top eight players. All of these restrictions meant that Toronto and Vancouver had limited money to operate with and a limited pool of players to choose from.

Still, after the expansion draft on June 24, Isiah Thomas was satisfied that, given the limitations, he and his staff had put together the beginnings of a quality roster. The key move was a trade that Thomas worked out in conjunction with the draft. He traded the player whom the Raptors chose with their number-one pick to the Golden State Warriors for a total of five players. The man Thomas traded was B. J. Armstrong, a shooting guard from the Chicago Bulls and clearly the prize of the expansion draft. But, in return for Armstrong, Thomas got five players who were much younger than the twenty-eight-year-old Armstrong, players who had the potential to develop into solid contributors to an expansion team.

Adding in the five from the trade, the Raptors emerged from the expansion draft with eighteen players. It was a roster that was heavy on big men, on centres and power forwards, and short on point guards. In fact, there was just a single player, B. J. Tyler from the Philadelphia 76ers, who had the potential to start at the point in the NBA. This seemed a serious gap in the Raptors' early makeup.

But Isiah Thomas had someone in mind to fill the gap.

The draft of college players in which all of the NBA teams would take part was scheduled for June 28. Shortly before that date, Thomas flew a young man into Toronto. This visit didn't take place precisely under a cone of silence, but neither did Thomas trumpet the event. The Raptors held the seventh pick in the college draft, and, when the media quizzed Thomas and other Raptors executives about which player they favoured, various names were bandied about. Kevin Garnett looked interesting, the big high-school kid from Chicago who was bypassing college and entering the draft. Thomas and the Raptors mentioned Garnett with much praise. They talked about Cherokee Parks, the centre from the University of North Carolina, and there was passing reference to Ed O'Bannon, the UCLA forward. But when reporters brought up Damon Stoudamire, the point guard from the University of Arizona, people around the Raptors offices got a little vague. Probably not a high pick, they said, probably not a strong possibility for the Raptors. Of course, if a reporter discovered that Isiah Thomas, one of the all-time great point guards, was really high on Damon Stoudamire, likewise a point guard, then everyone's interest, the media's, other NBA teams', would perk up. So, when Thomas flew Stoudamire to Toronto before the draft, he preferred to do it on the quiet.

Thomas and Brendan Malone had breakfast with Stoudamire in the lobby restaurant at the Westin Harbour Castle. They already knew plenty about the young guy. They'd watched him play on TV or in person, studied the Raptors' scouting reports, reviewed videos of his Arizona games. But talking to him at the Harbour Castle, getting to know him, seeing him up close, they warmed right up to the kid. He was bright, keen on an NBA career, and – this was the part that most got to the older basketball men – he exuded self-assurance. Without being a pain in the neck about it, the kid had confidence in his own basketball talents.

"When I came out of the restaurant behind Damon," Malone remembers, "he was walking up the steps on his tiptoes, and I could hear 'Yankee Doodle Dandy' in my head, because he reminded me so much of Jimmy Cagney playing George M. Cohan in the movie. Of course Damon, being a kid, didn't know who Jimmy Cagney was. I told him, and he said, 'Well, this Cagney must have been a tough guy.'"

Malone and Thomas took Stoudamire to a basketball court at the University of Toronto and put him through a workout. Stoudamire ran the floor, shot the ball, displayed his quickness and his skills. On the sidelines, Thomas oohed and Malone aahed.

"What Damon showed us," Malone says of that time in the U. of T. gym, "was, with his speed, his talent, his confidence, he was the whole package at point guard."

The NBA college draft took place on a Wednesday afternoon, June 28, at the SkyDome. It was a gala event – international TV coverage, twenty thousand fans in the building, David Stern presiding over the announcement of the selections, all the potential top picks waiting in the green room with their moms and their agents.

Golden State had the first pick and chose Joe Smith, a forward from the University of Maryland. The process worked purposefully through the list. Kevin Garnett, the Chicago high-school kid, went fifth to Minnesota, and then the Vancouver Grizzlies, picking sixth, chose a huge centre from

Oklahoma State named Bryant Reeves. Now the excitement level rose in the SkyDome. It was the Raptors' turn, and almost everyone in the building, all the fans, expected Toronto to choose Ed O'Bannon. They *knew* Ed O'Bannon. He was the forward who had led UCLA to the NCAA championship a few weeks earlier. It had to be O'Bannon. He was a star.

All of a sudden, David Stern was standing on the platform, in front of the TV cameras, with this husky little guy, practically a midget compared with the giants who'd gone before him. And this kid, way under six feet, he was the Raptors' draft choice. The fans in the SkyDome couldn't believe it.

Boooo!

The fans gave Damon Stoudamire the raspberry. Damon Stoudamire? Where was Ed O'Bannon? (He later went to the New Jersey Nets as the ninth pick.) Where was *anybody* the fans had heard of? Not this pipsqueak kid. The fans didn't *know* Damon Stoudamire.

But Isiah Thomas and Brendan Malone knew him, which, for the moment, was all that mattered.

On July 1, in a labour dispute, the NBA owners locked out the players. The argument between the teams and the NBA Players' Association centred mainly on the size of the payments to players in the sale of various NBA rights and on a cap on salaries for rookie players. Since the two sides took positions at almost opposite extremes, the lockout threatened to be a long one, possibly even threatening the 1995-96 schedule. There might be a whole season with no NBA basketball.

During the lockout, everything for the Raptors, as for the other teams, went on hold. No trades, no signing of free-agent players, no summer leagues where present or future Raptors could strut their stuff. It was a stagnant period and a particular handicap for a new team in its first building phase. "I didn't feel like a real coach as long as the lockout was on," Brendan Malone says. And Isiah Thomas ran into a personal problem. He had sunk a hole in the ground for his new house on Old Colony Road, started putting in the basement. But with the lockout, who knew what would happen? He called off construction, and later got rid of the lot. When things became more stable, somewhere down the line, he'd *buy* a house.

On September 18, the lockout ended, not without bitterness on many players' parts, and the Raptors got into gear. By the time the team went to training camp at Copps Coliseum in Hamilton on October 6, Thomas had added six new free agents. Altogether, through the expansion draft and the college draft, through free agency and the Golden State trade, Malone and his assistant coaches had twenty-two players to assess. The assistants were three: Bob Zuffelato, the man who also served as director of scouting; John Shumate, a Notre Dame graduate who had played in the NBA for seven years and had coached in college ball, most recently as head coach at Southern Methodist University; and Darrell Walker, a veteran of eleven years in the NBA, one of them with Malone and Isiah Thomas at Detroit, who was taking his first coaching job of any sort with the Raptors.

At training camp, the coaches discovered that there were no absolute stiffs among the players. But circumstances took some guys out of the picture. In Thomas Hamilton's case, avoirdupois was the circumstance. He was a very tall young man, seven-foot-three. Also a very heavy young man, about four hundred pounds. "There's a player inside that body," Malone said when the Raptors waived Hamilton.

Injuries were another circumstance. B. J. Tyler, the point guard acquired in the expansion draft, fell asleep with an ice bag strapped to his sore left leg. When he woke up, the leg burned and throbbed. The doctors told him the ice bag had done nerve damage to the leg. B. J. couldn't play basketball on that leg, not for a while.

Tony Massenburg's injury came about in a more conventional way. Massenburg was a power forward, the Raptors' second choice after B. J. Armstrong in the expansion draft, and, in a pre-season game against the Vancouver Grizzlies in Winnipeg, he came down hard and awkwardly on his left foot. A bone was broken in it, and Massenburg was put on the shelf for several weeks.

Some players, during the pre-season, almost *played* – or non-played – themselves off the team. Ed Pinckney was one of these. He was the power forward, the Raptors' tenth choice in the expansion draft, a veteran who should have wrapped up a spot on the team's roster. "But he had vanished out there, doing nothing that you'd notice," Malone says. Malone took Pinckney aside for a chat, and in the Raptors' first pre-season game, against the Philadelphia 76ers in Halifax, Pinckney went in for Massenburg in the later part of the game and produced seven points and seven rebounds. Now he was more visible.

Malone and Isiah Thomas seriously disagreed over one player during the pre-season. He was Chris Whitney, a point guard whom Thomas had picked up as a free agent. Malone liked Whitney. He liked him so much that, early on, before Damon Stoudamire found his stride, Malone called Whitney the best point guard in training camp. Malone wanted Whitney on the permanent team as backup at the point. Stoudamire would start, Whitney would give him breathers. Isiah Thomas disagreed.

Thomas had a couple of reasons for his position. For one thing, there were salary-cap complications. Of the players he had signed, thirteen had contracts requiring that they be paid for the length of their contracts – whether they made the team or not. If the Raptors didn't keep them, Thomas essentially had three options: trade them – if they were tradable; make a deal to buy out their contracts; or pay them not to play, thus adding to the amount that built up under the salary cap. Chris Whitney's salary would be in the low range, well below a million dollars, but it would add to the money under the cap.

Thomas's second reason was that he wanted other, younger guys to get experience as backup point guard. Jimmy King was one, and perhaps Martin Lewis was another. King, twenty-two years old, had come from the University of Michigan as Toronto's second-round choice in the college draft, and, though his experience was mainly at shooting guard, he was a good ball handler who might develop at the point. Martin Lewis was even younger than King, a twenty-year-old kid fresh out of Seward County Community College in Liberal, Kansas. Thomas had acquired him in the trade with Golden State, and he was another youngster whom Thomas wanted to see in NBA play, possibly at point guard, during the regular season. The idea, as Thomas said to Malone, was to give the kids some action on the floor, expose them to the NBA, judge whether they're real players. That was how an expansion team got built, by putting everybody on the floor, by sorting out the guys who made a real team.

So Chris Whitney was waived from the Raptors, and Brendan Malone didn't especially like it.

In such ways, over the course of the training camp and the pre-season games, from October 6 to the final cut-down day on November 2, the Raptors arrived at their first roster of players. These were the twelve guys who would dress for the opening game, plus four others whom the team could retain under various legitimate league pretexts.

In the latter category, B. J. Tyler and Tony Massenburg went on the injured list. So did Vincenzo Esposito, a free agent from the Italian league. Martin Lewis was suspended with pay, which meant he could stick around Toronto, draw his salary, and stand by to be called into action. One of the players who was waived, Dwayne Whitfield, was also promised a future spot. He was another player who'd arrived in the Golden State trade, a twenty-three-year-old power forward who showed signs of developing into the real thing.

The twelve-man roster included both of the young guys who came in the college draft, Damon Stoudamire and Jimmy King. Then there were two players from the deal with Golden State, small forward Carlos Rogers and centre forward Victor Alexander, though the latter seemed to have problems; he was a tad on the heavy side, and, earlier, when Isiah Thomas had tried to trade him to the Cleveland Cavaliers for a guard named Harold Miner, the deal had been cancelled after Cleveland doctors ran an MRI of Alexander's right leg and found a ruptured tendon he had never noticed.

Of the players Thomas selected in the expansion draft, six made the team. Ed Pinckney was one. Small forward Willie Anderson and power forward John Salley were two more. All three of these men were NBA veterans, either over thirty years old (Pinckney and Salley) or close to it (Anderson). Oliver Miller, Acie Earl, and Zan Tabak, all capable of playing centre or power forward, formed the younger contingent. John Bitove had been pulling for Tabak to make the final roster. "He's Croatian," Bitove explained, "and we've got a big Croatian community in Toronto that loves basketball."

The last two players, the ones who rounded off the team, both arrived in Toronto by way of free agency. One was another over-thirty veteran, shooting guard Alvin Robertson, and the other was the twenty-five-year-old small forward Tracy Murray. He arrived late with the team, so late that he didn't make the first edition of the Raptors' media guide, and his arrival made a story instructive in the ways, sometimes quick and instinctive, that a basketball team is put together.

On November 1, Isiah Thomas was late for lunch in the dining room at the SkyDome Hotel. The men who were waiting for Thomas could catch glimpses of their man through the dining-room window. He was way off to the right and down below on the basketball court on the SkyDome's floor, and he was talking with one last player left on the court, talking to the player and watching him shoot baskets.

When Thomas arrived in the dining room, he ordered a glass of orange juice and identified the player down on the court.

"That's Tracy Murray," Thomas said. "He just came in last night, and this morning was the first chance we've had to look at him."

And?

"Oh, he's on the team. He's going to be a Raptor."

Just like that? One morning's workout and the guy makes the roster?

"Well, you know, it really doesn't take long to recognize a player. Tracy's a player." Thomas gave his charming smile. "I guess we're just about ready to start the season."

6

THE COACH

Brendan Malone was turning the pages of a book about the Toronto Maple Leafs. He stopped at a photo section, shots of the players from the 1960s, and his finger hovered over the faces in the photographs.

"This guy, this's Allan Stanley," he said. "Here's Frank Mahovlich, the Big M. Johnny Bower. Bob Pulford. Here's Dave Keon in this picture." Malone went on, not misidentifying a single player. "That's Bob Nevin. I remember him when he got traded to New York. They were my team, the Rangers. When I was a kid, I had a dream of playing for them. Playing hockey in the NHL."

Malone grew up, one of four children of Irish immigrants, his dad a freight-car unloader, in the Astoria section of Queens, up at the top of the borough, west of La Guardia Airport. There wasn't a decent hockey rink in the neighbourhood, but a tennis court nearby used to freeze over in the winter. Malone and his pals played on it. And once, one glorious day, a special day for kids in New York who loved hockey, he played at the Garden. Madison Square Garden.

"I wore my father's work gloves with little sticks taped on them for protection," Malone remembers. "And for pads, I used magazines inside my stockings. It was kind of primitive equipment, but the point was, when you finally played ice hockey on nice ice, it was a great thing."

As a kid, Malone played basketball too, and, eventually, when he was sixteen, hockey faded in favour of basketball. He played for his school team, Rice High. And at college, Iona in New York State, he made both the freshman and the varsity teams – as a walk-on, he's careful to point out, not as a recruited player. Brendan Malone wants you to know he wasn't a basketball star.

But he discovered early that he could teach and coach the game. "That's where I really feel like I belong," he says. "In a gym, teaching kids how to play basketball." In his early twenties, he coached CYO basketball in New York City, then moved on, equipped with a master's in physical education from NYU, to a job as phys-ed director and basketball coach at Power Memorial High. It was a solid New York basketball school – Lew Alcindor, later Kareem Abdul-Jabbar, graduated from it shortly before Malone arrived – and, in his nine years at Power, Malone's teams won two city championships. Three times, he was named Coach of the Year.

College basketball programs hear about successful young guys like Malone, and he climbed up the scale of universities from Fordham to Yale to Syracuse, all as an assistant coach. Syracuse put Malone among the big boys, in the major leagues of college basketball. Six years at Syracuse followed, then two as head coach at University of Rhode Island. Malone's reputation for meticulous game planning, for teaching, as an xs and os man, kept spreading. The NBA beckoned, the New York Knicks. Malone was an assistant under a couple of near-genius-level coaches, Hubie Brown and Rick Patino. Another genius type, Chuck Daly, offered him an assistant's position with the Detroit Pistons in the summer of 1988. The timing couldn't have been better.

"We won NBA championships my first two years, two great years," Malone says. "The two years after that, we were competitive, but, in the next three years, we weren't. The teams that won played defence and rebounded. The later teams didn't work on defence, didn't rebound, played selfishly, and didn't win. That's the way it always is in basketball. Selfishness doesn't win."

During his seven years with the Pistons, Malone settled his family into a large house in Birmingham, an upscale community northwest of Detroit. Malone and his wife, Maureen, have six children, ranging in age from the late teens to just thirty. In photographs, the Malone offspring make an extraordinarily handsome group. That would come from Maureen's side of the family. While Malone's face is full of appealing deadpan Irish character, no one would mistake him for an older Liam Neeson. One of the handsome Malone kids is carrying on the family business. He's Michael, an assistant basketball coach at Providence College.

(On the subject of Brendan Malone's appearance, he's one coach who should be exempted from a particular NBA rule. The league, ever-vigilant about image, requires its coaches to wear suits and ties during games. Thus, men in $1,500 Armanis, assistants as well as head coaches, stalk the sidelines. Some coaches, Miami's Pat Riley most obviously, suggest the male models in *Vanity Fair* advertisements. But Malone is one of those guys who doesn't suit, as it were, a suit. In warmup outfits, which he wears at practices and on most other occasions away from the court, he looks positively natty. He looks natural and attractive. But in a suit? His body wasn't built for one. Or maybe he should speak to Pat Riley about a new tailor.)

The major spinoff from Malone's work with the Pistons was, of course, his connection to Isiah Thomas, which led to the Raptors' head-coaching job. In Toronto, Malone lived on his own, without family, in digs at the Westin Harbour Castle Hotel. Maureen remained in Birmingham to be with the youngest Malone, Shannon, while she studied her way through her senior year at high school. It made, Malone said, for a lonely time in Toronto. He took lots of long walks.

But on this special night, Friday, November 3, putting aside the loneliness, joined by his entire family, who travelled to Toronto for the game, he was about to experience one of the proudest moments of his career in basketball. He was stepping onto the floor of the SkyDome for the first time in a regular-season game, his Raptors against the New Jersey Nets, as one of the twenty-nine head coaches in the National Basketball Association.

Four lithe, muscular guys swaggered onto the basketball court dressed in loincloths. They were supposed to represent figures from a prehistoric age, back when dinosaurs roamed the planet. Except, if you looked closely, one of the four guys sported body decor from a much later stage of civilization: tiny rings dangling from his pierced nipples. The four bore on their shoulders a covered platform, a palanquin, and, upon it, there rested a large object shaped like an egg. The bearers made a show – *everything* was a show – of lowering the platform at centre court. A few moments of puzzled suspense hung in the air, while something inside the plastic egg began cracking its way out. The egg split in two, and, from the halves, there emerged, bounding, the Raptor. The team mascot. The fuzzy red thing with the large white incisors, the white Raptors basketball uniform, the white footgear that looked like a cross between furry slippers and Air Jordans.

"Basketball fans!" Herbie Kuhn, the stadium announcer, boomed into his mike. "Meet your *Raptor!*"

The 33,306 people in the SkyDome met a whole lot more before this first NBA basketball game got under way. They met rhythmic gymnasts and a squad of tumblers. They met the Raptor Dance Pack. They met the great-great-grandson of Dr. James Naismith, the YMCA director from Almonte, Ontario, who invented basketball in a gym at Springfield, Massachusetts, in December 1891. The great-great-grandson's name was Jeffrey, and he took part in the night's ceremonial opening tipoff. The band Barenaked Ladies sang "O Canada" *a cappella*, with a couple of lines in French. And the Temptations – minus, of course, the two lates, David Ruffin and Eddie Kendricks – sang "The Star-Spangled Banner." (They also sang, at half time, a more contemporary anthem, "My Girl," with all the over-forties in the crowd – a very large segment – bopping along.) An RCMP colour guard marched across the floor, a giant inflated Raptor hung over the court, fireworks erupted. Noise, balloons, music, spectacle. NBA total entertainment.

Brendan Malone thought all the pre-game whoopee was fabulous. "It was like a Hollywood extravaganza," he says. "I'll remember that night for my whole life." Part of the reason for his delight may have been that he'd felt tight all day, opening-night tension, and the pre-game show offered a small reprieve from the inevitable, from the basketball game. In that spirit, Malone strolled over to the media section, two long levels of tables running from the Raptors bench north to the visiting-team bench. He stopped where a broadcaster from New Jersey had set up, a guy Malone knew from his years around the league.

"You know what?" Malone said. "We should call off the game and play it tomorrow. This is a *great* show."

David Stern was giggling. The giggles, as he watched what was happening at the south end of the floor, erupted into a guffaw. The commissioner and a few other bigwigs from NBA head office in New York had flown to Toronto for the opener, and now Stern was laughing.

It was the balloons that got to him. Not the balloons themselves, long, narrow, twisty ones, but where the balloons were waving. Raptor staff had handed them out to fans in the seats in the south end behind the basket. The idea was that the fans would wave them whenever a Nets player stepped to the foul line for a free throw, thereby distracting the player from his shot. It was a familiar practice in all basketball arenas. But these balloons, in the hands of the fans at the south end, were, for the first half, at the *wrong* end. When the fans waved them, they'd be distracting their own Raptor players, whose offensive basket in that half was the south basket.

"This is a very novel concept for the league, John," Stern said to John Bitove. "Is it something new you're creating in Toronto?"

Stern couldn't resist rubbing it in. "If it works," he said, "we'll have to try it out in the other arenas."

Bitove grinned a little. "Okay, okay."

"Keep me posted on how it goes," Stern said. He wasn't ready to let Bitove forget this one. "You might be on to something."

Ed Pinckney, the Raptor power forward, jumped the ball for the tipoff that began the game. Pinckney had the job because of a couple of circumstances. One was that Oliver Miller, who would normally have started at centre and taken the jump, had been suspended for one game as a result of a small fracas he got into during a pre-season game. And the other was that Zan Tabak, who played centre in Miller's place, wasn't much of a jumper. So Pinckney took the jump, won it, and tipped the ball to Tabak.

Everybody on the floor, the ten players, fell into the nervous scramble for position that seems to come at the beginning of every basketball game. The offence was organizing itself for the first foray into the other guys' end. And the defensive people moved into place, getting a line on the players they were assigned to guard. The game was under way in the measured, careful manner that starts all – almost all – basketball games.

Tabak held the ball for a couple of beats, then passed it to Stoudamire and ran towards the New Jersey basket. Stoudamire took his time, brought the ball carefully into the Nets' zone. Stoudamire was watching his teammates run through a pattern, waiting for a shooter to spring open. Alvin Robertson was at the top of the key, twenty-five feet out from the basket. His man was playing off him, giving Robertson plenty of room, almost daring him to shoot, if he got the chance, from so far out. The ball went to Robertson. He thought about it for a second, thought about shooting, then he put the ball in the air. The shot was good. Three points. The time clock showed 11:83. Only seventeen seconds had gone by since the tipoff, and the Raptors were up by three.

The shot, as things turned out, set the tone. Set the tone for the game and, more particularly, set it for Alvin Robertson. He had a magnificent night of basketball. He was supposed to be a defensive whiz. And he *was* a defensive whiz in this game, keeping his man away from the basket, diving for loose balls, making five steals. But he was also hotter at the offensive end than anyone expected, even Brendan Malone. Maybe it was the encouragement of that first shot. It went in, so Robertson kept on firing. He took fourteen shots during the game, was good on eleven of them, two out of three on three-pointers, six of eight from the free-throw line. That added up to thirty points, high for the Raptors on the night. His seven rebounds were another team high. Robertson was a major reason that the Raptors won their opening game with ease, 94–79, never trailing through the entire four quarters.

It was a wonderful game for Robertson, and who would have dreamed it? After all, the man had spent that morning making an appearance downtown in the criminal courts. Not much happened, just an adjournment of his case and a continuance of his $3,000 bail, but it was part of an ugly episode.

The previous Saturday night, at the SkyDome Hotel, a woman complained that Robertson had assaulted her. The cops charged Robertson, threw him in the slammer, and held him overnight. When he was released on bail the next morning, newspaper photographers greeted him, and the papers ran humiliating pictures of Robertson ducking out of court, Robertson being led by a policeman, Robertson looking wan and sheepish and embarrassed.

This was the point at which the coach, Brendan Malone, became crucial. Was Robertson through as a Raptor? Was basketball through with him? The decision was hardly Malone's alone, but he was part of it.

"Alvin came to me and he asked if he could play," Malone says. "I said,

'Why not?' Just because Alvin was charged didn't mean he was guilty. There's a process to these things. Let it run and, until then, let Alvin play basketball."

And, for the opening game, Robertson played about as well as he ever could.

It was a swell night for Malone. George Rautins kidded him from a row of seats up behind the Raptors' bench. "Hey, Brendan, relax!" George kept yelling. "You're winning! Relax!" Malone heard the shouting, which George kept up on and off for much of the game. "It's your moment, Brendan! Take it easy!" But Malone didn't figure out who the shouter was until the fourth quarter. Then he smiled a broad smile and kidded back. "The only time you relax is when the game's over," he shouted at George.

George Rautins used to be a fine basketball player around Toronto, back in the 1970s. His younger brother Leo was even better. Leo won a scholarship to Syracuse, where Malone coached him. Later, Leo was a first-round draft pick by the Philadelphia 76ers. Later still, beginning on this very night, he was the colour commentator for telecasts of Raptors games. Malone had met George at Leo's wedding; they'd sat at the same table during the reception. He thought George was a great guy. And he got a kick out of George's cheerful razzing at the Nets game.

"It was typical of the way the night went for the team and for me personally," Malone says. "Everything was positive."

After the game, Darrell Walker, the assistant coach, chased down the game ball. He made a small ceremony out of presenting it to the person Walker thought deserved it most. He presented it to Brendan Malone.

Five days later, on November 8, after the Raptors got back to Toronto from their first two games on the road, two losses, in Indianapolis to the Pacers and in Chicago to the Bulls, Malone remained, despite the losses, enthusiastic. Malone's an up-beat guy by nature.

"The Friday night we won against the Nets here, and the very next night, we took it in the ass against the Pacers," Malone said. "The Pacers, you gotta remember, are one of the élite teams in the league, only one win away from the Eastern Conference championship last year, and they went in front of us by twenty-four points in the first half in the Saturday-night game. Then Damon Stoudamire picked us up all by himself in the second half. He started attacking the basket. We called plays that opened up the floor for Damon. We just let him play 'cause I knew their guards couldn't cover Damon one-on-one. He was beating them off the dribble. So we went from twenty-four points down to leading the Pacers by four. It was amazing. I can still see Damon punching the air after we went ahead, the ecstatic look on his face. The kid is really competitive. Well, unfortunately, later in the game, we turned the ball over a lot and finally lost."

The score was Pacers 97, Raptors 89. Stoudamire scored twenty-six points.

"In Chicago, I knew that Michael Jordan was gonna be guarding Damon. Before the game, I said to Damon, 'Damon, you're gonna attack him. Attack Michael Jordan.' And he did. He surprised Michael. He shot over him; he went around him. Michael could *not* guard Damon Stoudamire. Up until the third quarter, we were ahead, and people were sayin', Look at this *expansion* team takin' it to the Bulls. Eventually Michael Jordan did his Superman act on offence, and Chicago won. But that game and the Pacers game set a level for us. It showed we got a team that can be competitive in this league."

Five weeks further on, in the early afternoon of December 13, when Brendan Malone talked about his players, a new emotion seemed to have entered his voice. It might have been admiration, but it sounded more like affection. This could have little to do with winning basketball games; the Raptors' record, though it glowed with a handful of rewarding victories – the one at home over Seattle, for example, another on the road in Vancouver – showed more losses, fifteen, than wins, seven. But if it wasn't success in the W–L columns that accounted for Malone's show of affection, what was it? As best one could judge, as Malone chatted in his raspy monotone, it sprang from the doting pleasure he drew in a group of players who had apparently taken to heart Malone's own belief in hard work and competitive effort.

"Alvin, start with him," Malone said, sitting on a chair at the side of the SkyDome court after practice. "Alvin Robertson missed the first two days of training camp in October, but, after he got there, the intensity level in the whole place shot right up. That's Alvin. Now we're starting to call him 'The Raptor' because he embodies the spirit of the animal on our uniforms. Aggressive, you know, full tilt, a guy you can't ever discourage."

Malone raised his hand and held up one finger, then a second. "Second is Tracy Murray. He wants to show he belongs, because he didn't get to play much at Portland or Houston. So he comes into games and he gets the ball and right away he shoots it. He's impatient. He takes some shots before he's set. But he doesn't *need* to do that. We're gonna go to him *anyhow*. We're gonna get him the ball. He's a shooter. He tries his best to be a defender, but his forte is shooting. He lives for shooting the ball. And he hates coming out of games. He gets very angry when I send somebody in for him. I tell him, Don't try to show me up, just come out of the game and don't piss me off. He apologizes every time he does it, but he keeps on doing it, because he wants to play so bad."

Malone ticked off more players on his fingers. "Damon. Oliver Miller at centre. Willie Anderson, six-foot-seven and he can play the 2 or 3. Tabak backing up at the 4 and the 5. And Eddie Pinckney, what a long way he's come, not doing much in training camp, and now he's probably our most consistent frontline player. He's outstanding as an offensive rebounder. He got there by working hard. It isn't like that with everybody. Carlos Rogers, right now, isn't playing much and he's sulking. But the main group of guys are Alvin and Damon, Pinckney, Miller and Willie, Tabak and Tracy off the bench. Them, I count on."

Malone paused and developed a smile that, for an Irishman, was close to seraphic.

"I *love* that particular team," he said.

7

THE OTHER HALF

As it happened, later on the same day, Wednesday, December 13, there was a gala evening party in celebration of Allan Slaight and Emmanuelle Gattuso, and it was Slaight himself, the co-guest of honour, who, in the end, provided the night's principal entertainment. In his hands, it turned into something clever and dazzling.

This took place at the home of Julian and Anna Porter (he's a litigation lawyer; she's head of Key Porter Books) in the upper-middle-class Moore Park district of Toronto. The occasion was to mark the nuptials of Slaight and Gattuso, which had actually taken place the previous July 17 on Martha's Vineyard. The guest list reflected the media and entertainment side of Slaight's life rather than the basketball side. For example: Norman Jewison (movie director), Allan Fotheringham (columnist), Sylvia Fraser (novelist), Laurier LaPierre (TV personality), Peter Worthington (author and columnist).

After the cheeses, before the coffee, and during the wine, Julian Porter called on Slaight for a display of his magical powers. Slaight announced that he wasn't going to perform conventional stuff on this night. He was going to do something called mind transference. That got the room's attention.

The show began with Slaight appropriating eight books, apparently chosen at random, from the Porter shelves. He picked his way among the guests and distributed the eight books to eight people, also apparently chosen at random.

"Open your books to a place," Slaight commanded the eight. "Any place. You choose it. Each person select your own spot . . . Okay, got it? Everybody on a place? . . . All right, all I ask of each of you is that you concentrate on the top paragraph of the page on the left side. Now, don't memorize the paragraph. Just read it to yourself and get the general gist of it in your minds."

A moment or two passed while the chosen eight did their not-quite-memory work.

"Okay, Michael, you first," Slaight said to one of the eight, Michael de Pencier (president, Key Publications), keeping his distance from de Pencier, no peeking over his shoulders or other sneaky moves. "Now, your paragraph, Michael, I see something about romance, nothing sexy, but there's a handsome man and a beautiful woman in the paragraph, and they may be doing something intimate. Not sex, but affection."

"They're kissing," de Pencier said, smiling an impressed smile.

"Kissing?" Slaight said. "That's close enough."

"Yes, it is," de Pencier said. "Certainly is."

Slaight moved in turn to each of the other seven participants, and over the following few minutes, he guessed (guessed? mind read? mind *transferred?*) the contents of all seven paragraphs of the seven books to the satisfaction of the seven participants.

The guests cheered. Slaight bowed modestly, and announced another demonstration, also in the realm of mind transference. This one required two books and two participants. The latter appeared to be picked at random, as usual; the former did not. One book was a fat tome, title unannounced, the other was the *Oxford American Dictionary*. Slaight handed the tome to Susie Loewen (vice-chair of the board, the Royal Ontario Museum) and the dictionary to Patrick Watson (broadcaster and former CBC chair).

"Susie, open your book at any page," Slaight instructed. "Now, all I want you to do is look at your page and count up to the third line from the bottom . . . Done? Okay, pick out the longest word in that line, but don't say it out loud. Just memorize it."

Slaight turned to Watson and the *Oxford American Dictionary*.

"Patrick," he said, "open the dictionary at page forty-nine, okay? The right-hand column. Run your hand down twenty-two lines. Got that? Your finger should be on a word. Is that correct? A word that is followed by a definition?"

Watson nodded. "Correct."

"I don't want you to read the word itself," Slaight said, speaking slowly. "But read aloud from the dictionary the definition of the word."

Watson read, "'A person who prepares and serves alcoholic drinks at a bar.'"

"Good, good," Slaight said. He turned back to Susie Loewen. "Now, Susie, would you tell us the word from your page, the word you've memorized, the longest word in the third line from the bottom? What's the word?"

"Bartender."

You might think there's a connection between Allan Slaight the magician and Allan Slaight the communications mogul. Some qualities common to the two fields he's mastered? A higher level of mental discipline, perhaps? Or something much more mystical, a power to penetrate people's minds and read their very desires? Slaight isn't really biting on that one.

"Something I do in magic that makes me a better businessman?" he says. "Well, it's tenuous, but maybe two things. In magic, you develop the ability to influence people. That's useful in business. And then, in magic you have to be able to concentrate pretty fiercely and memorize certain things. That carries over to business, too."

Whether Slaight is displaying modesty in his analysis, or not revealing something more esoteric and mysterious, the fact is that magic seized him more than a half-century ago, long before he even thought about the communications business. He was eight years old and growing up in Galt, Ontario, when his parents took him for a pre-Christmas tour of Eaton's toy department in Toronto. Little Allan happened to walk past a stand operated by Johnny Giordmaine, a short Maltese gentleman in a black tux, who was demonstrating tricks from an Eaton's magic set.

"That was the moment," Slaight says. "I stopped in front of Johnny and stood there most of the rest of the day. I didn't care about the electric trains or the toy soldiers. All I wanted was to do magic like Johnny. All I wanted for Christmas was one of those sets of tricks."

He got it, and, to this day, magic remains a Slaight passion. He performs his own repertoire from the arts of the great conjurors and prestidigitators. And he's become a scholar of magic, accumulating a vast library of books on the subject, which he stores at his home in long rows of shelves in a room that seems almost a work of magic itself. (So does the entire Slaight house; it's a former dry-cleaning plant, on a back alley in north Toronto, which, unlikely as it seems, has been transformed into a residence that takes a deep bow to the architectural style of sixteenth-century Palladio.)

Back in Galt in the 1930s, Slaight's father, known to one and all as J.E., was the advertising manager of the *Galt Reporter*. Slaight's younger brother, Brian, exposed to the workings of the newspaper, found printer's ink coursing through his veins; he went into the business as soon as he was old enough and ended his newspaper career decades later as CEO of the Thomson chain. Allan didn't take to print, but, when J.E. moved the family west in 1946 and bought radio station CHAB in Moose Jaw, Saskatchewan, Allan found his calling.

"The station was up on the fourth floor of the local hotel, which also happened to be the top floor," Slaight says. "The first time I went up there, sixteen years old, never been in a radio station until then, I was absolutely smitten."

Before Slaight was out of his teens, he had married his first wife, Ada Mitchell, and was holding down a job as a news reporter at CFRN in Edmonton. He worked his way through the other two stations in town, as news reporter and sports commentator at CJCA and as news director and sales manager at CHED. Then he lit out for the big time, becoming program director at CHUM in Toronto.

In the year Slaight arrived, 1958, the Elliott–Haynes survey of Toronto radio listeners showed CHUM far back in the ratings. CKEY led all Toronto stations with 35 per cent of the audience, CFRB trailed at 28 per cent, and CHUM limped behind most of the commercial stations with 15 per cent. A year later, after Slaight had done some major tinkering with a Top-40 format, Elliott–Haynes came out with dramatic new numbers: CFRB hung in with its customary 28 per cent, but now CKEY had plummeted to 15 per cent and CHUM had zoomed to 33 per cent. Under Slaight, it stayed in that lofty area for the next decade.

In the 1970s, Slaight made a career zig-zag out of radio and into television. Global TV hired him as president and CEO to effect a rescue operation on a business that was losing a million and a half bucks every month. Slaight got down to the task at hand, but in the process, he discovered that it was radio that had smitten him, not TV.

"Radio is more fun than television, and certainly a lot more difficult to run," Slaight says. "In TV, you buy your programs, schedule them, build a good news department, and that covers all the bases. In radio, you live and die with the ratings. You have to keep changing and adjusting. That's what makes it so fascinating."

Slaight bid adieu to Global in 1977 and set about adding to the store of radio stations he had begun accumulating seven years earlier. CFGM in Richmond Hill, Ontario, a country station Slaight bought with the financial support of, among other backers, his pal Gordon Lightfoot. CFOX in Montreal. A station in Sarnia, Ontario. Q107, a new-concept Toronto rock station he started up in 1976.

All of this, and other dabbling in radio, was mere prelude to Slaight's master stroke in ownership: his purchase in 1985 of Conrad Black's Standard Broadcasting Corporation. Now he was sole owner of the largest privately held communications company in the country. What more could he ask, a guy whose first taste of radio came in a tiny station on the top floor of a hotel in Moose Jaw? Standard owned seven radio stations when Slaight bought the company; today, across Canada, it has thirteen – plus a giant share of the Canadian market in home videocassettes, video games, outdoor signs, and transit advertising.

When John Bitove came knocking on Slaight's door in early 1993, Slaight made an immediate connection between his business and Bitove's proposed business.

"It was fairly basic," he says. "In basketball, you have to please people, which is the same as in radio. And in both, you've got to be really inventive at marketing. How could I not say, Yes, I'm in?"

So, in no time at all, Slaight became the other half, the guy who owned most of the part of the basketball team that John Bitove didn't own.

On December 14, the Thursday night after the party at the Porter house, Allan Slaight took three friends to a Raptors game. Slaight's tickets are for seats on the floor, front row centre, so close to the action that you can feel the breeze off the players running the court. These seats are roughly in the same spot that Spike Lee sits for Knicks games at Madison Square Garden, where Jack Nicholson sits for Lakers games at the Great Western Forum. It's celebrity territory – except, on this night at the SkyDome, there were no celebrities in sight, unless you counted Senator Trevor Eyton (who happened to have been Slaight's legal adviser when he started buying radio stations in the 1970s).

The tickets for Slaight's seats list the section as simply "VIP." A polite kid in a security uniform escorts you to the section, gives the cushioned seats a cleaning swipe, and hands you a "Raptor Rap Sheet," which brings you up to the minute on player injuries and other crucial information. The tickets for Slaight's seats list the price, too: $150 per ticket. Slaight has four of them for all forty-one home games.

The Indiana Pacers supplied tonight's opposition. This was the solid team that had gone to the Eastern Conference final in each of the previous two seasons, losing in seven games to New York in 1994 and in the same number to the Orlando Magic in '95. The Pacers depended largely on two players – the All-Star shooting guard Reggie Miller and the centre Rik Smits – together with a bunch of smart role players and a coach, Larry Brown, who taught tenacious defence and who was accustomed to coming out on top (twenty-two winning seasons in twenty-three years as a college and pro head coach, with one NCAA championship at the University of Kansas in 1988).

Rik Smits trotted onto the SkyDome floor to begin the game. He was seven-foot-four, about 265 pounds, and his face gave off the gloom of a character in one of Janwillem Van de Wetering's Amsterdam crime novels. That was only appropriate, since Smits is as Dutch as windmills, dikes, and pessimism. He grew up in the city of Eindhoven, and was recruited for basketball by Marist, a tiny college in Poughkeepsie, New York. In 1988, the Pacers made him their first-draft pick, but it took Smits many years to blossom into NBA maturity. During the growing period, he bore much abuse from home fans at the Market Square Arena in Indianapolis and from the local basketball press, where one mocking sportswriter nicknamed him "Reek Smits."

Smits endured the calumny with the poker face he was born with and ultimately broke through to something very like stardom in the 1994-95 season. In particular, he won his spurs in the two playoff series that year against the New York Knicks and the Orlando Magic. In the first game of the Eastern Conference semis with New York, Smits dominated Patrick Ewing, thirty-four points to eleven, and he continued through the playoffs to go at least even with Ewing and to match up strongly against Orlando's Shaq O'Neal.

Smits had at last placed himself among the top six or seven of the league's centres, and he'd managed it with his sense of humour, as well as his dour expression, intact. On the very night of the game against the Raptors, all callers to the Indianapolis office of David Brenner, the Pacers public-relations director, were greeted by a charmingly tongue-in-cheek message: "Hi, this is Rik Smits of the Indiana Pacers, and I'm answering David Brenner's phone. I finally get some respect the last season against Hakeem, Shaq, the Admiral, and Patrick Ewing, then David makes me leave this message. So I lose respect. Oh well, do me a favour and leave David a message at the beep."

At about the six-minute mark of the first quarter of the Raptors–Pacers game, Alvin Robertson drove on the Pacer basket. The ball rimmed out. Robertson thought Indiana guard Mark Jackson had hit him on the arm, and he looked to the nearest referee, Michael Smith, pleading for the foul call. He didn't get it.

"Aw, fuck, man!" Robertson said to Smith.

Indiana grabbed the rebound and raced down court.

Thirty seconds later, Robertson again drove the Indiana basket. Same thing. He missed, and he thought Jackson had fouled him. He gave Smith his pleading look. Smith called no foul.

"Aw, fuck *you*, man!" Robertson burst out at Smith.

"That's a technical!" Smith shouted back. His hands went up in a T to signal the technical foul against Robertson.

Alvin Robertson had just demonstrated what separated a harmless profanity from an insult that demanded a technical. It was the second-person singular pronoun.

The Robertson blip aside, the Raptors did just about everything right in the first three quarters of the game. They ran and hustled and kept beating Indiana to the ball. On defence, the only guy the Raptors couldn't do much about was Rik Smits. For the early part of the game, Indiana's offence consisted mostly of tossing the ball to Smits at the high or low post and watching while he scored on hook shots and little jumpers. But, in those first three quarters, the Raptors had far-more-balanced scoring than the Pacers, and they led Indiana at the half by nine points and were still up by eight at the end of the third period.

Willie Anderson, among the Raptors, was having a particularly interesting game. He was a canny player. Indeed, canniness was a requisite for Anderson, given his medical history. He'd come out of the University of Georgia as the San Antonio Spurs' first-round draft pick in 1988 and promptly provided the Spurs with plenty of offence while playing mostly the number 2 position. On those rare occasions when the Spurs showed up on television in the late 1980s and early 1990s – San Antonio not being considered a large TV draw in those years – Anderson was the guy you'd notice, with the soft touch on his outside shot and with the authentic explosiveness in his drives to the basket. Unfortunately for Anderson, it was the explosiveness that practically vanished when he encountered his terrible leg problems.

They began with stress fractures in both shins. He suffered them in pre-season games in 1990-91. But he kept on playing, and his scoring average kept on dropping, until 1992, when doctors, to preserve his faltering career, inserted metal rods in both legs. It's a comment on Anderson's courage that he stayed in basketball, but, in the 1994-95 season, two things happened to him, both bad. He lost his starting job to Vinny Del Negro, and the Spurs left him exposed in the expansion draft.

Anderson arrived in Toronto as damaged goods, but he also brought plenty of admirable qualities with him. He was polite, articulate, and thoughtful, unselfish as a teammate, and he was patient with journalists who asked what might be mildly stupid questions. Was the SkyDome a difficult stadium to shoot in? Well, Anderson answered, the place had too much space, too much crowd and other movement behind the baskets to make it really comfortable for shooters. But, he went on, he'd worked out a strategy: he focused on the front rim of the basket as a way of blocking out the distracting scenery in the stands and in the large empty beyond of the SkyDome. Anderson knew how to compensate and adjust. He may have lost the speed to blow by people on his drives to the basket, but now he had developed a very long first step. That seemed to help him get past defenders. And he still had his soft outside shot.

All of these things were working nicely for Anderson in the Indiana game. He took four shots from three-point range and hit on three of them. And on his bursts to the basket, he was forcing the Pacers to foul him; he went to the free-throw line six times and made good on five of the shots. Anderson was hitting on this night.

The trouble was, he stopped hitting in the fourth quarter. So did the other Raptors. Maybe it was fatigue – Brendan Malone used only six players for virtually the entire game – or maybe it was the Indiana defence. It finally kicked in. It forced numerous Raptor turnovers, and it harried the Toronto guys into terrible shooting, five for twenty in the last quarter. At the same time, the Pacers started to get offence from people other than Rik Smits. Ricky Pierce, for one. He was a tough-looking, back-alley sort of mug with a marvellous outside touch, and he knocked down six of nine shots down the stretch. Almost by himself, he turned the tide of the game.

The Raptors were down by three, with 17.8 seconds left in the game, and Oliver Miller was inbounding the ball from the sideline just inside the Indiana zone. Dale Davis was assigned to guard Miller, but, instead of facing Miller, Davis turned his back on him, checking out the positions of the other players on the floor. The whistle blew to start play. Davis's back was still turned to Miller.

Rik Smits said later in the dressing room that he sensed what was going to happen, what Miller's next move would be, but that he couldn't get his mouth working in time to shout a warning to Dale Davis.

So Smits and everybody else watched as Miller, puckish, wily Oliver, bounced the ball off Davis's rear end, stepped inside the line, and caught the ball on one bounce off the rebound from the Davis bum. If Jim Carrey ever makes a basketball movie, this play will be included. It looked silly, surprising, and cute. On the floor, in the brief confusion that followed Miller's audacity, Tracy Murray shook loose all by himself in the corner to Miller's right. Miller hit Murray with a pass. Murray put the ball up, a three-pointer and a tie game if it swished in. It didn't. It bounced off the rim. But here was the resourceful Miller waiting under-neath to grab the rebound and stuff the ball through the hoop.

Raptors down by one, and the crowd was going nuts.

Indiana brought the ball up the floor, and Willie Anderson fouled Reggie Miller. Miller hit one of two.

Raptors down by two.

Damon Stoudamire drove on the Pacer basket and was fouled. Stoudamire stepped to the free-throw line. This was heavy pressure once again on the rookie: fewer than three seconds on the clock, his team two points behind, and he had two foul shots to tie the game. The crowd went into a hush. First shot, good. Big roar from the crowd. Second shot, good. *Huge* roar from the crowd.

Tie game, with 3.4 seconds left. Indiana called a timeout to plan a final play. As the five Raptors on the floor walked to their bench, people in the courtside seats stood and clapped them each step of the walk. The applause spread through the building. This, everybody seemed to agree, was thrilling stuff.

Derrick McKey inbounded the ball for the Pacers on the Toronto side of the centre line in front of the officials' table. Who would get the final shot? Reggie Miller was on the floor. The shot would probably be his. He'd had a lousy night, 2–9 shooting, but he was the Pacers' go-to guy, the clutch shooter.

It wasn't him. McKey threw the ball directly to Rik Smits. Oliver Miller was covering Smits. Miller played behind Smits, between him and the basket. Smits stepped out a couple of feet to meet McKey's inbounds pass, but Miller didn't move with him. Maybe another Raptor was supposed to switch off his man and pick up Smits. Whatever, Smits was left alone.

Was the big guy actually going to shoot? Was that the play? A centre putting up a jump shot from several feet out? Well, why not? Smits had popped in a few of them on this night, and, in the fourth game of the playoff series against Orlando the previous spring, Smits had hit a jumper at the buzzer for the win. With him, a shot like that was hardly unheard of.

Smits, ball in hand, back to the basket, turned and dribbled in the direction of the hoop. They were high, big-man dribbles, bouncing five feet from hand to floor and back again. Smits dribbled twice, two of these strange, floating, monster bounces. They carried him within fifteen feet of the basket, into the left edges of the key.

Would regulation time run out? Would the buzzer sound before Smits arrived at the spot he wanted to shoot from and got off his shot? Smits raised the ball in his hands, over his head, slightly in front of his body, which was tilting forward in a Tower-of-Pisa slant. The time clock over the basket read .02. The ball rolled off Smits's fingers and into the air. It rose, arced, flattened, and dropped towards the basket. The buzzer went off. The clock registered .00. And the ball fell through the basket, all net, no rim. Time had expired, but Smits had released the shot before the buzzer sounded. The shot counted.

Pacers 102, Raptors 100.

After the game, Allan Slaight took his guests to the Mercer Street Grill, a small and shiny bistro a few blocks north of the SkyDome. Slaight ordered a large martini. He was pumped up. Of course, Slaight is pumped up much of the time. "Allan isn't a type-A personality," Emmanuelle Gattuso says. "He's a type-AAA personality." But on this night, it wasn't the drive of business that had him on a high. It was the joy of the two and a half hours he'd just spent at the SkyDome.

"The game I saw in Phoenix almost three years ago, my first basketball game," he said, "it was a thrill, but it was nothing compared to the feeling I get at the Raptors games. Now, it's my city, my team, I know some of the players. It's fantastic. And everybody, the players plus the Raptor staff, they give you a wonderful show. The stuff that goes on during timeouts and half time, the contests, the people coming out of the stands to do crazy things, I love all that. And then you get a basketball game like tonight's. Was that exciting or what? This is as good as I ever imagined when I agreed to get into it. It's magical."

And that's a word, coming from Allan Slaight, that isn't meant lightly.

8

THE CAPTAIN

Ed Pinckney was asked, almost four years after the event, about a particular game he played in during his time with the Boston Celtics: Sunday afternoon, March 15, 1992, Celtics versus the Portland Trail Blazers at the Boston Garden on national television. It turned out to be a sensationally exciting game.

Portland was formidable that season, the team of Clyde Drexler, Buck Williams, Terry Porter, *et al.*, the team that would finish with the best record in the entire Western Conference, 57–25, and would go to the NBA final, losing to Chicago in six games. For Boston, the great front line of Larry Bird, Robert Parish, and Kevin McHale was getting long in the tooth, suffering frequent injuries, but the team was still good enough to eventually tie with the New York Knicks for first place in the Atlantic Division of the Eastern Conference and reach the Atlantic semi-finals before Cleveland bounced them in seven games.

Pinckney was a role player on that Celtics team. He got a lot of minutes when Bird or McHale or both were injured, but, when they were in playing health, Coach Chris Ford sent him onto the floor mostly to spell one or other of the superstars. And that was Pinckney's job in the Portland game, to be the guy who gave Bird and McHale a breather. But *what* a breather. The game went into double overtime, and it was Pinckney who came up big – gigantic, even – in the second overtime period.

Through the entire game, Boston played catchup. The Blazers, affecting a noticeable swagger, knew they were the better team, expected to win, and continued to hold a lead deep into the fourth quarter. But Boston insisted on hanging close, and, with the clock running out on regulation time and Portland up by three, Larry Bird, who would score an amazing forty-nine points on the afternoon, took a pass on the left side of the court, right at the three-point line in Portland's end. On a tape of the game, Bird looks off-balance, his feet tangled as he avoids falling over the three-point line. Still, he got off the ball a millisecond before the buzzer sounded, and the ball swished through for a most unlikely three. Tie game.

At the end of the first overtime period, Boston pulled off a similar game-rescuing strike. This time it was the small forward Kevin Gamble who hit a long jumper from the right corner for two points at the buzzer that again tied the game.

With three minutes left in the second overtime period, Boston was clinging to a precarious two-point lead when Kevin McHale fouled Clyde Drexler. It was McHale's sixth personal, and he was gone from the game. Pinckney replaced him. Drexler sank both free throws, and the score was once more deadlocked.

John Bagley, playing point guard for Boston, brought the ball up court. Pinckney trotted almost unobtrusively along the left side, then accelerated into position under the basket and to the left. Jerome Kersey was supposed to be guarding him, but Pinckney shook loose briefly from Kersey. Bagley spotted him all alone and fired a pass at chest level. Pinckney in one smooth, practised motion put in the layup. The score became 138–136 Celtics, and they would never fall behind again.

A minute and a half later, with Boston ahead by six points, Pinckney saw that Larry Bird, with the ball at the left of the Portland zone, was double-teamed. That meant Boston had an open man. Pinckney, alert, made sure it was him. He broke for the Blazers' basket, unchecked, and took a zippy Bird pass for an overhead reverse dunk, a thunderous shot. Boston up by eight. Portland scrambled to get back in the game. A three-pointer closed part of the gap. The Blazers got even closer. But Pinckney scored two more points, both on free throws, and he grabbed the last rebound under the Boston basket at the buzzer to clinch the stunning

Celtics win, 152–148. In three minutes of play, he'd scored the points that made the difference.

That, Pinckney was told, four years later, was a wonderful piece of work he'd performed.

"*That* game, yeah, it was a lotta fun," Pinckney answered. "I remember it because Portland took us for granted and we ended up beating them."

Well, *you* had the answer to Portland in the second overtime.

"Another reason I remember that game, you know, Larry Bird was just back from an injury. He had terrible trouble with his lower back, but he played anyway, and he scored a whole bunch of points for us."

Uh-huh, but what it all came down to in the overtime was *your* baskets.

"In the last part of regulation time, we kept fouling them, and they kept missing. We were kinda lucky we won that game. We got lucky."

Yes, but . . . well, never mind.

One of the writers covering the Raptors for the *Toronto Sun* had described Pinckney in an earlier conversation as "the most complete human being on the team," and among Pinckney's qualities – intelligence would turn out to be one, plus a natural bent for leadership and an unexpected gentleness – was apparently a built-in humility. The man was so self-effacing that he couldn't bring himself to reminisce about one of his own terrific moments on the basketball floor. Maybe it was this innate modesty that kept him from becoming an authentic NBA star.

Pinckney's dad was a big man, six-foot-two, a construction worker, and it was from this side of the family that Ed got his size. But Pinckney was as tall as his father by the time he was fourteen and entering his freshman year at Adlai Stevenson High in the Bronx. Then he started *really* growing.

"I went up seven, eight inches in four years," Pinckney remembers. "It was funny, I started out as point guard on the school team, and when I kept getting taller, I went through all the positions, point guard, 2 guard, the 3, 4, and at the end, I was the centre. It was funny, all that growing, but it was also very hard on my ankles."

It was as if Pinckney's ankles were saying, Hey, what's the load up there? Are we supposed to carry *that*? Supposed to, but couldn't. His spindly ankles didn't keep pace with the rest of his growing body, and that caused trouble on the court. Pinckney had a wonderful season as a junior, and he expected more of the same as a senior, a strong season that would attract scholarship offers from major universities. It didn't work out that way.

"My last years, I really messed up my ankles," Pinckney says. "A lot of times, I played hurt. People came to see me play, recruiters and coaches, but I'd play a half, then sprain an ankle – or *re*sprain it, more likely – and either I couldn't finish up or I'd be hurting out there. So I didn't get highly recruited for college."

One school that did pay attention to Pinckney was Villanova, a Philadelphia university with about eleven thousand students. Villanova, on Philly's ritzy Main Line, was overwhelmingly white (98 per cent), suburban, preppy, and upper-middle-class. Pinckney was none of those. "But I had a good feeling about the guys on the basketball team," he says.

Pinckney declared for Villanova, and discovered it wasn't a school that tolerated athletes who were too dim to cope with standards that required all baccalaureate candidates to handle one language, one math or science, a course in Western civilization, and some philosophy. So, along with everything else, notably a lot of basketball, Ed Pinckney got a sound education.

Villanova played in the Big East, a conference of such traditional basketball powers as Georgetown, Syracuse, and St. John's. Against those schools, Villanova often struggled. Still, during Pinckney's four years, Villanova enjoyed its small moments of triumph. There was the game in February 1983, playing against the Georgetown Hoyas, which were led by the mighty seven-foot centre Patrick Ewing, when Pinckney scored twenty-seven points and pulled down twenty-two rebounds in a one-point Villanova upset, 68–67. "This is my finest hour as a player," Pinckney said after the game. Little did he know.

In Pinckney's senior year, 1984-85, Villanova had an overall 25–10 record. That wasn't bad, not when the school played most of its games within the Big East, which was particularly strong that year. Georgetown, still with Ewing, set the standard. It was a team, coming off an NCAA championship the preceding year, that lost just two games all season, won the Big East tournament, and entered the NCAAs as the number-one seed. Villanova made the NCAAs, too, one of sixty-four colleges that would compete for the national championship. But no one counted on Villanova sticking around for long.

So which two teams were left to play in the final after a month of competition? Georgetown, as predicted, and Villanova, as very much not predicted. The championship game figured to be a pushover for the Hoyas, a blowout. After all, Georgetown had already whipped Villanova twice earlier that season. But on April Fools' Day at the Rupp Arena in Lexington, Kentucky, Villanova played what that night's TV colour commentator, Billy Packer, called "a perfect game." It helped a whole lot that a little guy named Harold Jensen came off the Villanova bench to hit five key baskets on five shots. But mostly Villanova owed its victory to aggressive defence, and to an offence built on patience and teamwork. The Villanova players, under enormous pressure, never lost their cool, and, in the victory that brought the national championship, it was Ed Pinckney who was the most cool, the most patient, the most aggressive. He was named the tournament's Most Valuable Player.

"Oh yeah, by far that was the most memorable game I ever played," Pinckney says today. "It was very tight all the way, a very physical game. But, you know, I can't remember the score."

For the record, it was Villanova 66, Georgetown 64.

It wasn't that Pinckney hadn't travelled much. During his Villanova years, he toured with the American team in the 1983 Pan-American Games (gold-medal winners) and in the same year's World Championships (silver medal). He even made it to Toronto for a couple of visits as a teenager in the company of two or three of his six sisters (he has no brothers). But Phoenix, way out there, as a new home? Playing for the Suns, who had one player fresh from testifying about drug trafficking before a grand jury that later indicted two other Phoenix players? Was this a promising place to launch a pro basketball career?

Probably not. But Phoenix took Pinckney as its first choice in the 1985 draft, the tenth pick overall, and he found himself on a team whose management was cleaning house of the snorters and sniffers and whose rookie coach, John Wetzel, was searching desperately for a system that accommodated the ever-shifting personnel. Wetzel mispositioned Pinckney at small forward instead of power forward. "I could play defensively against the other 3s," he remembers, "but I couldn't score from that position."

At the end of his second unrewarding season with Phoenix – both of them wound up with the Suns far out of the playoffs – Pinckney was traded to the Sacramento Kings, one of only three teams in the Western Conference that was in worse shape than the Suns. "With the Kings," Pinckney says, "we had a constant turnover in coaches, in players, and a lot of competition among guys for playing time, which wasn't always healthy." Sacramento went a miserable 29 – 53 in 1986-87, and, on a personal level, word was getting around that Pinckney might be "an underachiever," maybe even "lazy."

On the latter subject, Pinckney says, "The most important influence on my life was my father. His message was contained in the way he led his life: work hard. And that was an important thing for me, because I wasn't the type of player who always played to my potential. But over time I learned."

Pinckney's major NBA learning time began on February 23, 1989, when Sacramento bundled him into a trade with Boston: Pinckney and a reserve centre, Joe Kleine, for the marvellous shooting guard Danny Ainge, and another reserve centre, Brad Lohaus. The trade was the Celtics' idea. They had lost Larry Bird to injuries for a couple of months and were frantic for a big man up front, even if it meant surrendering Ainge. Pinckney, they figured, could be the guy for the job. He was – and he wasn't.

Pinckney performed competently filling in for Bird, and, the following season, he worked himself into the regular rotation of the eight Celtics who handled most of the playing time. But nobody on the Boston coaching staff entirely defined Pinckney's role on the floor. That took a couple more seasons, and it developed mostly by a process of elimination. Scoring went first.

"Partway through my second year in Boston," Pinckney says, "I realized I was like about the twentieth option on offence. It wasn't even a question of scoring any more."

Then what?

In November 1990, a Celtics assistant coach named Don Casey, a man who had coached at Temple University in Philadelphia and had therefore seen Pinckney in his finest college form, took Ed aside after a Boston practice in the gym at Hellenic College for a long heart-to-heart chat. Casey told Pinckney he'd reached the point where his basketball career hung in the balance, that he had to work hard, very hard, and that he must concentrate all his skills and athleticism on two particular aspects of the game, defence and rebounding, especially offensive rebounding. When the Celtics went into their set offence, the plays would be run to the strong side of the floor, the side where the scorers were positioned, McHale, Reggie Lewis, Robert Parish, and the rest. Pinckney would play the weak side. When his teammates missed a shot, his job was to grab the offensive rebound, keep the play alive, fire the ball back out for another play, or maybe, if the circumstances were right, score himself on a putback off the missed shot. If Pinckney pulled down eight or nine rebounds a game, if he defended against his own man, kept the opposition's power forward off the boards, he'd be earning his pay. That was what Boston asked of him.

Well, at last. There was nothing deep or profound in any of this, nothing that was really new to Pinckney. But the talk with Casey stabilized his approach to the game. So many NBA players – guys who weren't immediately stars or weren't lucky enough to join a team with a system that embraced their talents – endured such an odyssey in the league, such a long journey. Looking for a niche, fitting into a team plan. That was the case with Ed Pinckney. He'd never expected it to be this way, not for a guy who went tenth in the entire college draft, even ahead of Karl Malone, who just happened to develop into the quintessential NBA power forward with the Utah Jazz. But that was the luck of the draw in pro basketball, and Pinckney, this nice guy, dealt with his fate.

"Even in bad times when he wasn't playing, Eddie always kept his composure," said Joe Kleine, a teammate in both Sacramento and Boston. "He was always all right emotionally."

And with the Celtics, Pinckney did what his dad had done. He worked hard. He worked on his rebounding. He developed the style that he still displayed when he later joined the Raptors. Pinckney didn't depend on power. His was rebounding based on a rough sort of art and on relentless activity. He kept on the move under the basket, swarming, jumping, diving. Bigger men might try to bump and bat him out of the way. Pinckney slipped and weaved. He wanted the ball. He wanted a job.

In the 1991-92 season, averaging twenty-three minutes a game in eighty-one games, his stats worked out to seven rebounds per game, four of them offensive, plus a useful 7.8 points. The Boston fans voted him the prize as the player who "best represented Celtics pride."

Not too shabby for a man who'd been on an odyssey that once seemed without end.

Back in August 1983, between Pinckney's sophomore and junior years at Villanova, he had played basketball in a Philadelphia summer league. This was playground ball, on an outdoor court in the city, an urban scene of asphalt, traffic, guys in the hood hanging a little.

One day in the middle of a game, somebody, somewhere in the area, somewhere very close, fired a handgun.

Everybody took off. The players didn't pause to check whose argument it was, who was shooting at what. They ran. They flew across streets, through backyards, over hedges.

Ed Pinckney came to a fence. He wasn't about to detour around it. The only thing on Ed's mind was putting distance between himself and the guy back there with the gun. He was going over the damned fence. He soared up, up . . . and not quite cleanly over. His foot caught the top of the fence, and he came down hard on the other side. His left leg took the jolt, right in the knee. He kept running, but by now he was hobbling.

Pinckney's knee had to be operated on, with some surgical removal of cartilage around his kneecap. But he recovered quickly and missed no basketball at Villanova and none in his early years as a pro. The knee bothered him not at all, until almost a decade later in the autumn of 1992, when the fall over the fence caught up with him.

"By then," Pinckney says, "playing a lotta minutes over the years, all the wear and tear, I was getting terrible swelling in that same left knee."

On November 20, just as the new season was getting under way, the Celtics doctors performed arthroscopic surgery on the knee. In medical terms, they did "a lateral release and debridement of an osteochondral defect on the left lateral femoral condyle." In layman's language, the surgeons took some debris out of the cartilage around the kneecap in order to free up the knee to move properly. In anybody's words, Ed Pinckney could play no basketball in the 1992-93 season.

One sunny event lightened up this otherwise gloomy period. A few days before the knee operation was deemed unavoidable, the Celtics had signed Pinckney to a new contract. It covered three years at $1.6 million per annum, and all three years were guaranteed, which meant that, wherever Pinckney played during the three seasons through to the end of 1995-96 – indeed, whether he played or not – the team that owned his contract, the Celtics or anyone else, had to pay him his $1.6 million per annum.

Pinckney returned to the Celtics in the fall of 1993, sound of knee and eager to pull down the rebounds and play the tough defence. There was just one hitch: in his absence, the Celtics had signed a new and gifted power forward. He was Dino Radja of Croatia, a guy deemed to be the second-best player in all of Europe after Toni Kukoc, who later went to the Chicago Bulls. Radja was two inches taller than Pinckney, four years younger, and a player who was a natural at putting the ball in the basket. Radja got the job as starting power forward. Pinckney sat on the bench.

How did Pinckney react to this crusher of a development?

"Ed never showed any sign of being upset," Radja said three years later, during a Celtics visit to the SkyDome. "He kind of guided me through the NBA. He was the one who told me how to play the other guys in the league, what their strengths and weaknesses were. I considered him a great friend."

Radja finished the season averaging twenty-seven minutes a game, seven rebounds, and fifteen points. Pinckney's stats were twenty-one minutes, six rebounds and five points.

In the late spring of 1994, Boston appointed a new general manager, M. L. Carr, and his first player move was to deem Pinckney expendable and trade him to the Milwaukee Bucks. Pinckney's seniority and savvy were appreciated by his new team, and he was named the Bucks' co-captain and its representative on the Players' Association. But the Milwaukee coach, Mike Dunleavy, couldn't find a spot for him in the player rotation, and Pinckney's numbers for the 1994-95 season dwindled to the minuscule category: eleven minutes per game, three rebounds, 2.3 points. He didn't play at all in twenty games, including eight of the last thirteen. No surprise, Milwaukee left him unprotected in the 1995 expansion draft, and the Raptors snapped him up. Well, not exactly *snapped* him up. Took him in the tenth round, the nineteenth selection.

On the late afternoon of Sunday, December 17, 1995, three days after the heart-breaker of a loss to Indiana, the Orlando Magic arrived at the SkyDome. This was the team of two young superstars – Shaquille O'Neal, centre, and Anfernee Hardaway, point guard – the team that had gone all the way to the NBA final the previous season before losing to the Houston Rockets. Ed Pinckney's thinking before the Raptors took on the excellent Magic was this:

"Every time a team like Orlando comes in here, people say, This is the one that's gonna be ugly, this is the one where the Raptors are gonna get killed. But, you know, Houston was in here, and we only lost on a basket at the buzzer. Seattle? We *beat* Seattle. And we've gone down to the wire with a lotta other good teams. So nobody on our team's thinking in terms of getting killed, and Orlando shouldn't be thinking they got an automatic two points playing us. I'm just saying we're gonna be in the ball game."

At the five-minute mark of the game's first quarter, with the Raptors two points in front, 13–11, Damon Stoudamire brought the ball into Orlando's end. Stoudamire set off a string of quick passes that moved the ball around the perimeter: Stoudamire to Alvin Robertson to Carlos Rogers in the left corner, then back to Robertson. While this was going on, the Magic made a switch on defence. The power forward, Donald Royal, jumped out at Robertson, and the guard, Nick Anderson, moved back to cover Royal's man, Ed Pinckney. That gave Pinckney a mismatch. He had three inches in height on Anderson. Robertson spotted the mismatch and whipped the ball in to Pinckney under the basket. Pinckney, standing just in front of the hoop, went up with a backward over-the-head dunk that caught Anderson flat-footed. Pinckney jammed the ball home. It was a repeat of the great shot he'd made off the Larry Bird pass in the Boston–Portland game in March 1992. And what the basket against Orlando produced wasn't just *any* two points. It was two with joy and gusto and panache. A huge grin spread across

Pinckney's face, and, as he ran back down court, he slapped palms – *whap* – with Alvin Robertson.

The turning point in a basketball game isn't supposed to happen halfway through the first quarter, but the Pinckney jam came close to qualifying. The Raptors had been running hard from the start of the game. They were aggressive, seemed assured, showed unusual poise. They were beating Orlando to the ball at crucial moments. The Magic had a number of players who liked to shoot from outside, and, when they missed, they often gave up long rebounds. The Raptors were getting to those rebounds fast and taking off on three-on-two breaks that yielded points. The game was going that way from the start, a Raptors kind of game.

And when Ed Pinckney threw down his jam, the rest of the team seemed to kick it up another notch. Inspired, they ran harder, executed more deftly, guarded more sharply on defence. They came out of the first quarter five points ahead, and pushed it to an astounding twenty-point lead at the half. They didn't let down in the second half either, and came away at the end of the game, against one of the top two or three teams in the league, with a 110–93 win.

Afterwards, quite long after the Raptors' dressing room grew quieter, after the celebration more or less died away – "This is *unbelievable*," Tracy Murray kept saying, Tracy Murray who hit for sixteen points coming off the bench – Pinckney talked a little more analytically about the Raptors' unexpected win.

"Two things meant a lot, two things that people watching the game might not know about. One is this stigma about being an expansion team. Like, we're *expansion*, and we don't get any *respect*. Guys on the team don't like that feeling. A lot of us know the players on the other teams that come here, personal friends of ours, and we don't want them thinking, Well, yeah, here's an easy game against *these* guys. We know they're thinking that, and it makes us play harder.

"And the other thing is our coaches. They were smart, you know, at the beginning of the season. They got everybody on the team organized. Coach Malone and his assistants told us where we're supposed to be on the floor, where we go for certain plays, what we have to do, what the system is, all that stuff. The coaches had things worked out early in the year, and that isn't always the case in this league. I've been with teams where players spend a whole year with a new coach trying to find out what their roles are. It's not like that here."

What Pinckney didn't mention – is this familiar? – was his own part in the game. He played thirty-five minutes against Orlando, grabbed eleven rebounds, which was more than double the number recorded by the next-most-proficient Raptor rebounder, and he scored fourteen points, including the electrifying first-quarter reverse dunk.

What, Pinckney was asked, did he like least about life in the NBA?

No hesitation.

"I don't like eating in different restaurants all the time. I like home-cooked meals. I like *seeing* my food cooked. My wife's a very good cook."

In Toronto, Pinckney wasn't seeing much of his food cooked, not unless he cooked it himself. He lived alone in a downtown apartment, while his wife, Rose, and their four kids – three sons, one daughter – stayed behind in the Milwaukee family home. It was ironic about that "family" home. It was the *only* home Ed and Rose had owned in their nine years of marriage. They got married during Ed's second season in Phoenix, and, everywhere they lived, Phoenix, Sacramento, Boston, they rented. In Milwaukee, they got a deal and bought. Who was to guess that Ed would have a short and mostly lousy stay with the Bucks? The whole family might have moved to Toronto, except the NBA lockout during the summer of 1995 put basketball on hold, and, by the time that was settled, the Pinckney kids were in Milwaukee schools. So much for family life in the NBA.

Beginning early in the Raptors' season, Rose flew to Toronto for visits. She's petite, has a pretty, heart-shaped face, and met her future husband when the two were students at Villanova. Rose makes a charming contrast to the lower-key Ed. She's vivacious, outgoing, a talker, an organizer. It was she, even though she wasn't a constant presence in Toronto, who brought together the other Raptor wives and girlfriends for social occasions, for good-works projects. She oversaw the women's campaign to help the Daily Bread Food Bank at Christmastime. She wanted to do something for the city where her husband lived and worked.

When Rose wasn't providing company, Pinckney led a grass widower's existence. He played basketball. He practised. He rented videos and watched them at the apartment. Read novels. His taste in the latter ran to thrillers. And away from the basketball court, Pinckney also had duties connected to the game, since, as he had been in Milwaukee, he was both the Raptors' captain and the team's representative on the Players' Association. The other guys, it was clear, looked up to Ed.

Pinckney was talking about leadership.

"I try to lead in a quiet way. I'm not real vocal. I don't yell at the guys. So my style of leadership on the floor and off the floor is more quiet. Besides, there're really many leaders on our team. John Salley's a leader. Alvin Robertson. Willie Anderson. Those guys have been around the NBA for a long time. They've played with great teams and with poorer teams. They've been starters and they've played coming off the bench. They know all the different situations in basketball, and, if a younger guy asks them questions about a certain situation, they've been there, Alvin and Willie, and they know the answers."

As Pinckney talked, he was sitting in a chair at the side of the court in the empty SkyDome. Practice had ended thirty minutes earlier, and Pinckney had showered and changed into a stylish outfit of chocolate-brown windbreaker and medium-brown slacks. Tracy Murray trotted past. Murray had stayed out on the floor to tape a segment for a half-time feature on a future Raptors telecast.

"Hey, man," Pinckney called to Murray. "That you that left your wallet in your shoe in the locker room?"

Murray thought about it. "Maybe I did."

"Your wallet in your *shoe* in the *locker room?*"

"Guess so, man."

Pinckney's voice was low but stern. "Never leave your wallet out like that, man. Never."

"I'm gonna get to it right away," Murray said, and left on the run for the locker room.

Pinckney gave his sweet smile. "Right there, that was an example of what I call quiet leadership *off* the basketball floor."

9

THE REST OF
THE PACKAGE

Partway through the first quarter of the Raptors' game against the Charlotte Hornets at the SkyDome on Tuesday night, January 9, 1996, Larry Johnson, Charlotte's massive power forward, stepped to the free-throw line to shoot two fouls. He hit the first and missed the second. In the instant after the missed second shot pinged off the rim of the basket, a voice over the SkyDome's sound system said, "Oh, I'm sorry. Did that break your concentration?"

The voice, medium-pitched and drenched in irony, sounded familiar. So did the line.

In Quentin Tarantino's 1994 movie, *Pulp Fiction*, Samuel L. Jackson played a heavy named Jules Winnfield. He and another heavy, Vincent Vega, played by John Travolta, handled collections, enforcements, and other such violent matters for Los Angeles drug dealer Marcellus Wallace. Their immediate assignment, when the audience first encounters Jules and Vincent early in the movie, was to lean on three young guys, Marvin, Brett, and Roger, who had reneged on a deal with Marcellus. The heavies went calling on the young guys at their apartment. The young guys were terrified at the sight of Jules and Vincent, and Brett launched into an explanation and an apology for the way he and his friends had messed up the drug deal. Brett was into the second sentence of his speech when Jules reached inside his jacket, took out a gun, and shot Roger three times in the chest. In the stunned silence that followed, with Brett shaking in terror, Jules said to Brett, "Oh, I'm sorry. Did that break your concentration?"

This was the line, the sound bite, that had been played over the SkyDome sound system when Larry Johnson missed his second free throw. Playing the sound bite was the idea of the Raptors' Events and Operations division. And the Charlotte game wasn't the first time that Events and Operations had used the Samuel L. Jackson line when somebody from an opposing team missed a free throw.

Back on December 12, in a game against the Boston Celtics, the clip had whipped up a piece of controversy. Even though the Celtics won the game, their coach and general manager, M. L. Carr, had been so ticked off at the playing of the Jackson line that he made a formal complaint to the NBA offices in New York.

"If the league fines us," said Isiah Thomas, who loved the line, "I'm personally paying."

The league didn't fine the Raptors, but it suggested that maybe playing Samuel L. Jackson wasn't the best idea in the world. But the people at Events and Operations decided, in effect, to heck with the spoilsports. This was entertainment. This was show biz. This was the rest of the NBA package.

Near the end of the first quarter in the game against Charlotte, Toronto called a timeout, and, on the floor, three Raptors employees escorted a tall, casual gent in a grey sweater to the three-point line at the south end of the court. Herbie Kuhn, the Raptors announcer, called on the crowd to welcome the casual gent. He was about to take part in the Principal Shootout.

In the Principal Shootout, which was one of the contests held at every Raptors game, a principal of a Toronto high school stood at the three-point line and was given twenty-four seconds to hit a basket. Any principal who swished a ball through the hoop won a cash prize for his or her high school from the contest's sponsor, AST Computer.

It sounded simple, even simple-minded, but, as John Bitove says, "With the crowd, it's the most anticipated, most popular contest we do. The people in the seats go bananas." No doubt much of the appeal lay in the sight of those universal authority figures, high-school principals, looking so inept in public. Invariably the principals' shooting form was abysmal: lunging one-armed underhand shots, shots that left the left foot waggling in the air in a manner that suggested Charlie Chaplin about to dive into a swimming pool. The principals were good sports making fools of themselves, and everybody in the audience relished the spectacle.

The casual gent in the grey sweater was the principal of a north suburban Metro school, and, as he put up his first shot, it became instantly clear that he offered something different from his colleagues in the category of form. He was a left-hander with a smooth motion, and he was getting good height on the ball, a bit of rotation. The shots were headed on target, but were falling just achingly short. The crowd got behind him, cheering for him to bang home a shot, groaning when the ball needed a couple of inches more in distance. The principal adjusted his delivery, and, on his fifth shot, the ball dropped cleanly through the hoop.

The principal high-fived one of the Raptors employees, and in the SkyDome, with most people standing, everybody applauding, the place was as noisy as it had been all evening. John Bitove had it right – the crowd went bananas for the Principal Shootout.

Further along in the game against Charlotte, late in the second quarter, the Hornets called a timeout, and the Raptor bounded onto the floor. This was the team mascot, a fuzzy, comical, non-lethal version of the prehistoric velociraptor. He'd been around the SkyDome all night, doing mini-bits of funny business. He teased the players, fooled around with little kids, took running slides on the floor, performed backward flips, and generally behaved like a cute, acrobatic throwback to the Triassic period 220 million years before.

Inside the Raptor costume was another cute and acrobatic guy. His name was Ryan Bonne, he was in his early twenties, and he had an appealingly earnest face, which he never showed to his public. "If I took my Raptor head off in a place where kids might see," Bonne says, "they'd be shocked. It would be like Santa removing his beard."

Apart from taking his job very seriously, Bonne had many other qualifications for playing the childish-but-complex Raptor. His Winnipeg high-school class had voted him Most Likely to Make It to Hollywood. He held a degree in theatre arts from the University of Winnipeg.

He was a former Canadian junior trampoline champ. And he thought Jim Carrey in *Ace Ventura, Pet Detective* represented a high mark in comic genius.

At this point in the Toronto–Charlotte game, the Raptor was about to attempt the most difficult and spectacular trick in his repertoire. He was going to dunk the ball off a springboard. This was a part of the act that was a staple in all basketball mascot routines. It was introduced in the late 1980s by the Phoenix Gorilla, the mascot of the Phoenix Suns, and was later picked up by every self-respecting mascot around the league. Bonne was good at it. He rehearsed his dunks a couple of dozen times before each game, and he always displayed precision and terrific athleticism when he embarked on what was, after all, a slightly dangerous trick.

The Raptor began the stunt with a long running start. Assistants had assembled a springboard opposite the basket at the north end of the floor, and the Raptor set off at full speed from just outside the centre line in the south end. In his right hand, he carried a ball that was a bit smaller than a basketball, painted in Raptors colours, and he ran with short, stuttery steps. He reached the springboard and flung himself at it. His feet led the way into the board, but his body immediately took over and propelled itself high in the air towards the basket. At the same time, the Raptor's right hand came around and slammed the ball at the hoop in the motion of a guy wielding a tomahawk. The Raptor was on a flight that was at once scarifying, magnificent, kind of nutty, and undeniably the province of a true acrobat.

Alas, the Raptor's attempted dunk hit the rim. He missed the shot. He'd done everything right except finish off the routine with a basket. Whatever emotions Ryan Bonne was feeling inside the costume, the Raptor who faced the crowd in the SkyDome remained the same jaunty mascot, and the crowd loved him as much in failure as in success. The fans gave the Raptor a big hand.

As the Toronto players returned to the floor after the timeout, Herbie Kuhn on the public-address system welcomed back "your Toron-toe *Raaap*-tors." This was not Herbie Kuhn at peak volume. He saved that for the beginning of the game and for crunch times in the fourth quarter. Those were the occasions when he opened up, when he gave full vent to his voice, when the thick veins in his neck threatened to pop their moorings, when he let fly in introducing, with a little dip in the first word and with conscientious separation of the vowels on the second two, "YO-OR TOR-ON-TOE RAAAAAAP-TORS." It always brought the house down.

Herbie – everybody knew him as "Herbie" – was built along the lines of an old-time football linebacker, not very tall but thick and blocky through the middle. He had a shaved head, rubbery face, and especially thick neck muscles. In his late twenties, he lived with his mom and dad and a dog named Princess in the family home in the Beach neighbourhood of Toronto. He was affable and loved the limelight. On some nights at the SkyDome, he seemed to sign more autographs than most players.

Herbie got into the sports-announcing business by doing the football games at Montreal's Vanier College, where he was studying languages and literature. His breakthrough into a status close to the big time came when he was hired to handle twelve of the fifty-four games at the World Championship of Basketball. The man who hired him, Brian Cooper, liked Herbie's potential, liked his affinity for a more hyper approach to stadium announcing than fans at Maple Leafs hockey games or Blue Jays baseball games were accustomed to. And when Cooper joined the Raptors, he took Herbie along, favouring him over the fifty other announcers who applied for the Raptors job.

"I didn't want an announcer who blended in," Cooper says. "I wanted someone who stood out. I wanted an announcer who would become an integral part of the whole entertainment package. As a matter of fact, we had to hold Herbie back at the beginning of the season. He was going overboard. But now he's developed into a personality that makes most of the fans want to cheer along with him. Maybe not everybody likes his style, but everybody *talks* about it."

Among his other attributes, Herbie knows basketball. That's a necessity, since announcing duties require him to interpret the referees' calls on fouls and other developments on the floor and to pass them on immediately to the fans. His pronunciation of players' names, even the unfamiliar surnames of players from Lithuania and Serbia, is invariably bang on. His languages studies at Vanier come in handy here, and Herbie takes pride in, for example, getting the name of the Raptors' Vincenzo Esposito just right. It's Es-pah-si-to, not Es-po-see-toe as in hockey's Phil and Tony.

But, most of all, Herbie functions as in-house cheerleader. He pushes the fans' buttons. Keeps them from sitting on their hands. When Herbie introduces Damon Stoudamire at the beginning of the game – DA-MON STOOOOO-DA-MIRE – the people in the SkyDome know a star player is on the floor. That's how Herbie operates. He'll do anything for the home team.

At the Charlotte game, he allowed his shaved head to be painted with the Hornets logo, a sizzling grey, mauve, and white hornet. The Raptors' TV broadcast of the game opened with a closeup of Herbie's dome. Herbie was a gamer.

The Samuel L. Jackson clip, the Principal Shootout, the Raptor, Herbie the announcer, all fall under the umbrella concept of NBA total entertainment. All were the immediate brainchildren of the Raptors' Events and Operations division. And Brian Cooper had worked out a theoretical basis that embraced and justified all of them, all of the nutty contests and extravagant characters.

Cooper is the head of Events and Operations, a Raptors vice-president. He's a lanky fortyish man with a personal energy field that radiates for blocks. He got his first large taste of combining entertainment and sports when he was CEO of the Toronto Argos in the early 1990s. Those were the years when John Candy was an Argo co-owner, when the team became as famous for bringing the Blues Brothers to Toronto as for winning the Grey Cup. Not surprisingly, it occurred to John Bitove, when he was putting together the Raptors front office, that Cooper made a natural fit to run the show-business end of the team.

"Just think of this," Cooper said in his office one day. "People go home, and they can watch fifty-seven channels on their TV set. They can switch around and watch four sitcoms at once, click from one to the other and get the gist of them all. They can have a channel changer in one hand and play a computer gameboard with the other. They can do all that, and then they go to a sporting event, and what happens? The sporting event seems one-dimensional to them."

Well, maybe Brian Cooper, him and his restless dynamic, can simultaneously absorb "Friends," "Frasier," "Roseanne," and "Larroquette" and tap a computer board. Maybe others would suffer a case of terminal attention-span disorder. But let that pass. Where does he take the concept from there?

"So the idea at Raptors games is to offer people a comparable level of stimulation to what they can get at home," Cooper said. "You put a family at a game. The dad is watching the pick-and-roll play on the floor. The six-year-old is thinking, Wow, the Raptor just went by on a scooter waving a big flag. The mom is thinking about the fantastic steps the Dance Pack just performed. And the sixteen-year-old is looking up at the scoreboard to watch the Homer Simpson clip on Raptorvision. That's a definition of entertainment for the whole family."

And the game? The actual basketball game?

"The point is not to interfere with the integrity of the sport. The point is to enhance the sport. You give the fans something that is different and stimulating and enjoyable without getting in the way of the individual game. That's tricky. But it's helped by the fact that basketball has a natural stage. The floor allows you to focus everybody's attention. Which is what we do with the contests, the Dance Pack, the Raptor's dunks, and all the other stuff we come up with. The Explorers? They're very popular. The Ford Raptors Explorers, guys who get out there with a giant sling-shot and rocket small packages of T-shirts and socks way up into the stands. Fans love the Explorers."

Cooper's responsibilities reach out to areas that, according to some definitions, wouldn't normally come under the heading of entertainment. The national anthems, for example.

"You go to some sports events and you get the same guy singing the national anthem at every game. We don't want that. We want variety. We want somebody different every night. We want Canadian every night. So we've brought in blues singers. We brought in Salome Bey, Bare-naked Ladies. We brought Danosh Bennett out of the Dance Pack. She's a dyna-mite singer. And we had this kid Ashley MacIsaac from the Maritimes on the violin. He *played* the national anthem. John Salley and Oliver Miller listened to him, sort of old-time fiddle, and the look on their faces was, Oh, no, what's going on *here*?"

Cooper raised his hands as if in surrender. "Well, we don't always satisfy *everybody*."

Meanwhile, as the game between the Raptors and the Charlotte Hornets continued, as the half ended in a tie score, 45–45, a most peculiar statis-tic showed up on the Official Scorer's Report. It revealed that, in the first half, the Raptors committed eleven personal fouls, which sent the Hornets to the free-throw line for eighteen shots. By very stark contrast, the Hornets had been detected in only two fouls, which gave the Raptors two free throws. Both were by Damon Stoudamire, and he missed both. It was a vivid disparity, eighteen free throws for one team and two for another. But that was the way the three referees had called it, and the only thing that saved the Raptors was the feebleness of the Hornets at the free-throw line. They hit only ten of their eighteen shots. If they'd made all eighteen, the Raptors would have trailed at the half by eight points.

The number-one beneficiary of the foul calls was Charlotte's power forward Larry Johnson. He was six-foot-seven, 260 pounds, as packed in muscle as the Incredible Hulk, and his postup game had a furious inevitability to it. He would take the ball down low, rock back and forth like the singers in a Snoop Doggy Dog video, then turn and blast the short distance to the basket. Raptor players would scatter in the way that the Lilliputians tumbled off Gulliver.

But with all the body contact, it seemed difficult from the press seats to judge who fouled whom. Was Johnson guilty of charging? Or was a Raptor defender guilty of blocking? The referees on the floor apparently didn't think it was at all challenging to finger the responsible parties. They called no fouls in the half on Larry Johnson, and six fouls in total on the three Raptors who, at different times, were supposed to be guarding Johnson – Tony Massenburg, Ed Pinckney, and Zan Tabak. Fortunately for the Raptors, Johnson's shooting eye was dimmed from the foul line. He made only six free throws in ten attempts. But he was five for nine on his postup charges to the basket. That gave him eighteen points in the half, which was high for the game.

In the intermission between the first half and the second, a slim, handsome young man named Andrew Carter from Binghamton, New York, brought his act to the SkyDome floor. He went to work with a narrow, trimmed tree branch, actually two or three branches fitted together to form a pole about fifteen feet long.

Carter began the act by making a basketball spin on his finger. Then he transferred the ball, still spinning, to the narrow end of the branch. Slowly, gingerly, he raised the branch in the air over the centre of the court, the ball still rotating at the top, until the branch was extended to its full length. Carter carried the branch and the ball to the north end of the court, lowered the ball on a slant to within five or six feet of the basket, and dropped it through the net. He got a big round of applause from the crowd.

But young Mr. Carter wasn't finished. He adjusted another piece of branch into his fifteen-foot pole, until now it reached a length close to twenty feet. He had, as it were, raised the stakes, and, once again, he lifted the spinning basketball high in the air, escorted it to the south end of the floor, held it wavering and trembling ten feet from the basket. The logistics – twenty-foot pole, spinning basketball, ten-foot drop to a narrow basket – seemed sure to defeat the attempt. But, apparently against the odds, Carter released the ball at just the right moment to allow it to plunge crisply inside the basket's rim.

It was all very impressive in the way that people who can burp a recognizable version of "Beer Barrel Polka" are impressive.

Brian Cooper believes that Events and Operations can have an impact on the progress of a basketball game on the floor. Naturally the impact favours the Raptors. The Samuel L. Jackson clip was a small example. By playing the clip after a visiting player has missed a free throw, it may make that player, or another player on the opposing team, misplace his concentration the next time he steps to the free-throw line. But a better – and larger – instance of the effect that Events and Operations might exert on the game comes through the programming of music on the sound system.

During a game, Cooper sits on a small platform behind the media section. From there, through a network of earphones and microphones, he's plugged into eleven people who control the Events and Operations schedule for the game. He's in touch with the video people, with the audio crew, with Herbie Kuhn, with a key operator named Jamie Nishino, who sits beside Herbie and actually calls most of the directions for the evening's routines ("Get the principal ready for the Shootout on the next timeout"). In addition to the eleven people on the communications link, another twenty Raptors employees are scattered around the edges of the floor waiting to be instructed into action ("Bring out the principal *now*"). All of these members of the crew work from a document called a "Raptors Game Operations Game Log." The Log, which has been meticulously drawn up in the days before the game, runs to about five pages and contains an abbreviated description and the timing of all the evening's entertainment events. Nothing is left to chance.

Well, almost nothing. Cooper cuts himself plenty of slack when it comes to the music. Throughout the game, during lulls in play, the sound system blasts short clips of dozens of songs, and Cooper has a play list of hundreds of tunes to select from. He dictates the choice of most songs from his platform perch, and audience entertainment is one obvious factor that figures in his selection.

"At the beginning of the season," Cooper says, "our music was too hip-hop. We were too hip for the room. It's largely a Waspy crowd, and they have to relate to at least some of the music. So we broadened our mix, a little of everything, mainstream rock, summer songs, cutting edge, James Brown. There's even a Bruce Cockburn track on the list."

But, entertainment aside, it's Cooper's view that he can program music that translates directly to what's happening – and what might happen – in the basketball game.

"I've got a group of songs I call Pavlov songs. I play them, and I *know* I'm going to get a reaction from the crowd. For example, if the Raptors come off two baskets in a row and the second one's either a slam dunk or a three-pointer, then there's an intensity on the floor and in the crowd. We don't want to lose that intensity, and there are certain songs I can go to that'll help to maintain the mood. I play "Dancing in the Street" or "Pipe Dreams" or "Devil with a Blue Dress On." Real up-tempo, exciting, high-intensity music. And the crowd stays in the game. The music doesn't let the crowd out of the excitement, and that's gotta help our players down on the floor."

The supreme moment in Cooper's programming occurs in the last quarter. "We never schedule much of anything in the fourth quarter," he says. "We load the contests and the corporate stuff into the first three quarters, and then we let the flow of the game dictate what we do at the end."

If the game is close in the last minutes, if the Raptors are hanging tough, or even leading, Cooper swings into what he calls the Twenty-Minute Workout. It's actually only ninety seconds long, but, in the interests of urging on the fans, it may feel like twenty minutes.

"Suppose there's a minute left, and a timeout's been called on the floor," Cooper says. "Okay, the Raptor comes on. He does a flip one way.

Then he runs down the other way, and he does a slam dunk off the trampoline. Then we switch up to the Raptormeter on the scoreboard, the thing with the needle that measures the noise volume in the building. Herbie says, 'Come on, Toronto, let's welcome your *Rap-tors*.' By this time, the place is bedlam. Everybody's up and yelling. The needle on the Raptormeter is going right off the index. The pitch is so loud inside the SkyDome that it's bound to affect the other team. They have to be thinking of the crowd. So we've helped the flow of the game."

In the game against Charlotte, the Hornets were in front of the Raptors by one point, 87–86. The clock showed 29.7 seconds left in the game. Charlotte called a timeout.

And Cooper signalled for the Twenty-Minute Workout. The Raptor did his back flip. He raced down the floor for a slam dunk off the trampoline. Oops, he missed again. But Herbie urged the crowd to make some noise, and the needle on the Raptormeter swung to the breaking point. The place was a mass of sound.

Play resumed, and Charlotte's guard, Dell Curry, put up a three-pointer. He missed. The crowd's cheering may have thrown him off his shot. Unfortunately, Alvin Robertson was called by a referee for fouling Curry in the act of shooting. Since it had been an attempted three-pointer, Curry got three free throws. He made two of them. The score was 89–86 in favour of the Hornets.

Tony Massenburg came back with a dunk. That put Toronto down by one point with :12.7 left to play.

Charlotte brought the ball up court, and one of the referees whistled Robertson for a hold on Curry, who hit one of his two free throws. Now the score was 90–88.

Oliver Miller inbounded the ball to Willie Anderson, who whirled around and shot, a potential two-pointer to tie the game. The ball rimmed out, and Anderson, hurrying to grab his own rebound, was called for an offensive foul against Curry. Curry sank both of his free throws for a 92–88 Charlotte lead.

Damon Stoudamire nailed a three-pointer at the buzzer, and the game ended with Toronto losing by one point.

Cooper wore a rueful smile. "We almost got them home," he said.

The weird pattern of fouls that began in the first half had continued through the second half, and, by the end of the game, the Hornets had gone to the free-throw line forty-one times, compared with just three times for the Raptors. Toronto had missed all three of its foul shots, thereby setting a league record. No other NBA team in history had ever gone through an entire game without making a single point on free throws. That was interesting, but what was puzzling was the enormous disparity in foul calls. How could the referees call so many fouls against one team and so few against its opponent in the same game?

In the dressing room after the game, Ed Pinckney put the weirdness in perspective.

"When you're a young team, you don't get the calls," he said. "When I first came into the league, Maurice Lucas of the Lakers threw me to the ground, and there was no foul. The ref told me, 'Welcome to the NBA. Now get up.'"

10

MICHAEL

The first item out of the ordinary at the game on Thursday night, January 18, apart from the size of the crowd, was the signage. Not just the existence of the signs that the fans had made at home and brought to the game – until tonight, the SkyDome had been virtually a sign-free zone – but the fact that by far the majority of the signs were directed, admiringly, at the visiting team, at the Chicago Bulls. "Welcome to Raptor Land, Michael." And, "Chicago's Bull Roar." And, for Dennis Rodman, "Dennis the Rebound Menace." Just one lonely piece of pro-Toronto encouragement waved among all the Chicago banners, a far-out salute: "Korea Loves the Raptors."

As for the size of the crowd, the game drew the largest turnout so far this season in any NBA city, the most people *ever* to see a basketball game in Canada – not just in the SkyDome but anywhere in the country. The attendance numbered 36,118, not counting the seventy-one extra requests for media credentials to the game. And the vast majority of these people in the SkyDome, fans and press, practically *all* of them had come to see one player, to see Michael Jordan.

To be sure, Chicago offered other attractions on the floor – the versatile forward Scottie Pippen, the Croatian marvel, Toni Kukoc, power forward Dennis Rodman, who was the league's premier rebounder and its most shameless exhibitionist. The general Bulls excellence was an appeal, too. Their record stood at a stunning thirty-two wins and three losses coming into the game. And there was speculation that this team could equal or surpass the all-time NBA season record of 69–13, which was held by the 1971-72 Los Angeles Lakers of Wilt Chamberlain, Jerry West, and company. The Bulls – and Bulls T-shirts, caps, and windbreakers – were very hot items. But it was Michael Jordan who supplied most of the heat, who was the reason why everybody in the SkyDome was going a little gaga. Here was the greatest basketball player of the age, probably at this moment the most famous person in the entire world.

"This is one of those events you want to be able to tell your grand-children about," John Bitove said before the game. "'I saw Michael play here once.'"

There was something else out of the ordinary: the Jumbotron, in constant use during the baseball season but almost always kept dark on basketball nights, was in operation. It was the huge screen beyond the north end of the court on which Brian Cooper's gang could play around with movie clips and short videos, with live-camera footage of players and fans right there in the SkyDome.

Just before the opening tipoff, a clip from a movie started to roll on the Jumbotron. It showed a large bull – an animal bull, not a Chicago Bull – as a set of thick straps lifted it, helpless, into the air. A boy, ten or eleven years old, sitting just above the press row, watching the screen, let out a screech of happy recognition. He knew the movie clip. His screech was echoed by more soprano screeches around the building. The kids in the crowd – those very young people whom the Raptors hoped to make their paying customers of the future – understood what was coming on the screen. The strapped bull was lowered from the air into a large hole in the ground. A line of print superimposed on the film labelled the hole in the ground "The Raptors' Pit." But the kids already knew that. They got the symbolism of the film clip. They'd seen it all before. The clip was from the raptors' feeding scene in *Jurassic Park*.

Michael Jordan had a quiet first half. He didn't hit his first basket until there were two minutes and twelve seconds left in the opening quarter. It was a fallaway jumper over Damon Stoudamire. At that moment, Stoudamire happened to be guarding Jordan on a defensive switch. Alvin

Robertson, the Raptors' maniac on defence, was assigned to Jordan for almost the entire game, and he performed an effective job in the first half. Jordan took only ten shots, hit on four of them, and ended the half with a measly ten points.

Stoudamire, meanwhile, was a busy bee on offence. On the very first Raptors' offensive play of the game, with Michael Jordan guarding him, Stoudamire beat Jordan off the dribble, went around him, and found Zan Tabak free under the Bulls' basket with a sizzling pass. Tabak dropped in the layup. Stoudamire had eight such assists in the half, setting up his teammates for sure baskets, and, at half time, the Raptors surprisingly led the Bulls by seven points.

At 8:53 of the third quarter, Michael Jordan had the ball, facing the Raptor basket, about fifteen feet in front of it and slightly to the right. Alvin Robertson, both hands reaching out, guarded Jordan closely. Zan Tabak dropped off his man and moved over to double-team Jordan with Robertson. Jordan was crouched, right hand bouncing the ball, nothing else moving. There was no body language to read what he had in mind. He took the first step with his left foot, veering slightly left, outside of both Robertson and Tabak. The first step was so quick, so sudden, that Robertson rocked back on his heels for an instant. He was the very illustration of a man caught off-guard. As for Tabak, he was out of the picture in the split second that Jordan set off. In three more strides after the first step, Jordan was around Robertson and on a free route to the basket. He left his feet, rose to the hoop, rose a little more, covering six or seven feet in the air. And he slammed the ball through the rim.

What Jordan had just done was something of immense audacity and imagination, and it suggested that B. J. Armstrong might have been on the right track seven years earlier. Armstrong was the guard whom the Raptors had drafted and traded away the previous summer, but, before that, Armstrong had been a Michael Jordan teammate on the Bulls for six seasons. In Armstrong's rookie year, 1989-90, he was so daunted at the prospect of keeping professional company on the court with Jordan that he had gone to a library and checked out two books, one about Einstein and the other about Mozart. Armstrong's reasoning was that books about two geniuses might help him to understand a third genius, the one he played alongside every night.

The irony in Jordan's elegant attack on the Raptor basket was that he didn't do much of that sort of thing any more. He rarely drove the hoop these days. Indeed, the drive around Robertson and Tabak was his first of this game and, as it would turn out, the last.

Soaring flights to the basket like that one had once been the cornerstone of Jordan's offensive style. He performed them in games, in Nike commercials, no doubt in his sleep. But now he'd trimmed back on the spectacular air game. Partly it was a matter of age. He was thirty-two years old – thirty-three on February 17 – and he'd lost a half step in speed and gained a little more respect for gravity. And partly it was a matter of precaution. Driving the basket was dangerous for an older guy, all those arms and bodies lying in wait, eager to pound on Jordan. He no longer risked that ambush, at least not as often, at least not when he didn't have to. He had changed his game.

Now he was primarily an outside shooter. When Jordan had entered the NBA from the University of North Carolina in 1984, he had had an indifferent jumper. He didn't need a better one, not with the sensational things he could do with the ball in the air. But over the years, with practice, he acquired a jump shot. A *great* jump shot. He could hit from anywhere on the court. And he invented ways of putting up his jumper that were unstoppable.

For example, there was, as he demonstrated towards the end of the third quarter, his turnaround fallaway jumper. It began with Jordan taking the ball in the high post, near the top of the paint. Alvin Robertson was behind Jordan, between Jordan and the basket, waving his arms, bumping Jordan a little. Jordan faked to go right, faked to go left. He went neither way. Instead, he whirled around on the spot and pushed himself into the air in a motion away from the defender, backwards from Robertson. At the same time, falling backwards, he released his shot in a graceful arc. It was not blockable, this shot, not by anyone under seven-foot-six, a height Alvin Robertson fell shy of by more than a foot. The ball, feathery light in the air, fell cleanly through the basket. A turnaround fallaway jumper. Jordan allowed himself a small smile at the loveliness of the shot. Robertson smiled, too.

In recent months, Dennis Rodman's hair had been green and it had been a shade of red that matched the colour of the Bulls' jerseys. Now, at the

SkyDome, it was blond. The constant dyeing seemed to be wasting his hair away. At the moment, it looked like a withered patch of yellow steel wool glued to his skull.

The tattoos were creepy, too. Many NBA players had taken up the wearing of tattoos in the last few seasons. Some had even done it with discretion and taste; Damon Stoudamire's Mighty Mouse wasn't exactly art, but it added a whimsical touch. But Rodman's tattoos ran from wrist to shoulder on both arms, a mélange of crosses, suns, and heavy-metal images that suggested he had fallen under the needle of the crazed tattooist Bruce Dern played in the 1980 movie *Tattoo*.

But the tattoos and dye jobs formed part of the image that Rodman seemed so intent on cultivating. So did the sex with Madonna, the hanging out at the gay dance club in Chicago called the Crowbar, the dropping of $30,000 in thirty days at the Las Vegas gaming tables, the occasional outbreaks of cross-dressing. Dennis was a wild and crazy guy. Or a cagey and mercenary guy – his publicized weirdness would help the sales of the autobiography, *Bad as I Wanna Be*, scheduled for publication in May. Or maybe, at thirty-four, Dennis was just a guy looking to get a life.

Thank goodness for rebounding. It kept Rodman employed. He had been the best at it in the NBA for the previous four years, averaging a league-leading 18.7, 18.3, 17.3, and 16.8 rebounds per game. He wasn't quite up to those numbers this season, about 14.5 per game, but his average was still better than anybody else's.

Rodman was short to be such a superb rebounder, six-foot-eight. But he had exceptionally long arms, and he appeared to be in marvellous condition, not an ounce of body fat in sight under those tattoos. He seemed to be a tireless runner, too, though he had a peculiar running style: he lifted his knees high in the air, almost to his hips, like a man dashing through a flooded basement.

At about the mid-point of the third quarter in the game at the SkyDome, Rodman prepared to offer an example of his rebounding technique. Michael Jordan was getting set for a shot from the top of the Raptors' key. Rodman had stationed himself in the crowd that was pushing and shoving under the basket. His immediate location among the pushers and shovers was just to the left of the basket and three or four feet in front. Oliver Miller was to his left and Tony Massenburg to the right. Rodman seemed to be in a good spot to grab the rebound if Jordan missed his shot. But he apparently wasn't satisfied. At the moment Jordan put the ball in the air, Rodman began yanking and pulling at Massenburg to get on the other side of the man. Why? What did Rodman know that everybody else didn't?

Quite a lot, as it happened.

Jordan's shot hit the rim on the right side. The ball bounded in the same direction, to the right of the basket, and, when it came down within grabbing range, it was Rodman, leaping at a slight backwards angle, who snatched the rebound. He seemed to have reasoned, when the ball was in the air split seconds after leaving Jordan's hands, where it would bounce, if it bounced at all. Maybe Rodman read the spin on Jordan's shot. Maybe he'd seen so many Jordan jumpers in games and practices that he could predict which way a missed shot would fly. Either way, it was a slick piece of anticipation. Great execution, too, since, after Rodman seized the rebound, he fired the ball to Scottie Pippen on the left wing, and Pippen drove the basket for a layup.

Jordan scored thirteen points in the third quarter, and Chicago went into the fourth quarter with a 67–64 lead. But the Raptors were sticking with the Bulls, and, when Tracy Murray buried a three-pointer at 4:03 of the period, Toronto nosed in front 83–81.

Chicago brought the ball down the floor, and Jordan tried once again to post up Robertson for his fallaway jumper. Robertson fouled Jordan, who sank both free throws. Tie game.

Steve Kerr had now taken over from Jordan the task of guarding Damon Stoudamire. Kerr had a fascinating and tragic background. He was born in Beirut, where, many years later, his father, the president of the American University, was assassinated by Arab terrorists. Two days after the assassination, while Steve was waiting to fly from the United States to the funeral, grief-stricken, he played in a basketball game for his school, the University of Arizona. He led the team to an upset victory, and, only a freshman, became an instant legend on his campus. That was in 1984. Twelve years later, still looking like a college freshman, boyish, clean-cut, Kerr was a Bull, a determined player, perhaps the best three-point shooter in the league, and maybe a touch slow to guard Damon Stoudamire, who hit a basket over him to put Toronto back in front by two.

With the Bulls returning to the offence, Scottie Pippen promptly knocked down a three-pointer from the right corner, and, when the Raptors failed to score on their next trip into the Chicago end, the Bulls called a timeout. They led by one point, 86–85, the clock showed 2:02 remaining, and the crowd knew it was watching a honey of a basketball game.

Near the end of the timeout, Michael Jordan sauntered over to the officials' table. He stopped in front of the two women who kept the records of the game's statistics. Both women were about thirty, dressed in official Raptor jackets. Jordan wore a half-grin, and, even with beads of sweat dotting his shaved head, he looked cool, relaxed, healthy, and attractive.

"You're not getting all my steals," he said to the two women.

It took a second or two for the women to get their tongues moving.

"We've got one steal for you," the woman on the left said.

Jordan held up two fingers. "It should be two."

The first thought that came to the minds of those eavesdropping on this small drama was, How did Jordan *know?* How did he know what the official game statistics showed? Had he taken time during the game to check the sheet? Did he keep track of such minutiae? Apparently so.

But that matter wasn't nearly so interesting as the reaction of the two scoring officials. They stared at Jordan as an early generation of females must have regarded Elvis or, even earlier, Frank Sinatra. They were on the verge of swooning. And when Jordan turned away, back to the game, the two women looked at one another and broke into giggles of relief and awe and gratitude.

Jordan stepped onto the floor, and behind him, he left two women all atremble in his wake. It probably happened every day.

At 1:48, Alvin Robertson again fouled Jordan, who potted his two free throws. Bulls up by three.

Damon Stoudamire brought the ball up court. Before the game, Steve Kerr had said that, in the Bulls' last game against the Raptors, in Chicago, the defence had played off Stoudamire until he got well into the Bulls' zone. But that allowed the Raptors to get too easily into their offence. So, for this game, the Bulls' defence was meeting Stoudamire much earlier.

It's September 1993, and these pleased gentlemen are announcing that they're the new owners of the NBA franchise in Toronto: left to right, David Peterson, John Bitove, Jr., Allan Slaight, and Borden Osmak of Scotiabank.

Smiling John Bitove, Jr., president of the newly named Raptors, introduces his new executive vice-president, basketball, smiling Isiah Thomas. It's May 1995.

Here's the brain trust of the 1995-96 Raptors: left to right, trainer John Lally, head coach Brendan Malone, assistant coaches John Shumate, Darrell Walker, and Bob Zuffelato.

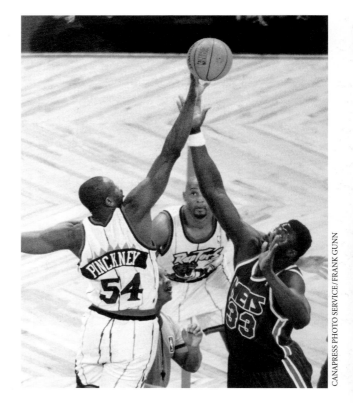

The opening tip in the opening game of the 1995-96 season at the SkyDome, New Jersey Nets versus the Raptors. Ed Pinckney jumps the ball against Yinka Dare, while Alvin Robertson waits for the action to begin.

Brian Cooper, the Raptors' man in charge of events and operations, embraces one of the stars of his basketball shows, the mighty Raptor.

Herbie Kuhn, the public-address announcer, gives his all for the Raptors. That includes his skull, which is painted with a ban-the-Bulls symbol. The Chicago Bulls, that is.

The Raptors' high-scoring forward, Tracy Murray, goes aloft for two over the Houston Rockets' Chucky Brown.

Centre Oliver Miller gets high, too, feathering a delicate shot over Sean Rooks of the Minnesota Timberwolves.

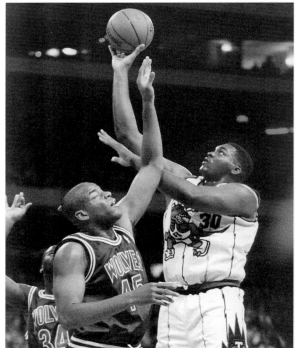

Croatia's gift to the Raptors, centre Zan Tabak, drives to the basket, breezing past Boston Celtics forward Eric Williams on the way.

A Carlos Rogers specialty – he's number 34 – is the block. Here he gets ready to apply one to an attempted shot by New Jersey's Kevin Edwards.

Michael Jordan (right) finds Raptor Damon Stoudamire a pesky guy to guard.
Meanwhile, Zan Tabak, steady as a monument, sets a pick for Stoudamire to roll around.

Raptors guard Alvin Robertson, intent on getting off his shot, ignores the histrionics of Boston's Dino Radja.

Willie Anderson, Toronto's small forward, shows the elegance of his form as he shoots over, once again, Boston's Radja.

To celebrate his selection as the NBA Rookie-of-the-Year, Damon Stoudamire got a Michael Jordan haircut. That's Toronto's new head coach, Darrell Walker, joining in the celebration.

These two men are looking deep into the Raptors' future: Toronto's top draft pick, Marcus Camby, of the University of Massachusetts, and his coach, Darrell Walker.

The only trouble with the new strategy was that Stoudamire happened to be hitting almost every shot he took, no matter where he was on the floor. Which is what he proceeded to do at :56 of the fourth quarter. With Kerr guarding him closely, Stoudamire still sank a two-pointer to narrow the score to 88–87 for Chicago.

On the Bulls' next possession, Robertson pressed Jordan. Kept him off-balance. Jordan put up his shot anyway. It missed. Chicago recovered the rebound. Pippen fired a pass from the right side to Rodman in the middle of the court to Luc Longley, Chicago's big, bulky, Australian-born centre, under the left side of the basket. The passes had been so crisp and swift that the Raptors, thrown momentarily off their defence, didn't have a man near Longley. He dropped in the layup and restored the Chicago lead to three points.

This time down the floor for the Raptors, Kerr harassed Stoudamire into a missed shot, and the Bulls broke for the Toronto end. Jordan took a pass to the right of the basket just outside the paint. He was facing the hoop, and Robertson seemed to have him blanketed. No way Jordan could put up a shot. But he did, a fallaway jumper, and it swished through the basket. A miracle shot.

Brendan Malone called a Raptors timeout. The game clock showed 24.2 seconds left, with Chicago up, 92–87.

A scene from *Animal House* rolled on the Jumbotron. It was the sequence where John Belushi, playing Bluto Blutarsky, was exhorting his frat brothers to take action. "It ain't over till I say it's over! So let's get going!" At the end of the speech, the brothers charged out of the frat house primed for bear.

Stoudamire had the ball about twelve feet from the Bulls' basket. Steve Kerr was all over him. Luc Longley moved out to double-team Stoudamire, huge, seven-foot-two Luc Longley. Stoudamire looked completely hemmed in, surrounded, bottled up. He took a small jump and released the ball in a very high arc over Kerr, over Longley's arms, which were stretched above his head to a height of about nine feet. The ball somehow cleared all the obstacles, skimmed Longley's fingertips, and, when it came down, it dropped straight through the basket. This game was coming down to a contest of miracle shots.

It was 92–89 Chicago, with :16.1 on the clock.

Oliver Miller fouled Longley, who, unaccountably, missed both free throws.

Still 92–89 Bulls, :04.6 on the clock.

Tony Massenburg inbounded the ball to Stoudamire, who was immediately fouled by Steve Kerr. It wasn't a shooting foul. Possession remained with the Raptors. Malone called a timeout. The clock showed 2.8 seconds left in the game.

During the timeout, a camera in the SkyDome feeding footage into the Jumbotron found a gorgeous blonde woman in a yellow sweater. She was standing up in her seat and dancing with a kind of cheerful fury, big smile, pumping arms, full-body shimmy. The camera stuck with her, showing her at ten times life size on the Jumbotron, and gradually, inside the stadium, where pandemonium had been reigning since the beginning of the second half, the crowd forgot about the basketball game and stared silently at the dancing blonde in the yellow sweater. In the Bulls huddle at the side of the floor, Coach Phil Jackson was drawing on a small chalk board a defence for his five starters against the Raptors' final play. One of the five starters wasn't paying the slightest attention to Jackson and his defence. Dennis Rodman, mouth hanging at half-mast, had his gaze fixed on the woman on the Jumbotron.

The day before the game, late on the Wednesday afternoon, Brendan Malone had sat in his small corner nook in the Raptors offices on lower Bay Street and talked about clutch shooting.

"There are players who can make every shot in practice," he said, "players who can hit their baskets in the first quarter, the second quarter, the third quarter. But the question is, Can they score in the last minute of the fourth quarter? Can they hit the basket when the game is on the line? That's the question you ask as a coach, and, if the answer is yes, then you've got a real basketball player. Isiah Thomas, his lifetime shooting average was 43 per cent. That's not particularly high. But in the fourth quarter, if the game was on the line, you went to Isiah, because that's when he scored. His percentage when the game was on the line was more like 70, 80 per cent. We need to have players like him on the Raptors."

For the final :02.8 of the game, Malone put Stoudamire, Robertson, Miller, Massenburg, and Murray on the floor. Of the five, Stoudamire and Murray were the closest thing to the sort of clutch shooter Malone needed. They were also the two most reliable three-point shooters. The Raptors had to have a three-pointer to tie the game. They could hope for a player to hit a two-pointer and to get fouled in the process of shooting, thereby allowing a free throw to tie. But that was very unlikely. No Bull player, recognizing a Raptor putting up a two-pointer, would risk fouling the shooter. The two-pointer would leave the Raptors a point short, and time would have run out on the clock.

Malone assigned Alvin Robertson to inbound the ball. Robertson was standing just inside the centre line in the Bulls' end in front of the officials' table. The four Raptors on the floor arranged themselves essentially in a line across the top of the paint near the Bulls' basket. When Robertson raised his hands to prepare himself for the toss-in – he had five seconds to get rid of the ball – Murray and Stoudamire feinted towards the Bulls' baseline, then turned and ran furiously towards points midway between the centre line and the top of the paint. Stoudamire was on a line closer to Robertson, Murray a few feet to Stoudamire's right. The plan was for Robertson to throw the ball to the guy who got free, Stoudamire or Murray, who would try for a tying three-pointer.

Neither man got free. Steve Kerr had Stoudamire in a straitjacket of coverage, and Scottie Pippen, with his long arms and his brainy sense of defence, was taking care of Murray. Robertson hesitated, looking for Stoudamire or Murray to break loose of the defenders, waiting until the last ticking half second. He could wait no longer.

Oliver Miller, close to the Bulls' basket, recognized Robertson's dilemma and ran back to help out. He reached a spot on Robertson's side of the court, a few feet outside the three-point line. He was all alone. Luc Longley, assigned to guard Miller, probably figured Miller wasn't much of a threat for a three-pointer and let him go.

Robertson had no choice. Miller was the only Raptor open. He tossed the ball to Miller. The clock began to tick down the instant the ball touched Miller's hands. He had 2.8 seconds to do something with the ball. He looked to his left for Stoudamire or Murray. They were still covered. Miller made a passing motion with the ball, but he didn't release it. His feet weren't in position for a shot. He looked slightly off-balance. The clock was down to :01.0. Miller had to do *something* with the ball.

He shot it.

He got the ball off before the clock ran out. If he scored, the shot would count. The ball passed through the air on a fairly low trajectory. And it came down on the basket's right rim.

The shot missed. The buzzer sounded. Game over. A whoosh of disappointment washed down from the crowd.

Bulls 92, Raptors 89.

In the Chicago dressing room after the game, Michael Jordan said, "What the fans on the road come to see is me get fifty and their team win."

That was an old line with Jordan. The first sighting of it in print, at least in a national magazine, came in the November 9, 1987, issue of *Sports Illustrated*. An old line but a good one. The three Toronto newspapers used it next day. Too bad Jordan hadn't quite delivered on the line: he'd scored *only* thirty-eight points, and the Bulls had won.

Jordan gave good interview. In the dressing room, he was barely visible through the thicket of cameras, microphones, and scribbling reporters. But in all the frenzy, he still looked cool, relaxed, healthy, and attractive. He was also accessible and articulate. What he said in the group interview, in his deep voice, wasn't profoundly insightful or outrageously funny, but for a guy improvising answers to the one-millionth interrogation of his life, he sounded astute and good-natured.

Just what you'd hope for from the most famous person in the world.

In the Raptors' dressing room, Tracy Murray had a bit of anger to unload about the fans in the SkyDome on this night.

"The crowd was disrespectful in the beginning," he said. "*Our* fans were cheering for *them*."

Murray had a point, but he might have taken it further. Many of the fans at the game had simply experienced a serious case of awe that Michael Jordan and friends were in their midst. They still felt dazzled and complimented that the NBA had settled in Toronto, and the additional thrill that the sport's greatest player and best team were actually playing a game that counted right there in the SkyDome was just too overwhelming. In another year or two, these fans would no doubt acquire a touch more sophistication about these things. They'd treat a Jordan visit as less of a celebrity occasion and more like a date on the regular NBA schedule – a very significant date – but still one in forty-one, not the *only* one. More people, in a year, would show up as basketball fans, as devotees of the game, as Raptors supporters. Which was a subject that Tracy Murray ultimately arrived at in his short speech of objection.

"I'm sure," he said, "we won some new fans with the way we played tonight."

Russ Granik didn't think more sophistication was called for in Toronto. He said, after the game, that he couldn't believe what he had just experienced. Russ Granik was positively glowing. This was the man who had been in the NBA for seventeen years, the league's chief operating officer, a man who probably thought he had experienced everything that was possible in professional basketball. But he had come to Toronto for the Bulls game, and he found something that, even for him, was fresh and unexpected.

"I was sitting there in the middle of the fourth quarter," he said, "and I thought to myself, I feel like I got into a spaceship, and, when I climbed out, I had no idea where I was, where the spaceship had dropped me. There was a building, it had thirty-six thousand people in it, the place was rocking, and the Chicago Bulls were neck and neck with an *expansion* team. Wherever that spaceship took me, it was a new and wonderful world."

11

HANDS

Alvin Robertson comes across in interviews – which is the only way for a journalist to get at least a small handle on him – as a moderate, reflective, reasoning kind of guy. He might pull down a mask during most conversations with strangers, seldom smiling, buttoning up emotionally. But he doesn't withhold his views when the subjects at hand relate to his profession as a basketball player. He apparently doesn't hold back in charity work, either; his résumé shows an impressive record of service in the NBA cities where he's played: an anti-drug cause in San Antonio, work for Easter Seals and the families of Desert Storm troops in Milwaukee. In Toronto, reflecting another side of the man, it was clear that his younger teammates looked his way for guidance in the game and that he possessed an active and analytical basketball mind. He was the sort, you felt confident, who would one day, after retirement from active play, make a smart and caring coach.

On an afternoon in mid-January, after a Raptors practice, Robertson, Damon Stoudamire, and Willie Anderson were eating a late lunch in the dining room at the SkyDome Hotel. They were spaced over two tables in an empty part of the room, just inside the entrance. A large, handsome woman came in, carrying a clipboard. She worked at the hotel, in charge of the housekeepers and other employees. She spotted the three Raptors.

She knew them and headed in their direction, three cute guys. When she reached their tables, she ignored Stoudamire and Anderson for the moment, but she wasn't about to pass on Alvin Robertson. On him, she laid a huge, affectionate, long, lingering hug.

You definitely get the impression, hanging around places that are Raptor territory, that women take to Robertson in a big way. In the SkyDome Hotel lobby, in the area outside the back door to the Raptors' dressing room after games, a gorgeous woman or two invariably settles on Alvin. None of the bachelor Raptors is exactly lacking female attention. But Robertson – the adorable guy with the Bambi eyes and the guileless expression – seems to be the one who draws the most glances.

All of which – Robertson's intelligence, his charity record, his status as a natural magnet for female admirers – makes it perplexing and troubling that it is he who has got himself into such grief over alleged assaults on women. There are four such charges facing Robertson: the one in late October 1995, arising out of the complaint by a woman after an incident in Robertson's room in the SkyDome Hotel, two more alleged assaults in San Antonio in November 1994, and another charge claiming a break-in at an ex-girlfriend's San Antonio home. It's a possibility that Robertson is innocent of these charges (in fact, he was later cleared of the Skydome Hotel charge). It's a certainty that he has expressed regret and remorse over the episodes that gave rise to the charges. But why did they take place at all? Why, of all people, of all players, Robertson?

One possible explanation may lie in the man's intensity on the basketball court. Maybe the ugly episodes with the women represent an eruption in the civilian world of the incredibly raw force that Robertson brings to his work in the basketball world. Robertson's play isn't violent, but it bristles with an energy that often seems on the brink of explosion on the court. It never happens *there*, on the court, apart from a burst of profanity or a smacking of the palms in frustration over a misfired play or a referee's bad call. Robertson doesn't lose control when he plays basketball. But maybe, just maybe, the intensity simmers inside, looking for an outlet, and maybe the outlet comes along in relations with women that go slightly wrong.

It's a theory, and an adjunct to the theory is that, on the basketball court, Robertson's specialty is in the area of the game that requires the most concentration, the most dedicated work, the highest *intensity*. Robertson is a great defensive player, one of the very best in recent NBA history. That doesn't mean he's a liability on offence. Far from it. With San Antonio and Milwaukee, he had seven straight years of scoring averages in the double digits, including one year, 1987-88, when he averaged 19.6 points over a full 82 games. The man can shoot. But it's in the tough, trenchant, often-tempestuous – not to mention largely unsung – area of defensive play that Robertson has made his reputation, set his records, and won his prizes.

Every aspect of basketball requires practice. Shooting, rebounding, passing. But those things are fun. They mean a guy is handling the ball. But defence? *That's* hard work. There's no ball-handling on defence. No glamour. No fun. Just a lot of dedication to the task at hand. This explains why coaches often have so much trouble getting their players' attention at practices when it's time to think about tightening up a team's defence.

As it happened, Robertson played basketball at a university, Arkansas, where the resident head coach, Eddie Sutton, was a defensive fanatic. In one of the Sutton drills, designated players went two hours straight doing nothing except defending. Robertson benefited greatly from Sutton's teaching, and he says today that defensive ability is the product of nothing more than a willingness to do the grunt stuff.

"Any player who thinks of himself as a good offensive player can make himself into a good defensive player," Robertson says. "He's just got to decide he's going to apply himself."

Robertson's implication is that not many players care to make the commitment. He does. That's how he earned his nickname, "Dog." It's short for dogged. On defence, Robertson never gives up.

All of these qualities – commitment, application, intensity – are especially necessary to perhaps the most difficult and, when it's done successfully, the most spectacular, defensive move. This is the steal, snatching the ball away from an offensive player. Robertson is a stealing master. The statistics prove it. Among all NBA players, active or retired, entering the 1995-96 season, Robertson ranked third on the list of those with the most steals; he trailed behind only Maurice Cheeks and John Stockton, and he would probably have been ahead of both of them if he hadn't missed the past two seasons with herniated-disk problems in his lower back. Robertson has also led the league in steals three times, and, in one of the years, 1985-86, he set the NBA's all-time single-season steals record with an amazing 301 thefts.

According to Robertson, it isn't anything so elusive as "instinct," not some sixth sense, that enables him to make so many steals. Successful stealing begins with something more ratiocinative, with something closer to basketball scholarship.

"You have to learn stealing," Robertson says. "You have to learn how to anticipate what a player is going to do with the ball. You pay attention to individual players and get an idea of certain moves they make when they get the ball. You anticipate their moves in certain situations, and you get yourself in a position to try for the steal. It takes hard work to learn the skill."

Robertson is definitely okay in the hard-work department.

Stealing also takes a willingness to risk the possibility that you'll miss the steal and make yourself look foolish, a willingness to lay yourself bare.

Robertson is okay in that department, too.

And stealing takes a high quotient of intensity. Cold, piercing intensity.

Robertson, it's clear, has plenty of that. Maybe, for better or worse, he has more of it than any player in the NBA.

At 10:23 of the first quarter in the game between the Raptors and the New Jersey Nets at the SkyDome on Tuesday night, January 23, New Jersey's power forward P. J. Brown tried a sixteen-foot jumper. It hit the rim, and the rebound went to the Nets small forward Armon Gilliam, who made the mistake of holding the ball low, at waist level. Suddenly – *very* suddenly as far as Gilliam was concerned – the ball was no longer in his hands. Alvin Robertson, who is five inches shorter than Gilliam, had slipped around Gilliam's right side, reached for the ball, which, at waist level, was accessible to the shorter Robertson, and ripped it free. Robertson whipped a pass to Damon Stoudamire, who was already streaking down court. Robertson took off right behind Stoudamire, who dribbled the length of the floor, then dished off to Robertson for a driving layup.

One steal for Robertson.

At 8:26 of the same quarter, the Nets' shooting guard Ed O'Bannon rebounded a missed Stoudamire jumper and passed the ball to P. J. Brown. Before Brown had much of a grip on the ball, Robertson seized it in his own hands. A steal. But Brown, not giving up, jarred the ball out of Robertson's hands. A steal for Brown. Brown turned to dribble. Robertson moved with him, and, with remarkable hand speed, before Brown could put the ball on the floor, Robertson snatched it back. Another steal for Robertson. He fed the ball to Willie Anderson, who drove for the layup. The ball rimmed out, and Brown got the rebound.

Two more steals for Robertson, making three altogether.

Still in the first quarter, 5:16, Vern Fleming, who had just replaced O'Bannon at shooting guard, was bringing the ball out of the Nets' end. He saw Gilliam up ahead on the right wing and passed the ball in his direction. What Fleming hadn't seen was Alvin Robertson lurking just off the line of the pass, waiting, anticipating. Robertson leaped out and intercepted the pass. He flipped the ball to Damon Stoudamire. Stoudamire scored on a layup.

For Robertson in the first quarter, that made four steals, which led directly to four Raptor points, and four happened to be the number by which Toronto led at the quarter's end. Robertson had no steals in the second quarter, but he deflected three or four New Jersey passes and generally disrupted the flow of the Nets' game. He also did a conspicuously splendid job of defending against his man. In the entire half, New Jersey's shooting guards, the guys Robertson was in charge of, managed just seven shots, and hit on one for a grand total of two points. And Robertson accomplished all of this while committing only a single foul.

The downside for the Raptors was that, even with Robertson's wonderful play, they let their lead over New Jersey slip away. At one time in the first quarter, the Raptors were up by ten points. At the end of the half, they were behind by four.

Tony Massenburg asserted himself in the third quarter.

Massenburg had returned to the lineup, recovered from the foot he had broken in the pre-season game against Vancouver, a month earlier. He played as backup to Ed Pinckney at power forward, gradually getting more minutes, and, by January, he was starting at the position, making Pinckney the backup. Massenburg gave Brendan Malone a couple of qualities that Pinckney didn't possess. Youth, for one thing; Massenburg was five years younger than Pinckney. Massenburg had more pure athleticism, and, on offence, he showed more variety in his moves to the basket than Pinckney did. And his outside shot, on the rare occasions that he took it, was slightly more reliable.

Massenburg was a good-natured guy. He went around with a smile. In really good moods, he effervesced – and when someone six-foot-nine and 245 pounds effervesces, it's powerful stuff. And he could get off a funny line. Indeed, a few days before the New Jersey game, at a Raptors practice, he produced the season's great piece of patter. It came when Brendan Malone was running the players through a five-on-five drill. Massenburg was guarding Carlos Rogers, and he kept denying Rogers the ball. He had Carlos Rogers's number.

"I don't call him sun because he shines!" Massenburg sang out at the top of his lungs after yet another slick defensive move on Rogers. "I call him son because he's *mine!*"

What made Massenburg's constant affability so striking was that his basketball career had frequently put him through the ringer. This began on a June night near the end of his freshman year at the University of Maryland. The day before, the Boston Celtics had taken his teammate, Len Bias, as the number-one pick in the college draft. Now, on the June night in the Maryland dorm, Bias was celebrating. He sampled a little cocaine. He overdosed. Friends rushed him to the hospital. Massenburg had been asleep in another room while the partying was going on, and, when someone wakened him with the frightening news, he joined the watch at the hospital. It didn't last much more than an hour. Len Bias died. And for the next three years, Massenburg played in a basketball program, Maryland's, that had disintegrated under the scandal and shame.

The San Antonio Spurs took Massenburg in the second round of the 1990 draft, the forty-third pick overall, but didn't give him much work in his rookie year, just small parts in thirty-five games, and let him go early the following season, on December 2, 1991. What happened to Massenburg over the following few weeks was so discouraging that it might have bottomed out his confidence forever. Charlotte signed him on December 11, kept him twenty-seven days, and released him. Boston picked him up on January 10, 1992, looked him over for twenty days, let him go. Same thing with Golden State: signed on February 13, checked out for twenty days, released. Just to round out a swell year, Massenburg travelled to Italy and played four games in the Italian league.

Looking for a mental pick-me-up, as well as a job, Massenburg stayed on in Europe for two seasons. The therapy worked. First with Unicaja–Mayoral of the Spanish league, then with Barcelona of the same league, he averaged more than fifteen points and more than eight rebounds in the two years. That fine showing got him a position on the Los Angeles Clippers for the 1994-95 season. Alas, the position wasn't the one he was accustomed to, centre rather than power forward, and the Clippers were a dreadful team, losing their first sixteen games and winning only seventeen on the year. But Massenburg produced nine points a game and six rebounds. Not bad for a player on a dog of a team. But apparently not good enough for the Clippers, who let him go to the Raptors in the expansion draft.

In the opening minutes of the game at the SkyDome against New Jersey on January 23, Massenburg played as if his low-self-esteem problems hadn't been altogether set at rest. He started the game at power forward, but, by 9:50 of the first quarter, he'd been whistled for his second foul, and Ed Pinckney replaced him. Massenburg returned in the second quarter, but didn't get himself untracked, and he ended the half with just two rebounds and three points.

Things changed dramatically in the third quarter.

At 11:04 of the quarter, right off the bat, Massenburg leaped to throw down a dunk. New Jersey's Kendall Gill fouled him. Massenburg went to the line and sank both free throws.

At 7:27, Willie Anderson missed a layup. Massenburg, rising in the air in the slicing manner of a shark breaking the ocean's surface, seized the rebound and laid the ball in the basket.

At 4:31, Massenburg missed a layup, jumped back to grab the rebound of his own miss, and tipped the ball through the hoop.

At 3:29, he took a pass from Willie Anderson to the right of the Nets' hoop and drove on the basket with the determination of a man bolting for a closing subway door. He scored on the layup.

That made eight points for Massenburg in the quarter, eight points with *authority*. He also pulled down four rebounds in the same in-your-face style, and the Raptors ended the third quarter with a three-point lead.

Meanwhile, as Massenburg chipped in his two bits' worth, Alvin Robertson continued to drive New Jersey mad with his defensive genius. There was more of the close guarding, more of the disruptive work, more stealing.

At 2:05 of the third quarter, Robertson once again suckered Vern Fleming. Fleming, looking for a chance to pass, saw his open teammate up ahead, but failed to see Robertson waiting for him to make the pass that Robertson had already anticipated. Robertson picked off the pass and scored on the Nets off a driving dunk.

Fifth steal for Robertson.

At :03.9, with the quarter winding down, Armon Gilliam tried a long upcourt pass in an effort to set up a basket before the buzzer sounded. Robertson intercepted the pass.

Sixth steal.

In the fourth quarter, at 3:55, with the Raptors up by four points, Damon Stoudamire shot from twenty-four feet out, a potential three-pointer. He missed. Shawn Bradley, the Nets centre, rebounded the ball and passed it to Gilliam. Robertson was on Gilliam in a flash, buzzing around the bigger man, flapping his hands at the ball, preventing Gilliam from getting off a pass. Gilliam tried to protect the ball. He held it out at his sides, over his head, low, high, in the middle. He couldn't shake this pest of a Robertson, and finally Robertson batted the ball free and leaped on it. A steal. Robertson shunted the ball to Damon Stoudamire, who passed it to Tracy Murray, who put up a twenty-one-foot jumper. The shot was good.

Seven steals for Robertson, a franchise record, the most steals by a Raptor in a single game.

The Tracy Murray basket that had come off Robertson's seventh steal put the Raptors in front by seven points, and that was the margin of the Raptor victory at the end of the game, 86–79, the team's twelfth win of the year against twenty-eight losses.

Afterwards, Brendan Malone's talk centred on Alvin Robertson.

"Alvin was the key person in the game," Malone said. "He's like a small Dennis Rodman in the sense that he shows you don't have to score to affect a game. How many points did Alvin have tonight? Four. But he was the guy who turned the game our way. He had the seven steals, plus twice as many deflections. All of those things allowed us to get into our offence and score some points. People watching the game may not realize it, but Alvin made the difference between winning and losing."

The court hearings against Robertson on the allegations of assault, in Toronto and in San Antonio, were adjourned to the months after the end of the basketball season.

12

THE MEDIA MAN

John Lashway was of two minds about the arrival of the Portland Trail Blazers for a game at the SkyDome on Monday, February 5. On the one hand, he would be greeting old friends among the Blazer players and officials. On the other hand, he was welcoming to Toronto the organization that, a little over a year earlier, had canned him from the job he'd held for almost nine years.

Lashway, thirty-six, slim, soft-spoken, with a beard and a full head of hair, both light brown and nicely styled, fills the office of executive director, communications, for the Raptors. That puts him in charge of two areas, the team's media service and its community-relations program. He handled the same general function for Portland until the moment, shortly after lunch on January 23, 1995, when Trail Blazer president Marshall Glickman appeared in the doorway of Lashway's office.

"I'm sorry about this, John," Glickman said, "but effective today you're no longer employed here."

"What? You're serious?"

"We're having budgetary problems. We've got to cut from the team's non-revenue-generating areas. Four people are going, and you're one of them."

When the early shock wore off, it became clear to Lashway that, for him, there was life after Portland in the NBA. People around the league knew and liked his work, and offers of positions poured in. He narrowed his choice to Houston or Toronto.

"It was really no contest between here and the Rockets," Lashway says. "When I came up to Toronto for an interview, I liked everything about the organization. And the other thing was, I wanted to go to an expansion team. I'd been in the business long enough that I'd done everything else. I'd been to two NBA finals. I'd worked six All-Star games. The only thing I hadn't done was expansion. This was my chance."

And, so far, the Raptors experience was panning out sufficiently well that Lashway had smoothed away the pain of his sudden leave-taking of the Blazers. "No hard feelings at all," he said. In fact, when he gave the matter second thoughts, he was kind of glad to see his old employer in his new town for the February 5 game.

"All I'd like," he said not long before the opening tipoff, "is for the Raptors to beat these guys."

Lashway's presence in the Raptors front office, an American occupying a central position in a Canadian organization, was part of John Bitove's overall plan.

"The idea," Bitove says, "was to get a mix of people with deep NBA experience, Americans, and, of local people, Canadians who knew the Toronto market."

So, most conspicuously, Bitove hired Isiah Thomas to run the basketball operations. Then he brought in another NBAer, Glen Grunwald, as Thomas's right-hand man; Grunwald, with a law degree from Northwestern, a master's in business administration from Indiana, and four years in the Denver Nuggets office, is billed as the Raptors' vice-president, legal affairs, and assistant general manager. Another vice-president, another Raptor with an NBA background, is Dan Durso. He came from twelve years of running the financial side of the Philadelphia 76ers and six years of the same with the Orlando Magic, and is now vice-president, finance, for the Raptors, the man in charge of contracts, budgeting, and other money matters. And then there's Lashway, the Raptors' chief of communications.

"Part of our job is to show the people here how the NBA works," Lashway says. "All of us, Isiah, Dan, me, have been around the league, and we're able to teach and structure and lead the rest of the Raptor group."

And a large chunk of the rest of Lashway's job is to deal with the Toronto media, which, as he was pointedly warned before he signed on with the Raptors, could be fractious.

How does a guy get into the business of dispensing sports information, compiling and distributing to the media reams of statistics and biographical data about athletes and their teams?

By starting very, very young.

"When I was a kid growing up in Eugene, Oregon, just nine or ten years old," John Lashway says, "I used to listen to all the games in all the sports on radio and TV, and I kept score books on everything I heard. You know how the play-by-play announcers say, 'For all of you keeping score at home . . .?' Well, I was the one they were talking about, the guy scoring at home. Golden State was my favourite basketball team, and Rick Barry was my favourite player. I kept charts scoring every game Barry ever played for the Warriors. I even recorded his points on a bar graph. My older brother said I was growing up in a fantasy world. I never thought that way, and here I am, years later, doing the same thing that I did back then, and getting paid very well to do it."

Lashway took a degree in public relations from the University of Oregon's School of Journalism, and, at the same time, he worked part-time handling sports information for the university. "I didn't know such a profession even existed, sports information," Lashway says. "I just knew I wanted to do it." On graduation, he went at the job full-time, and, after four years, the Portland Trail Blazers hired him. He was twenty-six years old and the second-youngest communications director in the NBA.

Almost a decade later, when Portland let Lashway go, he knew little about Toronto, a city he had never visited. "But I'd become a Toronto Maple Leafs hockey fan from watching them on TV in the NHL playoffs in the spring of 1993," Lashway says. "That was the year they kept reaching the seventh game in each series. I got on the Leafs bandwagon, and then somebody told me I looked like Wendel Clark without the scars. I guess when I finally arrived here, I was really ready for Toronto."

Once Lashway was settled into the Raptors offices, once the basketball season got under way, two Toronto groups came as a pleasant surprise to him. One group was the fans.

"Portland fans were famous for their support of the Trail Blazers," Lashway said in his office one afternoon just before the Portland game at the SkyDome. "We'd sold out at our arena, the Memorial Coliseum, for 810 consecutive games. That was the second-longest streak in sports, second to the Toronto Maple Leafs. The streak ended for Portland at the beginning of this season, but the point about the crowds was that the people came to the arena, then they sat on their hands. They supported the team, but they weren't great fans."

Toronto fans, Lashway has found so far, are different.

"Take the game against Washington back on January 13," he said. "The Bullets are an okay team, maybe a playoff team, but the night they came to the SkyDome, two of their stars were out with injuries. The night itself was terrible for weather, and the Leafs were at home and on TV. With all of that going against us, twenty-five thousand people still showed up for the Raptors, and they were loud, excited, and really into the game. Our fans are the best. I've been around all the NBA cities, and some fans are *not* supportive. Maybe the Toronto people are so great because the sport is new to the city. Maybe they won't be this great in the future. But right now, it sure is fun."

The second group that has surprised Lashway, mostly pleasantly in the end, is the media.

"The media here," he says, "had a reputation in the NBA as being unfair, unreasonably confrontational, and not well-liked. I was told by many people that that's how they were – tough, unduly tough. And when I came up here for my interview, I was led to believe that relations between this organization and the media were pretty terrible."

Lashway discovered a certain amount of truth in this accepted wisdom about the Toronto media.

"In one instance, there was a political agenda at work with a news-paper," he says. "Back in 1993, there were the three different groups bidding for the Toronto franchise, and one group had connections to the *Sun*. When that group didn't win, the *Sun* had an axe to grind, and they ground it."

Then there was a sort of knee-jerk anti-Raptor bias.

"When I got to Toronto, somebody gave me the news clips from the year the Blue Jays started here," Lashway says. "I read all the stories, stuff by Scott Morrison of the *Sun*, Dave Perkins of the *Star*, other people who are still around, and, if you took the words 'Blue Jays' out of the stories and substituted the word 'Raptors,' you'd get the same stories that were printed when we, the Raptors, started up. The issues that they were complaining about in the 1970s relating to baseball – stadium issues, season-ticket issues, price issues, issues about the competence of the office personnel – were the same ones they raised about us. It just seemed to be an automatic thing for the media to do."

But when Lashway began to deal personally with the members of the Toronto media, to meet them and know them, he found a much less intimidating and hostile bunch than he might have expected from advance notice.

"They're good people, friendly, nothing I could object to in the least," Lashway says. "And then of course the educational factor entered into the picture."

Toronto's sports press didn't know much about basketball. What's more, they confessed to Lashway their failings in this area. Even more, they asked him for help. They wanted basketball clinics. Lashway obliged.

"We put on two clinics for the media people," he says. "We set up chalk boards, videotapes. Isiah Thomas and Brendan Malone ran one of the clinics over at a high-school gym. They answered all the questions the reporters asked. What is an illegal defence? What is hand checking? The whole thing was very refreshing. A lot of times in a lot of cities, people from the media pretend they know, but they don't. In Toronto, the reporters came right out and admitted, We haven't a clue about certain things. So we tried to fill in the gaps."

One aspect of the Toronto media that Lashway, almost halfway into the season, found that he still hadn't entirely adjusted to was its size.

"We never had anything this big in Portland," he says. "You start with the three daily papers in Toronto, plus the *Hamilton Spectator*, all of them covering the team on an everyday basis. That number is very unusual where I come from. It's unusual in most NBA cities, except for New York and a couple of others. Plus there's more TV and radio in Toronto than I've ever seen in my life. A radio station like The Fan, I've met two guys from it who cover the games, and the other night I met a *third* guy. Three people from one station covering the team, it's amazing. Up here, the media just keeps coming at you in waves."

The media people assigned to the Raptors – from newspapers, radio, television – were generally agreed on a variety of matters that touched on their work. They agreed, by and large, that the *boeuf bourguignonne* was the tastiest dish served before games at the press buffet on the SkyDome's 300 level; that the sexiest member of the Raptors Dance Pack was Carla; that the players to go to for a fast, sure-fire quote were, first, Ed Pinckney and, second, Alvin Robertson. But apart from such issues, and apart from a camaraderie shared by everyone on the basketball beat – no member appeared to loathe another member – the media people were clearly differentiated by the medium for which they worked.

Print reporters, particularly the writers from the three Toronto newspapers and Canadian Press, formed the top level of the media hierarchy. They were the ones who had the space to be analytical – and critical – about the performances of the Raptors on the floor and of the bosses in the offices. They spent more time on the job, more time interviewing players, watching practices, probing Brendan Malone and Isiah Thomas for answers to troublesome questions. The TV and radio people, by contrast, confined in their reportage to short snaps of two minutes or less in the news reports on their stations, tended to move quickly and to spend little time hanging out. They restricted their questioning, if they asked anything at all, to soft topics: "How do you feel about playing your first game in two months, Tony?" There were notable exceptions: the guys from The Fan radio station were astute about basketball, and so were the CBC reporters, on the occasions when they showed up. But the print reporters as a group occupied the top of the media heap.

Brendan Malone's post-game press conferences, as an illustration of the media at work on different levels, fell into a regular pattern. These sessions were held in a SkyDome employees' lunchroom across the wide corridor from the Raptors' dressing room. The room was equipped with a microphone connected to a sound board that was monitored by a technician. Malone spoke into the mike, and, immediately behind him, fixed to the wall, was a shiny wooden board decorated with the Raptors logo. The board, gleaming in back of Malone as he stood in front of the cameras, made the locale look much grander on TV than it was in – rather grubbier – reality.

Malone, according to the pattern of the event, came across the corridor about ten minutes after the end of a game, stepped briskly to the microphone, and launched into a monologue of as long as five minutes, in which he offered his views on the game. He tended to be more windy after wins than after losses. Once he stopped, he was open to questions. At this point, unless some obviously crucial matter remained to be addressed, the TV people usually packed up their cameras and scurried across the corridor to shoot footage of the game's star Raptor. Some radio reporters likewise deserted Malone at this stage. The print representatives stayed. They had questions. They *always* had questions for the coach.

Doug Smith of Canadian Press was frequently first up to quiz Malone. His questions fell into the meat-and-potatoes category; he had a reliable instinct for homing in on the play or the strategy that might have made a difference in the game. Did Malone really intend Oliver Miller to take the jumper that missed at the third-quarter buzzer? Everybody scribbled the answers to Doug Smith's questions.

Mary Ormsby of the *Star* could be counted on to ask questions with an edge at those times when an edge was called for.

Craig Daniels of the *Sun* had the manner of a probing social worker, gentle but determined. His determination was born partly of a failing he saw in Malone's answering style. "He'll start to answer before I've finished asking the question," Daniels says. "The result is that he doesn't answer the question I'm really asking." Daniels tried not to let Malone get away with short-changing him. He asked the question again, the full question. He was persistent. He was a typical print person on the basketball beat.

An eclectic collection of reporters representing a variety of newspapers and magazines augmented the contingent from the establishment print. There was a writer from *Corriere Canadese*, an Italian-language Toronto weekly (this writer took scrupulous notes); a reporter from *Share*, a magazine for the local Caribbean audience (this reporter took no notes at all); an Argentinian writer and editor, who put out a Spanish-language monthly basketball magazine (this writer-editor was such a rabid Raptors fan that he had no time to lift a pencil or tap a keyboard).

Tom Tebbutt, a freelancer, an erudite fellow with a whimsical streak, was best known as the *Globe and Mail*'s tennis correspondent (he hadn't missed a French Open since 1978), but he was also a basketball fan who hoped to shop hoops stories to any market that occurred to him. He made a particular habit of dropping in on the visiting team's dressing room after games.

"The people in there are in a better mood because they're usually the winning team," Tebbutt says. "The coaches are always very nice to me, Doug Collins for Detroit, Brian Hill for Orlando. Lenny Wilkens, the Atlanta coach, talked to me for a half hour. The only exception was Mike Dunleavy, the Milwaukee coach. For some reason, he was terribly grouchy. And his team had *won* the game."

But, of all the print people on the Raptors scene, the one with the most off-beat responsibilities was Pierre Lebrun.

In *I Gave at the Office*, a very funny 1971 crime novel by Donald E. Westlake, a prolific American writer who specializes in very funny crime novels, the central character and narrator, Jay Fisher, has a bizarre job. He works for Townley Toomis, a highly popular radio and TV personality on a major U.S. network. One of Townley's many shows is a lunchtime radio program featuring his interviews with famous and almost-famous people. But Townley, being so busy, lacks the time to do the interviews himself. So Jay Fisher handles that part of things, sitting down with each famous or almost-famous guest at a quiet table in a New York restaurant called The Three Mafiosi and reading Townley's questions to the guest, who delivers his or her answers into a tape recorder. Later, Townley dubs in the questions between the guest's answers, and the show is broadcast as Townley's own work.

Pierre Lebrun's job was something like Jay Fisher's.

Lebrun, an easygoing guy from Ottawa, in his late twenties, worked for Canadian Press as Doug Smith's man in the *other* dressing room. Near the end of each basketball game, Smith tapped the lead to next day's CP story into his laptop. He showed the lead to Lebrun, letting him get the drift of the story that Smith intended to write. Then, after the final buzzer, Smith went to the Raptors' end of the building to ask questions of Brendan Malone and to quiz the players. Lebrun did the same thing at the other end of the building, in the visiting team's dressing room, where, guided by the lead to Smith's story, he got quotes from the coach and the players, and jotted them hurriedly in his notebook. Smith and Lebrun met up a few minutes later in the press room. Lebrun showed Smith his quotes. Smith rejected some, accepted others. The quotes he liked soon found their way into Smith's final account of the basketball game. Thus, Lebrun's interviews were often central to the story, but he got no byline.

But, the way Pierre Lebrun looked at it, there were rewards to his job, even if he alone was aware of them.

"My favourite interview was with Dennis Rodman after the Bulls game," he said one night by way of explanation. "That was because Rodman answered all the questions I asked and because he spoke in a very colourful vernacular. But mostly it was my favourite because all my quotes, every one of them, got into the final story. That was satisfying."

At 2:44 of the second quarter of the February 5 game between Toronto and Portland, Tracy Murray hit a twenty-one-foot jumper off a feed from Damon Stoudamire. The basket made the score 40–33 in favour of the Raptors, and, at seven points, they equalled their biggest lead of the game.

For the rest of the quarter, for the two minutes and forty-four seconds to the end of the half, nothing much happened to the Raptors that was good.

The first time down the court after Murray's jumper, the Raptors couldn't shake a man loose for a shot. They allowed the twenty-four-second clock to run out and turned the ball over to Portland.

The next time down the court, Willie Anderson made a bad pass, and the ball was intercepted by Arvydas Sabonis, the Trail Blazer centre.

Just past the one-minute mark, the Raptors brought the ball into the Portland end for a third time. Damon Stoudamire drove the basket for a layup. The Blazer power forward Buck Williams blocked it, and Portland recovered the ball.

And on a fourth trip down the floor, Stoudamire, dribbling the ball close to the sideline, inadvertently stepped out of bounds. The ball went over to the Trail Blazers.

In the meantime, while the Raptors were committing these four consecutive blunders, these wasted attempts at scoring, Portland registered four points, and the half closed with Toronto now leading by only three.

Damon Stoudamire had a brilliant third quarter. He took four shots, all jumpers, and hit on three of them. One was a three-pointer, and he went two-for-two from the free-throw line. That made nine points for the quarter. And he set up two other baskets, one with a sizzling pass that sent Oliver Miller in on a layup and another that cleared the way for an Alvin Robertson jumper.

Toronto led by five points at the end of the third quarter in an exciting game.

But the trouble, as far as the Raptors were concerned, was that Rod Strickland seemed to be heating up for the Trail Blazers. He too had nine points in the quarter. He too was rallying his team. Strickland was Portland's point guard and its most consistent shooter. Twenty-nine years old, six-foot-three, he played with remarkable ease. His moves were subtle, virtually anonymous, and his facial expression reflected zero emotion. He might have been churning with feelings inside – in fact, anger was probably seething through Strickland's psyche, because he had been carrying on a lengthy feud with Portland coach P. J. Carlesimo – but, from the outside, he appeared to be, rather disconcertingly for his opponents, Mr. Blank.

Strickland began the fourth quarter resting on the bench. He came into the game at 9:30. By this time, Toronto had built a nine-point lead on a gorgeous hook shot by Zan Tabak. Then Strickland got serious. Over the following seven minutes of play, he scored on a driving layup, an eight-foot jumper, a twelve-footer, two free throws, and a jump shot from fifteen feet. That tied the game with 1:23 left.

Strickland got significant help in this run from the league's most unlikely rookie. He was Arvydas Sabonis of Lithuania. Sabonis stood seven-foot-three, with a stolid, erect build, and had a haircut that looked like it wouldn't have been out of place on a Russian Politburo member, circa 1958. Portland had drafted Sabonis in 1987 when he starred for the Soviet National Team. But politics and money kept him in Europe, and it wasn't until a lucrative contract with Real Madrid of Spain ran out in 1995 that, at last, at age thirty-one, he elected to try the NBA.

Age and leg injuries had cost Sabonis much of his mobility, but he still showed Portland some nifty skills. He was a fine passer for a big man, adept at no-look and over-the-shoulder feeds in traffic to his teammates. He also had a smooth outside shot, and, with his enormous size, he was a rebounding force on the inside.

In the last quarter of the game against the Raptors, it was mainly

Sabonis's rebounding that stymied Toronto. He seemed to get position with ease on Oliver Miller, the Raptor centre, and to pick off rebounds at either end of the floor in the manner of a man catching butterflies with a net. He had three offensive rebounds in the quarter and four defensive rebounds. Miller had just a single rebound, on defence, during the whole quarter. It was Sabonis who meant that Portland controlled the boards and kept the ball to themselves.

All this sterling stuff by Sabonis and Strickland put Portland in front by two points at :39.3, when Sabonis scored on a fast-break layup. Toronto called a timeout, and set up a play for Damon Stoudamire. Under pressure, he hit an eight-foot running jumper. Tie game, 22.5 seconds to go, and Portland went into a timeout to arrange one last shot.

With time back in, Rod Strickland dribbled the ball to the top of Toronto's key. Alvin Robertson was guarding Strickland. Inside, under the basket, three Trail Blazer big men, including Sabonis, pushed and shoved for position. Behind Strickland, Portland's shooting guard, James Robinson, hung about by himself. Robinson was a third-year man, not a terrific outside shooter. In this game, he'd hit on only two of eight shots, one for five from three-point range. He didn't seem a threat.

Strickland dribbled in place at the top of the key, letting the clock run down. When it showed fewer than two seconds left, he began a drive towards the basket, veering slightly to his right. Robertson stuck with him. In mid-drive, Strickland unexpectedly – unexpected as far as any Raptor was concerned – turned back in mid-air and whipped the ball to James Robinson. No Raptor was within ten feet of Robinson. No one was guarding Robinson, who was standing about three feet beyond the three-point line. The clock showed .02 when Robinson put his jumper in the air. It was good.

Portland 90, Toronto 87.

One of John Lashway's duties as communications director is to escort Brendan Malone into the post-game press conferences. The purpose of this chore seems slightly mysterious. Lashway never says anything at the press sessions. He simply stands at the back of the room as Malone talks, and, when the last question has been asked, he waits to accompany Malone back to the Raptors' dressing room.

Ten minutes after the Portland game, Malone, with Lashway riding the point, walked into the press conference and stepped to the microphone. Steam might have been coming from Malone's ears. His mouth was a tight horizontal slit. When he talked, his lips barely moved, and his eyes seemed to rest deeper than usual in their sockets. Brendan Malone was very angry.

Instead of making his usual opening remarks, Malone waited for a question. Doug Smith asked it. "At the end," he asked, "did you plan to double-team Strickland?"

Malone got rid of that one in a hurry. "Alvin was on Strickland," he said. "We thought Strickland would go to the basket and pass it off to somebody to shoot a two. We just broke down defensively. James Robinson shouldn't have been that open."

Without waiting for another question, Malone rushed into what was really on his mind, what was making him so furious. "The moment of truth doesn't necessarily come at the end of a basketball game," he said. "You don't always lose them in the last few seconds. We lost this one in the last minutes of the second quarter. We had a good lead. Then the last four times down the court, we made bad shots or turned the ball over. We went down into their end four times and didn't get a basket. Not a single point. That's when we lost. We had a lead, and we didn't take the opportunity to drive the stake into their heart. Instead, we let them come back into the game, and then Rod Strickland took over. He's probably the most underrated point guard in the league. He should be on the All-Star team. We gave him a chance to beat us, and he took it."

Malone answered a few more questions, and gradually the room cleared of reporters, leaving Malone and John Lashway alone. Through the windows that looked into the room from the corridor, Malone could be seen tapping his fingers on the pages of the game's official play-by-play report. He kept pointing angrily at the pages and murmuring to Lashway, who nodded and said little. Lashway looked as though he were playing psychiatrist to Malone's troubled patient. Just another part of John Lashway's job as communications director of the Toronto Raptors.

13

TWO BIG KIDS

In the early afternoon of February 6, the day after the loss to Portland, the two young men sitting at the far right end of the row of dignitaries on stage in the auditorium of Vaughan Road Collegiate could have passed for a couple of students. Exceptionally tall students, yes, close to seven feet both of them, but they had the gawky shyness of kids who are put on display, still and solemn one moment, erupting into muffled giggles the next. They avoided eye contact with everyone, especially with the students who filled the seats in the auditorium in front of them. They paid attention only to one another, conferring in whispers behind their hands when other speakers were standing at the microphone in the centre of the stage. They whispered and frowned, gave one another quick grins, jiggled their long, long legs. They were nervous.

These two were Oliver Miller and Carlos Rogers, and they had come to Vaughan Road to speak to the school's students and to the younger kids who had been brought in from nearby J. R. Wilcox Public School. The players' appearance was part of the Raptors' Community Outreach Program. All of the Raptors players are required by the team to speak to at least one school group during the basketball season. B. J. Tyler, the backup guard who was on the injury list for the whole year, held the team record; by late January, he had addressed assemblies at no fewer than eight schools. Most players – Miller and Rogers fit into this category – settled for one or two appearances each. But no matter who spoke or how often, the subject was the same for everyone: stay in school. That was the theme: basketball stars, even if they looked like kids themselves, telling high-school students not to give up too soon on their education.

Vaughan Road probably qualifies as an inner-city school. It is situated in the City of York, a small, working-class and middle-class borough in northwest-central Metropolitan Toronto. The houses near the school are narrow and sturdy and mostly well cared for. The neighbourhood had once been heavily Italian, but now it had attracted a growing Caribbean community. The largest concentration of black shops in Metro lay just north and west of the school. And a fairly substantial percentage of Vaughan's students are black; when the school's senior girls' basketball team, City of York champs, was summoned to the stage for congratulations as part of the February 6 program, the team was made up of five black girls, three white. On the negative side of the local race picture, it was only three weeks earlier and a few blocks from the school that a Metro policeman had shot a man who was standing in Bathurst Street, waving a sword and apparently threatening to do some bloody business with it. The man with the sword was black, and the white policeman shot him dead.

Speaking of violent death, Rogers and Miller knew a thing or two about it from personal experience, specifically about murder. Rogers grew up in the Detroit projects, one of a very large family that got slightly smaller when an older brother, Kevin, fifteen years of age at the time, was gunned down by a kid in a street gang. Miller's brush with murder had come more recently. Just as the Raptors' training camp was beginning in the autumn, a judge in Fort Worth, Texas, had sentenced Oliver's father to thirty years in the penitentiary for killing another man. The victim was a real-estate agent who had cheated Miller senior out of $100,000 worth of land he had inherited. Mr. Miller went a little crazy and shot the swindler. All of this was established in court – the cheating, Miller's understandable rage, his loss of control, even that Miller may have been mentally ill – but the judge still put him away for thirty years without parole, long enough that the poor man would surely die behind bars.

With those sort of experiences in their pasts, what Rogers and Miller were going to say to the kids in the Vaughan Road auditorium had the potential to be very serious stuff.

Community relations – the thing that Rogers and Miller were about to become a part of – is a big deal with the Raptors. Seven employees work full-time or part-time on that branch of the team's operation, and, apart from arranging talks by players, the program embraces such worthy endeavours as the distribution of free tickets to underprivileged children, hefty donations to various kid-oriented charities, the staging of youth basketball tournaments, tie-ins with dozens of community groups, and a project with schools and the Metro Police.

The inspiration for the latter originated with a specific cop. He was Det. Const. David Stinson of 51 Division's youth bureau. Stinson was working with an eleven-year-old abused child when he hit on the notion of taking the child to a Raptors game. He called the Raptors, looking for a couple of tickets on the house, and James Williams, whose official Raptors title is community outreach coordinator, responded with two $113 courtside seats and with the idea of expanding the combination – police, kids, Raptors – into something on-going. The result was a sub-program called Courtside, Kids, Cops & Community, under which younger public-school children, chosen in groups of four from each school on the basis of such accomplishments as improved attendance, attitude, and academic excellence, are rewarded with prime tickets to a Raptors game. The kids have two chaperones for the evening, their teacher and a police officer from the neighbourhood.

James Williams, the outreach coordinator, was himself developing a modest fame in Toronto schools for his motivational talks. Williams is a tall, powerful man with a James Earl Jones voice, and one of his typical visits was to Shelter Bay School in Mississauga, west of Toronto, a school for kids from junior kindergarten to grade six. Williams's major prop during his talk was something he called a "pride sheet." It spelled out "PRIDE" vertically in large letters, and five more words extended across the sheet from each of the five letters that made up "PRIDE." The "R," for example, formed the first letter of "RESPECT." So Williams talked to the little kids about pride and how you earned it and displayed it, about respect and how you showed it for the people you met. And the kids soaked up every lesson that Williams preached.

"Our children heard from James that the values we talk about at the school are values that other people also aspire to," says Mac Campbell, Shelter Bay's principal. "He said the Raptors believe in these values, and, coming from James, that made a big impression on our kids. You can still see the effect around the school, because the kids went out and reproduced their own pride sheets."

No doubt the Raptors have practical motives of a commercial and public-relations nature for carrying on such admirable works. The kids of Mission Bay today could be the Raptors' season-ticket buyers of tomorrow. Or, if not customers or even fans, they would at least grow up thinking fondly of the Raptors. But, those factors aside, there is a strong feeling of altruism running through the team's Community Outreach Program, of a genuine sense of caring for kids, especially for kids who are growing up in tough circumstances. Indeed, people around the Raptors offices get positively messianic when they talk of community outreach. They slip into something close to hyperbole.

"I don't know if any organization in the history of professional sports," John Bitove said, "has spent the money or put the resources behind community relations like we have."

Or James Williams: "We're making an impact on these kids' lives not just for now, but forever."

Herbie Kuhn had come along to Vaughan Road Collegiate as master of ceremonies, Herbie, the announcer at Raptors home games, the guy whose voice could crack windows at one hundred feet.

"All right," Herbie said into the microphone, his voice operating at only half volume, "is everybody out there a *Raptors* fan?"

"YESSSS!"

"Then you *know* how I introduce the team at the SkyDome. You *know* what I say. So, right now, when I say, '*Toronto*,' I want you to scream, '*Raptors*.' Okay? Here goes . . . And *now*" – Herbie's voice ratcheted up a couple of decibels – "your *Toronto* . . ."

"RAPTORS!"

The auditorium rocked.

Once Herbie had the kids warmed up, Vaughan's principal took over, Terry Baytor, a proper but comfortable-looking man in his forties. He announced that he'd just reviewed the students' report cards for the first semester. Seventy-three students received honour marks, 80 or better, and twenty of those had scored over 90. The kids applauded politely. Baytor had another announcement: the Raptors were donating to the school 150 tickets for the Bulls game on March 24. The kids applauded wildly.

The mayor of York brought greetings. She was Frances Nunziata, not a politician whose oratorical style was Churchillian, or even Chrétien-esque. The kids were growing restless. A lady from the school board brought more greetings. The kids were beginning to mutter. Toby Cox, president of the student council, presented each of the people on the stage with a Vaughan Road sweater. For Rogers and Miller, the sweater sizes were marked on front in large letters: triple x. That got a big laugh from the kids.

Paul Jones stepped to the microphone. Jones, a handsome, thirtyish man, had a foot in both camps, basketball and education. A former teacher at a York junior school, he was now a vice-principal in the system. And in Toronto basketball, he had starred in high school (Oakwood Collegiate) and at university (York), and had become the colour commentator on CFRB's radio broadcasts of Raptors games. He talked to the Vaughan kids about Rogers and Miller, dropping tidbits of inside dope – that Rogers was the team's best chess player, Miller the best at dominoes. And then Jones introduced the first of the afternoon's two major speakers.

"I give you Carlos Rogers."

Just nine days earlier, on Sunday afternoon, January 21, Rogers had enjoyed his most satisfying fourteen minutes as a Raptor in the win over the Boston Celtics at the SkyDome. With a couple of minutes to go in the game's third quarter, the Raptor centre, Zan Tabak, had been whistled for his fourth foul. Brendan Malone wanted to get another big man into the game to replace Tabak. Tony Massenburg was already on the floor. Oliver Miller had been laid low by the flu. Who would Malone call on? Ed Pinckney? John Salley? Malone gave the wave to Rogers.

That was a surprising choice for a couple of reasons. One was that Rogers had hardly played much all year, getting into a mere twenty-three games for about twelve minutes a game. And, for another thing, Malone had been using Rogers mainly at small forward rather than at Rogers's own preferred positions of power forward or centre. But maybe Malone had a hunch, maybe he appreciated the way Rogers worked hard at practice, even if he was getting so little game action. Rogers went into the Celtics game, stayed in for all of the rest of it, fourteen minutes, and became one of the architects of the victory.

It wasn't his scoring that did the job; he got four points off two-for-five shooting. No, it was his ferocious and inventive defensive play. Rogers was all over the court. Six-foot-eleven, but skinny at 220 pounds and remarkably quick, he showed terrific speed and athleticism. He kept in the faces of the Celtics' big men, boxing out, rebounding (five of them), and, with eleven seconds to go, Rogers made a spectacular set of defensive moves that saved the Toronto win.

Damon Stoudamire had just hit a jumper that put the Raptors in front 97–95. The Celtics brought the ball up court. The pass went to Dino Radja at the left of the Toronto basket. Both Rogers and Massenburg jumped into double coverage on Radja, who whipped the ball to the uncovered Rick Fox on the other side of the basket. Fox went up for what appeared to be an easy layup that would tie the game. But Fox made a small tactical error. Going up for the shot, he pumped the ball, and double-pumped it, and, in the short second or two that the pumping took, Rogers flew across the space between the two players, leaped into the air above Fox, and swatted the ball from its upward path to the basket. The ball rebounded straight to Radja, six feet from the basket. He tried a jumper, but Massenburg and the swiftly recovering Rogers put such pressure on him that he missed the shot. Rogers grabbed the rebound, and the game was over.

Afterwards, Rogers was the noisiest guy in the locker room. Actually, that was no rarity. Even when he wasn't in a celebratory mood, as he was after the Celtics game, Rogers's voice, high-pitched, carrying, insistent, often rode over top of the room's steady babble. The voice could be abrasive, too, as it was most notably after an exhibition game against New Jersey when Rogers thought the statistics people should have credited him with more than the two official blocked shots he was awarded. That was Rogers, rancorous one night, joyous another, always in full voice.

A mercurial guy, but what else might he be coming out of a childhood as deprived as his? A home in a ghetto in northwest Detroit, and a dad, an angry man, who was one of two things, absent or abusive, a bully who beat up his kids. Family was mother, Jacqueline, and his eleven siblings (Carlos came tenth in line), reduced to ten in 1988 when his brother Kevin was murdered.

Carlos found comfort in basketball. He learned it as a little kid on the Dexter Davison playground and developed into an all-city, all-state star at Northwestern High. But to keep going, to take his basketball to the next level, Rogers needed two cracks at higher education. First he went to the University of Arkansas–Little Rock. He sat out his freshman year of basketball, because he didn't have the marks and was academically ineligible. He played in his sophomore year, not badly but not great. He transferred to Tennessee State, and again sat out his first season. Then, in seasons two and three at the school, he blossomed.

Before Rogers's arrival, Tennessee State had gone four straight seasons of twenty or more losses in each year. With Rogers, the school won its first-ever Ohio Valley Conference championship. Rogers himself was named the conference's Player of the Year twice, and racked up big, big numbers in his final year: 24.5 points, 11.5 rebounds, 3.0 blocked shots. This was clearly a guy headed for the NBA, but, as in all stages of Rogers's life, the step into pro basketball didn't come easily or flow smoothly.

In the 1994 college draft, the Seattle SuperSonics made Rogers their first pick, the tenth overall. That was heartening. But two months after the draft, Seattle moved Rogers out in a six-player trade with the Golden State Warriors. The trade was a rejection of sorts; Rogers hadn't played a single game in the NBA and already one team had passed on him. And it wasn't as if he didn't have other responsibilities, other worries. Back in Tennessee, there was a girlfriend and two little kids, Carlos's kids, Carlos, Jr., the toddler, and baby Ariel. Life was complex.

It got more turbulent at Golden State. Just signing a contract turned into a marathon, with Rogers's agent and the Warriors batting terms back and forth for two months. By the end of negotiations, Rogers had a nice contract – $8.5 million over nine years, all guaranteed – but he had missed all of the training camp and the exhibition season. Not a recommended way for a rookie to break in.

By the time Rogers finally joined the team, in November 1994, its makeup had changed in ways he didn't care for. Golden State had traded Chris Webber to Washington. Webber wasn't just a marvellous power forward, the number-one pick in the whole 1993 draft; he was also a pal of Rogers's, another Detroit guy, someone Rogers had played against in high school. Without Webber, Golden State's offence revolved mainly around its splendid outside shooters, Tim Hardaway, Latrell Sprewell, Chris Mullin. That didn't leave much for the guys inside, especially for a late-reporting rookie like Rogers.

Injuries got in the way, too. First, the strained lower back. It kept Rogers out for thirteen games in December and January. And an injured right ankle accounted for fifteen more missed games later on. The ankle was so bothersome that, after the season, Rogers had arthroscopic surgery to take out loose bone and cartilage.

Then there was his mouth. It wasn't injured. In fact, it was working overtime. Rogers didn't keep to himself the negative views he had of the Warriors' guard-oriented offence, of the selfishness he perceived in some of his teammates, guys, he thought, whose preoccupation was with their own stats at the expense of the team. Rogers spoke up, and he found himself in a feud with Tim Hardaway. That was the wrong teammate to tangle with. Hardaway was a player with credentials, five years in the league, a consistent twenty-point scorer, quick, clever, a leader, an all-star. Hardaway got very pissed with Rogers, and, almost a year later, when he came to Toronto for a Warriors game at the SkyDome on November 27, he still had no use for the guy.

"It's to [Rogers's] benefit to keep his mouth closed, but he can't," Hardaway said when he was asked about Carlos after the game. "He thinks he's a joker, but he's not."

But with Golden State in 1994-95, despite everything – despite the Hardaway feud, despite the injuries, despite the offensive system – Rogers grew more assured on the floor as each month passed. March was his second-best scoring month, with 10.6 points per game, and April was his best, 12.4. The guy was getting better, a bounding, athletic player, young, improving, probably teachable. Which had been good enough for Isiah Thomas, reason enough to deal B. J. Armstrong to Golden State for Rogers and three other guys.

In Toronto, Rogers didn't immediately find a place in Brendan Malone's regular rotation, but the move helped to bring a measure of stability to the rest of his life. The girlfriend back in Tennessee? Rogers broke up with her after eight years, but he got custody of the kids, Carlos, Jr., by now six years old, and Ariel, three. Rogers rented a good-sized house in Richmond Hill, north of Toronto, and set up an extended household: Carlos, his two kids, an older sister, Louise, and her three kids. Things were getting steady, secure, like a real family.

Rogers, in mustard-coloured trousers and a sweater in vertical stripes of beige and yellow, walked to the microphone in the Vaughan Road auditorium, and, in those four or five steps, he seemed to lose the nervousness he'd shown earlier and to take on a kind of detached confidence. He began to talk, without anything in front of him, no typed speech, no notes, and what he said, speaking for fifteen minutes without pauses or hesitation, almost without punctuation, in sentences that ran into one another, was a mix of the surreal and the gritty. He drew on much autobiography, the story of the kid from a ghetto. Up on the stage, he looked as if he had entered another world, one of memory.

"In my environment in Detroit, I watched a whole lotta guys fall by the wayside. They are the people who are doin' *nothing* today, the guys who say what they *coulda* been, the girls who say what they *woulda* done if they wouldn't have got pregnant, the guys who say, Man, I was the *baddest* basketball player in school. He's the same guy, the one who said that, who's sittin' on the corner today asking for some spare change."

The kids in the auditorium had laughed at first, fidgeting in their seats, not knowing where Rogers intended to take them. But the laughs gave way to silence, the fidgets to stillness. This, they seemed to be thinking, was heavy. This was real.

Rogers, at the microphone, in his rambling way, had arrived at a metaphor.

"You can paint your own picture. You can paint some roses and a nice mountain." His hands described the motion of painting. "Or you can paint a couple of garbage cans, 'cause if you don't take care of business here in school, that's exactly where you gonna end up. In the garbage cans.

"I've seen both sides of the picture in my own life. I was the first person in my family to go to college. The very first. And you know, in Detroit, it snows a lot. And when you go out in the snow, your mother tell you not to get your feet wet, so what you do, you step in the footsteps that's already in the snow. Step. Step. Step." Rogers lifted his feet to imitate a man walking in snow. "Except, when I went to college, I didn't have no footsteps to follow. Every step I took toward college was a new step to me. I didn't know where I was going. I didn't know if I was making the right decisions. But I knew I wanted to be a professional basketball player, so I knew I hadda go to college, and I made the sacrifices to get there."

Rogers reached back for an earlier chunk of autobiography.

"At first, I wanted to be a gangbanger when I was comin' up. I felt that was the direction I needed to go, 'cause that's where all the cool people were. Well, now, today, all the old cool people are *dead* or in jail for *life*."

Gangbangers? Some of the kids in the auditorium looked at one another. Like, was he talking about gangs where people deal drugs and do drive-by shootings and kill other people? He *was*. It wasn't movies. It was life Rogers was talking about. To some of the kids, especially the smaller children from J. R. Wilcox Public School, Rogers might have sounded as if he'd just arrived from Mars. Still, he was making a very large impression. The silence in the hall left no doubt of that.

"I will never see those old cool people again. But that's okay. Those are the people in your life that you have to recognize and let 'em go. There's a lotta people you gotta let go in life, a lotta people, 'cause they aren't gonna make it, and they're gonna take you down with them. That's the decision I had to make, choosing between them and the picture I painted in my mind of me as a professional basketball player. I made my choice, and I never looked back, because there's *nothin'* back there to look at."

Rogers had finished. At first there was a pause in the auditorium, a lull, and then the kids broke into a long, loud cheer.

Paul Jones, the Raptors' radio man, was back at the Vaughan Road microphone.

"This is a very special day for Carlos," Jones said. "And we're going to help him celebrate. Today is Carlos's birthday. He's twenty-five. So let's everyone join in singing 'Happy Birthday' to Carlos Rogers."

The students got into it, a few hundred kids belting out "Happy Birthday" to the bigger kid on the stage at the front of the hall.

Four days before Carlos Rogers's speech, on February 2, the Raptors had sunk a one-time payment of the better part of $4.19 million into its community-relations program. That wasn't how the expenditure was entered on the team's books, or the way it was announced to the media, but it was money invested in brushing up the Raptors' good name in the community. The millions went to John Salley. It bought out the year and a half left on Salley's contract with the Raptors and released him from the team. The official line from the Raptors offices was that Salley no longer fit into the team plans on the basketball floor. Maybe he didn't. *Probably* he didn't. But that wasn't the real story behind the spending of so much money.

One of John Salley's problems may have been that he came across as a trifle self-important. He was an engaging guy, always ready with a big smile and a quotable answer to a writer's question. At least it was quotable after it had been trimmed for length, since Salley tended to run on. He was a sharp dresser and paid particular attention to the way he smelled. "I believe in aromatherapy," he said in one of his quotable lines, and explained that, in the olfactory department, he favoured a combination of dewberry scented oil, patchouli, and sandalwood.

Scents and all, Salley had ambitions beyond basketball. He was going to be a businessman, and an actor. In business, he had been laying plans for years to market a brand of underwear called funKEe unDEe. The briefs, for both men and women, would feature exotic colours and clever lines written across the buttocks. "This underwear," Salley claimed, "will have attitude." In acting, Salley boasted one solid credit. He appeared in a Disney movie, shot in the summer of 1995, called *Eddie*. The movie, starring Whoopi Goldberg, cast Salley as a basketball player. Well, what else would a guy six-foot-eleven play?

All of this was applaudable, and yet there was a kind of puffery about Salley. Off the basketball court, he sometimes leaned to pontification. On the court, he often grabbed the centre of attention. Between plays, it was invariably Salley who waved players into position, whether they needed waving or not, who made a show of consulting the bench for instructions, whether Brendan Malone wanted Salley as a consultant or not. In one sense, this behaviour may have been leadership, as Ed Pinckney thought. In another sense, it was John Salley commanding the limelight.

Salley had begun his basketball career in hot-shot fashion. He grew up in Brooklyn, and, at Carnarsie High, he earned a big name as a New York high-school star, this tall kid with the incredibly long arms. The arms got him a nickname, "Spider," and Spider's long arms made him an ace shot-blocker. At Georgia Tech, the university that won him in a very active recruiting competition, he set the school's all-time shot-blocking record. The Detroit Pistons took him in the first round of the 1986 draft, eleventh overall, and Salley found himself on the Isiah Thomas–led team that won the two consecutive NBA championships. Salley was usually the second or third man off the bench for the team, in the rotation as a strong defensive player, a good rebounder, a very active shot-blocker. Scoring wasn't what the Pistons expected of Salley; he never finished a season in the NBA with a scoring average in double digits. Salley stuck around Detroit for six years, got traded to Miami for three more, and was picked up by Toronto in the expansion draft.

With the Raptors, at the beginning, Brendan Malone made fairly liberal use of Salley. He played twenty-four minutes coming off the bench in relief of Pinckney at power forward in the opening game against New Jersey, and, over the season's first eight games, he averaged ten points and six rebounds per game. But by December, he was getting fewer minutes on the floor, and, when Tony Massenburg recovered from his foot injury and rejoined the roster just before Christmas, Salley was given what seemed to be a permanent spot on the bench.

"I feel Pinckney and Massenburg have played better," Malone said when he was asked about Salley. "They give me more rebounds, and what I'm looking for is rebounds and low-post defence."

Talk about a cold shoulder from the coach. At practices in January, when Malone ran five-on-five drills, working on set plays, Salley was never one of the ten men on the floor. And when Malone put in substitutes for the drills, he would wave Victor Alexander to the floor, Vincenzo Esposito, guys way down the depth chart, but never Salley. How did he pass the time at practices? Pumping on the Exercycle at the side of the floor. And in games Salley remained anchored to the bench, appearing in no games in late December and none in January, except for a couple of minutes in a loss to the Magic in Orlando.

But it wasn't Salley's perceived shortcomings on the floor that ultimately cost him his job, that drove the Raptors to spend the big money that got rid of him. It was something else. It was the events of New Year's Eve.

When Salley had moved to Toronto at the beginning of the season, he did it with style. He and his wife, Natasha, rented a house in pricey

Forest Hill and enrolled their daughter, Giovanna, in Bishop Strachan, the exclusive girls' school, and Salley got busy making contacts around the city. He talked about opening a blues club. It'd be named Salley's Alley and would be in a building downtown at Adelaide and Duncan. Salley's Alley never came off. But the New Year's Eve party did. A couple of promoters approached the now-highly-visible Salley to lend his name to a gala soirée that would usher in 1996, and Salley threw himself into the project.

"It'll be called John Salley's New Year's Eve Bash," he announced in late November, "and it'll have hors d'oeuvres and champagne, and it'll be the best party Toronto has ever had."

The scene of the party was a large industrial building on a back street down near Toronto Harbour, in a wasteland of huge hydro transformers, a bulk grocery outlet, and docked freighters. Not exactly an inviting neighbourhood, but that didn't keep a couple of thousand guests at fifty dollars a head from joining Salley and Natasha at the bash.

And it went off as Salley had guaranteed: booze, throbbing music, tasty eats, balloons, and a noisy pyrotechnic show that featured exploding firecrackers.

So far, so gala. And then, at three o'clock in the morning of New Year's Day, as the party began to break up, as guests headed to the coat-check room, chaos took over. So did theft, crime, and phone calls to the police at 51 Division. It seemed that the coat-check employees, overwhelmed by customers, abandoned their duties and invited the guests to help themselves to their coats. Some guests helped themselves, sure enough, to *other* people's coats, to furs, to leather jackets, to anything that looked more chic than their own coats. These thieves, some with five or six garments over their arms, pushed out of the coat room and slipped into the night. The victims were left to wail and complain. And it didn't improve the melancholy situation when some of the men and women thought they heard a gunshot outside.

Page two of the next day's *Sun* tabloid, carried an account of the party's dismal ending under a large headline that read "Hoopla turns to melee." "Rowdies ruin Raptor's year-end party," the subhead elaborated. A half-page photograph accompanied the story. It showed a hapless gent, a guest from the party, wearing a smart jacket and slacks (note the absence of an overcoat on the chilly night) and shrugging gamely. Behind the gent was his car, nosed down a snowy incline onto the ice of Toronto Harbour. The picture conveyed more than a thousand words could the disorder and misdirection that had concluded John Salley's party.

The story and the photograph, the juxtaposition of words like "melee" with the word "Raptor," really made John Bitove's New Year. He read, he looked, and he was just a tad upset.

"That was the sort of publicity we didn't need or deserve," Bitove said a few weeks later, explaining his reaction. "Everybody around the Raptors has worked hard on doing good things for Toronto. We've got an image as a family-oriented, community-spirited organization, and it isn't just the image. That's the way we *are*. And the party ran against everything we represent."

The day after that, January 3, John Salley made an assay into damage control. The party, he said, ran as smooth as silk until the coat-check people unfortunately lost control. And that gunshot people talked about? It never happened. No gunshot. Which is where Salley should have stopped talking, but he didn't.

"In Detroit, at twelve midnight," he went on, "gunshots are the fireworks. Everybody walks out of their house and shoots guns."

No, no, John. In respectable Toronto, you don't *think* about guns, don't *mention* them, don't *suggest* that in other cities – in Detroit yet, perennial contender for murder capital of the United States – guns can be a form of innocent hijinks.

If Salley's goose wasn't cooked before he opened his mouth, now it was. It took another month of discussing and dickering in the Raptor offices, of looking into a trade for Salley, but, in the end, the team adopted the direct solution: pay the guy and let him go. John Salley got a cheque and his walking papers.

"That shows you how much community relations mean to us," John Bitove said a few days after Salley's departure. "We were willing to pay millions of dollars to keep them good and solid."

Maybe Bitove's talk about the Raptors' community program wasn't hyperbole after all.

Back at Vaughan Road Collegiate, Paul Jones introduced Oliver Miller to the students in the auditorium. Miller came forward, dressed in baggy jeans and a snazzy cloth-and-leather windbreaker. Given his enormous size, six-foot-nine and somewhere around three hundred pounds, he tended to loom up there on the stage, a touch of menace coming off his huge body. But his round face, seraphic, looking as if it hadn't lost its baby fat, wasn't at all threatening. It seemed almost adolescent, a fuzzy teenage face, and, at that moment, it radiated a small measure of uneasiness. Unlike his buddy Carlos Rogers – the two were best friends on the Raptors – Miller hadn't shed his nervousness at the prospect of making a speech.

On the basketball floor, in Raptors games, Miller seemed the team joker. He was the one who fooled around with the mascot before the games started, the one who nudged the player next to him and rolled his eyes when a gorgeous woman was singing the national anthems. There was one indelible image of Miller in his playful mode from a pre-season game against Atlanta at the SkyDome. In the second quarter, the referees called a timeout to get the stalled clock reset. The players trotted over to Brendan Malone for a conference – all except Miller. He stayed on the floor, under the Atlanta basket, alone with the basketball, and, for the entire timeout, he tried to bounce the ball off the floor at an angle that would make it fly up and through the hoop. Six times he bounced the ball. Twice it zoomed over the glass backboard. The other four times, it splatted against the glass and shot back to the floor. He played the little game as if he were by himself in the arena, just a kid and a ball and a trick shot. He never once looked at the crowd. Maybe he had forgotten the people were there. Or maybe not. He wore an impish grin.

Then there was the other Miller, the flip side of Oliver. He was the fellow who could freeze out an inquiring reporter in a manner that transcended disdain. And he was the guy, this flip-side Oliver, who could snap out in anger on the court. His two fracases with Shawn Bradley of, first, the Philadelphia 76ers, and then, after an early-season trade, the New Jersey Nets, offered one odd view of Oliver in a temper. Bradley made an utterly implausible opponent; at seven-foot-six and 240 pounds, he looked like a tall reed waiting for a wind to set him swaying, and he was a devoutly religious sort, so deep into the Mormon Church that he took two years out of college basketball in the early nineties to knock on doors in Australia. Miller wanted to duke it out with *this* guy? Uh-huh, twice.

Once during the pre-season at a game in Halifax, Oliver charged off the Raptors bench to engage Bradley, an episode that got Miller suspended by the league from the season's opening game. And again on January 23 at the SkyDome, Miller was prevented from seizing Bradley in a death embrace only when Brendan Malone rushed onto the floor and pried Oliver loose. Why did Miller erupt at Bradley? He wasn't saying. Perhaps he was just being the flip side of Oliver.

Of course, it could be argued that, particularly in the Halifax incident, Miller was sticking up for the team. When Miller ran from the bench, he was hurrying to the aid of his teammate John Salley, who was in a contretemps with the 76ers. Other Raptor benchwarmers accompanied Miller. To John Bitove, among others, "Oliver and the other guys were showing spunk. If you looked at the 76ers bench, their guys were just sitting there. They weren't running out to protect their team. Our guys were. Oliver was. It showed we had team spirit right from the start."

Nevertheless, it was baggage of this sort – getting into tussles, drawing suspensions – that almost kept the Raptors from drafting Miller from the Detroit Pistons, that made him Toronto's very last pick in the expansion draft, the twenty-sixth player chosen overall. Actually, it was at least two – maybe three – sorts of baggage that made the Raptors wary. One was his contract; the Pistons had signed him up in 1994 for a generous $10 million over four seasons. The second was his weight, which fluctuated from too much to wa-a-ay too much. And the third was perhaps a general suspicion that Miller might come up short in the character department.

"Oliver was the last one we wanted, the last one we took," John Bitove says. "That was because of his contract and because of his supposed attitude. But he's not only turned out to be a gem of a person, he's also a gem of a player."

There was never any doubt that Miller could play the game, play basketball and every other sport. Growing up in Fort Worth, Texas, he was sports smart, and his size, ample from childhood, didn't seem to get in the way.

"I've always been athletic for my size," he once explained. "Me and my cousins would go down to the country, to my grandma's in Teague, Texas, and we'd have our own Olympics. Hundred-yard dash. Hurdle old tires. My cousins were smaller than me, but I'd catch 'em."

The tension between avoirdupois and talent played itself out at each stop in Miller's basketball career, at Southwest High in Fort Worth, for four years at the University of Arkansas, at Phoenix where the Suns had taken him as the twenty-second pick in the 1993 draft, and at Detroit, when the Pistons signed him as a restricted free agent. All of Miller's coaches admired his skills, but all begged and pleaded with him to diet down below three hundred pounds – or threatened. Lugging all that weight up and down the floor, his coaches insisted, was holding him back from greatness. Big O, as he now styled himself, shrugged.

Miller showed improved numbers from season one to season two with the Suns, raising his scoring average from 5.6 to 9.2, his rebounding from 4.9 to 6.9. But Phoenix tired of the Oliver antics, especially of the on-going weight thing (at one point, Miller tipped in at a humongous 323 pounds). And he also apparently got himself into a couple of border-line incidents with women, nothing that resulted in any legal charges, just news reports that did little for Miller's reputation. It seemed to be the flip side of Oliver on display. Finally Phoenix let him go.

The story was similar at Detroit. No women troubles, but, on the court, it was a case of a nice-enough performance for a fat guy. Miller averaged 8.5 points and 7.4 rebounds and showed no signs of getting slimmer. At the end of the season, the Pistons exposed only one player to the expansion draft. It was Miller, and Toronto eventually took him.

When Miller arrived at the Raptors' training camp, he looked different – not precisely svelte, but not blubbery either. He seemed to have done a little slimming. "This summer I just decided to make a commitment," he said at his first press conference. "I am not a fat-assed guy."

On the floor, as he quickly established, he was a big guy who had the moves of a little guy. He was remarkably swift in his sneakers. Sure, he resembled one of the elephants in *Fantasia*, a large creature tippy-toeing on tiny feet, but, just as he did in his grandma's yard, he got there faster than many of the slim players who looked more like athletes.

Most of all, Miller possessed great mitts, "soft" hands as they say in basketball. He moved the ball like a magician, like an Allan Slaight, performing sleight of hand. Now you see it in Oliver's paws, now you see it zipped to the open man. Miller turned out to be a wonderful passer; through to the end of January, he was averaging almost two and a half assists per game, which was actually down from his high of 3.5 in his second season with Phoenix. Also in the deft-hands department, he was third on the Raptors in steals, behind only Alvin Robertson and Damon

Stoudamire. He led the team in blocked shots, was second in rebounds (to Ed Pinckney), and even though, at six-nine, he was short for a centre, he was proving that he deserved the pivot job on merit. He was, as John Bitove says, a gem of a player.

And now, on the stage at Vaughan Road Collegiate, he was about to go part of the way to demonstrating he might be a gem of a person.

"Coming after Martin Luther King, Jr., here," Miller began, grinning in the direction of Carlos Rogers, "I'm gonna keep this real simple and short."

And he did. Miller talked for only four minutes, but, in front of the Vaughan kids, edged a little by nervousness, he appeared sweet and sincere, artless, ingenuous. He gave the impression that he cared about the small message he was delivering, and everybody in the audience appeared to sense his honesty and not to question it for a minute.

"I was no angel in school," he said, "but I still got my education. It's not up to your friends what you're gonna be in life, just like it's not up to you what your friends are gonna be, unless you want to be not a good friend to them. It's up to each person. If you tell yourself, I want to be a doctor, I want to be a nurse, I want to be a housewife, then it's up to you to get there.

"The real world is not a place to play. It's serious out there. It's nothing to joke around with. But once you tell yourself that you want to be somebody, then you *can* be somebody. But if you tell yourself, Hey, I don't know what I want, maybe I'll just be a bum on the street, then that's what you're gonna be. It's not easy to be a professional basketball player. It's not easy to be a doctor. It takes a lotta time. It takes a lotta dedication. So, if you dedicate a lotta time to doing school work, you're gonna be some*body*.

"I told you I was gonna keep this short, and that is all I have to tell you."

As Miller turned away from the microphone, Carlos Rogers stood up, reached out, and embraced him, two big kids hugging on the stage at the high school. The other kids in the audience cheered for a very long time.

14

RECONFIGURATION

On the afternoon of Tuesday, February 20, John Bitove retreated to his tiny personal room behind the central working space at the Raptors offices on lower Bay Street. Raptor Central is laid out on an open plan. Bitove sits at a long desk facing east into the large room, while the desks and computers of other executives and administrators are squared around to face west in Bitove's direction. When Bitove needs a respite from all this facing and from the buzzing phones, he steps down from his desk and into the room at the rear. It's about the size of a kid's tree fort, and just as cosy. It's hung with pictures of Bitove's kids, decorated with bits of sports memorabilia, and furnished with an arrangement of sofas and coffee tables. It makes for an unwinding kind of place.

Which is what Bitove looked in need of. He had changed in a couple of ways in the previous few months. He was talking faster. Bitove's mouth always went at a lickety-split pace, but now he was up to full throttle, each sentence slam-dancing into the sentence in front. And Bitove had put on a few pounds, his face a little fuller, his belt digging gently into his waistline.

"I should get out and run, do something about my weight," he said. "But if I did, I'd only feel guilty. Nobody else around here takes time off, so how could I?"

Bitove and the Raptors, indeed all of the NBA, had recently come off the league's annual All-Star weekend, a time when teams traditionally pause, take a deep breath, prepare for the second part of the season and the dash to the playoffs. The All-Star game and its attendant festivities had been held this year in San Antonio from February 9 through 11. Only one Raptor player travelled to San Antonio; that was Damon Stoudamire, who was selected to play in the all-rookie game on the Saturday before the big Sunday game between two teams made up of the twelve best players from each of the Eastern and Western conferences.

No Raptor made the Eastern All-Star team, but Raptor management showed up *en masse*, Bitove, Isiah Thomas, Brendan Malone, and their wives. Malone went for pleasure, to treat Maureen to a tour of San Antonio, since it was one NBA city she'd never visited. But Bitove had management matters to discuss with his fellow owners. And Thomas focused on business of a particular urgency. The season's final day for trades between NBA teams lay less than two weeks away, on Thursday, February 22, and Thomas was anxious to take this last opportunity to make changes, to unload some of his older players, to pump more youth into the Raptors. He schmoozed in San Antonio, felt out the other general managers, checked what players were available, preferably young guys who might fit into the Toronto picture long term. Thomas closed no trades in San Antonio, but he got within sniffing distance of some possibilities.

The rest of the Raptors players, back in Toronto, eased into the five-day freedom from games and practices. Some left town on holidays. Ed Pinckney swept his wife, Rose, and their four kids off to Puerto Rico. Zan Tabak and his wife, Gorana, took in the shows in New York. And Tracy Murray, whose warm blood adjusted only grudgingly to Toronto winters, flew home to Los Angeles and the sun. Oliver Miller didn't go anywhere, but, shortly after the All-Star break, he felt a touch of vindication when he read the report of a Miami–New Jersey game. The Nets centre Shawn Bradley got into a rumble with the Heat's Alonzo Mourning. Shoving, punches, blood, the whole multi-foul package. See, Miller thought, it obviously wasn't me who instigated the two fights with Bradley. It was him who started the brawls. It was that pious beanpole Mormon.

Now, with the regular season resumed, with conditions restored to hectic normalcy, John Bitove sat in his little room and took stock of his basketball team's first three and a half months.

"Attendance, almost twenty-two thousand a game," he said. "That puts us third in the whole league, behind Charlotte and Chicago."

In group sales – that is, sales of tickets to groups of twenty people or more – the Raptors were in first place, way out in front, with more than a hundred thousand group sales as against an average for the rest of the league's teams of seventy-five thousand. And, in the peddling of team merchandise around the world – T-shirts, caps, and anything else that a team logo would fit on – the Raptors ranked fifth after Chicago, Orlando, Charlotte, and Phoenix.

"We're the new kid on the block and already we're ahead of the New Yorks, the Detroits, the L.A.s," Bitove said, speed-talking through his pleasure. "It shows that those kids at the focus group knew what they were doing when they voted for the Raptor name and the Raptor colours. People love the Raptor stuff in France, Russia, any country where they play basketball."

Bitove touched on the acquisition of the old Post Office Building and the construction on its site of the new basketball stadium, which was proving a real headache. "There are 138 agreements that have to be put in place before we get the shovels in the ground. It seems like every law firm in the city is working on one or other of our contracts. It's nuts, but in terms of the process it takes to get there, we're way ahead in time. Unfortunately, it's just not fast enough to please us."

And he mentioned the adjustment in team ownership that had taken place earlier in the winter. Isiah Thomas had exercised his option to buy into the team. He took 9 per cent. That meant the ownership now shook down to 39½ per cent each for the Bitove group and Allan Slaight, 10 per cent for the Bank of Nova Scotia, 9 for Thomas, and 1 each for David Peterson and Atlantic Packaging. Except, sadly, Phil Granovsky, the nice man who had played a small-but-significant role in the franchise pitch to the NBA expansion committee on September 20, 1993, no longer represented Atlantic on the Raptors board. Granovsky, who had wanted a piece of a professional sports team for so long, finally achieved his goal, and then, on December 24, 1995, had died of leukaemia.

As for Bitove's office relationship with his new partner, Isiah Thomas, the division of responsibilities, it was, Bitove said, clean-cut. "Isiah runs the basketball side, and I don't second-guess him," he said. "And it's vice versa over here, me running the business side, him not second-guessing me. We operate independently, but we respect each other's judgement."

Bitove leaned back on the sofa in his little room – a brief concession to relaxation, the leaning back, since Bitove is a habitual edge-of-the-chair sitter – and dwelt for a satisfying moment on the player drafts of the previous summer.

"We felt we'd be happy if we came out of the drafts with just one player who'd become a fixture on the team," Bitove said. "Just one guy who we'd embrace as a Raptor for the next six or seven years. But look what happened. We got Damon. We got Zan Tabak. Miller. Massenburg. Yeah, now there's a guy who's definitely a keeper. Tony Massenburg."

At the very moment John Bitove was talking in his hidey-hole, Isiah Thomas was proving the truth of Bitove's assessment. The two men split responsibilities and trusted one another. That was what Bitove had said. Split and trust and no second-guessing. At that very moment, Thomas was working the telephones, talking to the Philadelphia 76ers, cutting a deal with John Lucas, the 76ers coach and GM. It would take another day and a half to nail down the deal, right up to the early hours of the February 22 trading deadline, but, in the end, Thomas got the man he wanted, a second-year power forward and centre named Sharone Wright. In return, Thomas gave up two Raptor players. One of the two was Tony Massenburg.

Thomas had a couple of reasons for letting Massenburg, the former "keeper," go. For one thing, Massenburg may have wanted more money in his next Raptor contract than Thomas was willing to pay. But that was the minor reason. The major reason was that Sharone Wright, five and a half years younger than Massenburg, was a genuine postup player, some-thing the Raptors didn't have, a big strong guy who could take the ball in the low post with his back to the basket and use brute strength to force his way in for a layup or a short jumper. Thomas wanted one of those for the Raptors. And he got it, even if it was partly at the expense of Tony Massenburg.

Back in December, after a practice at the SkyDome, Ed Pinckney had been looking at a small item about himself in the *Toronto Star*. The article was mainly a list of Pinckney's preferences in everything from pizza (he liked it with pepperoni) to video games (he answered, appropriate to a man of his maturity, that he didn't play them). In the list, as his current favourite movie, he had named *Seven*, a dark thriller with Morgan Freeman and Brad Pitt.

"I should have changed that," Pinckney was saying. "*Seven* was good, but a movie I watched on video the other night was better, *Crimson Tide*." *Crimson Tide* was a submarine adventure story with Gene Hackman and Denzel Washington.

"Next year," Pinckney went on, "when they ask me the same questions for the newspaper, I'll get it right the first time."

Next year? Pinckney expected to be with the Raptors next year?

"I don't *expect* anything, not in this game," Pinckney said. "But I *hope* I'll be here."

At noon on February 22, in Salt Lake City, where the Raptors were having a shoot-around in preparation for their game that night against the Utah Jazz, the two players who had been traded to Philadelphia for Sharone Wright were informed of the trade and told to pack their bags. The first player was Tony Massenburg. And the second was Ed Pinckney.

Randi Bitove reached Rose Pinckney by phone in Milwaukee.

"Oh, Rose, I'm so sorry."

"Why didn't Isiah *tell* us?" Rose was crying. She said, "Ed and I loved Toronto so much. We loved the organization. And now to be traded *again*."

"We should make a rule," Randi said. "The rule should be that the team always has to speak to the wife first before there's a trade."

"Well, one thing," Rose said, "we're not giving up the apartment in Toronto, at least not until the lease runs out. Both of us love it up there. We loved Toronto."

She was still crying.

Rose Pinckney made a phone call of her own. It took a few days to get through to the person she wanted, but she caught Brendan Malone in his hotel room in Houston, where the Raptors were playing the Rockets on February 27.

Rose introduced herself and said, "Coach Malone, we didn't meet this year, but I want to thank you for giving my husband the opportunity to play. He'd lost his confidence in Milwaukee. It was that bad there, but you restored his confidence, and Ed began to enjoy the game again. We didn't know what to expect in Toronto. There was always talk that he shouldn't bring his family to the city because he might not last there. But you played him, and he got his confidence back. I just phoned to say thanks."

For a rare moment in his life, Brendan Malone was, briefly, speechless.

"A wife never phoned me like that," he says. "It makes you appreciate what players and families go through in professional basketball. Tough times, I tell ya."

Isiah Thomas made a second important trade: slick Willie Anderson and Victor Alexander, the overweight fellow who had spent the season on the injury list, to the New York Knicks for Doug Christie and Herb Williams. Christie was, like Anderson, a swing man, able to play off guard, small forward, and, in a pinch – as for instance when Damon Stoudamire needed a rest – point guard. The difference between the two men was in years; Christie was younger than Anderson by four of them. Thomas was seriously striving for youth on the Raptors, and, in the end, the trade turned out to be a two-man affair, Christie for Anderson. That was because neither Williams nor Alexander stuck with their new teams. The Knicks, deciding Alexander wasn't the player they hoped for – another strong presence inside – let him go after three weeks. The Raptors didn't take that long with Herb Williams, a centre. He played in one game for the Raptors, thirty-one minutes against Utah, then, partly on the basis of senior citizenry – Williams was thirty-eight – he was released. But he landed on his feet when the Knicks signed him up once again.

Doug Christie, walking down the corridor from the trainer's room to the dressing room in the SkyDome before a game in early March, wearing only a pair of underwear shorts, had a body that needed Judith Krantz's vocabulary to describe. "Sculpted." "Wide shoulders tapering to narrow waist." "Discreet ridges of muscle across the stomach." A Gen-X Adonis, that was Doug Christie. He stood six-foot-six, weighed two hundred pounds, and was twenty-five years old, but his face made him look younger, the fresh face of a college sophomore.

When Christie sat at his locker to talk, his body language spoke of a certain defensiveness, arms sometimes folded as if to close himself off, eyes avoiding contact with his interviewer's eyes. Maybe not so odd. Christie has encountered more than a fair share of trials in his life. He grew up in an inner-city neighbourhood in Seattle. He didn't know his father, a longshoreman, until he reached his teens. His mother raised him, but she had to work long hours, and young Doug was a latch-key kid.

Coming out of Pepperdine University in 1992, Christie was drafted by his home-town team, the SuperSonics. That didn't work out. It was a difference of opinion over salary; Christie dug in his heels, and Seattle traded him to the Lakers. Things didn't click in L.A., either, though he produced not-bad numbers in the 65 games he played in 1993-94, 23.3 minutes per game, 10.3 points, 2.1 assists, 3.6 rebounds. The Lakers traded him in 1994 to New York, where it was more of the same, a matter of not pleasing the coaches or poor chemistry, something out of kilter. The Knicks traded him to the Raptors.

Four trades in four seasons – Christie had the record of a problem case. He didn't think that was fair. "I work hard," he said. "In fact, I'm sort of a workout-aholic. And I try to get along with teammates and coaches."

Brendan Malone didn't think Christie was a problem, either.

"When I knew Christie was coming here, I phoned my friend Don Chaney for advice," Malone said. Chaney was a Knicks assistant coach who had been the head coach in Detroit during a couple of Malone's seasons with the Pistons. "Don said Christie's a good kid. He said the one thing is, on the court, you have to teach Doug to go at different speeds, because he always wants to go at one speed – very fast – and, as a result of that, he has a tendency to turn the ball over. That's what Chaney said, and it looks like he was right. It's the way Christie's been in his time with us. But if he plays at different speeds and takes care of the ball, he'll be all right."

Malone liked other things about Christie's game. "Very fast hands. He can steal the ball. He can post up against most guards. His shot, though, he needs work on his shot."

In Christie's first few games at the SkyDome, from early March to the middle of the month, he showed some of the strengths Malone spoke of, some of the weaknesses, some of the perceived weaknesses that turned out to be not so feeble after all. And, most of all, from an aesthetic point of view, he showed that he was an exciting player, electrifying at times, a speedy adornment to the team, a guy who played basketball with a sense of drama.

The game against Denver on Monday night, March 18, a 122–114 loss for the Raptors, was typical of Christie in all his facets. He started the game at the off guard and played twenty-two minutes. He might have had more minutes, but his eagerness got him into foul trouble. And an old bugaboo, too much speed leading to turnovers, appeared to do him in. He had four turnovers, and, what with one thing and another, the fouls and the turnovers, Malone had to sit him down in favour of Jimmy King. But, on the positive side, Christie shot with a deadly eye, hitting five of six, two of them from the three-point line. He made one steal, pulled in three rebounds, played fair defence.

And, in all things, he presented himself in ways that were a pleasure to the eye. On one of his baskets, he spotted an opening in the defence, breezed past the man who was guarding him, took off to the hoop in a flight that resembled a karate move, slammed the ball through the basket, grabbed the rim with both hands, and, for an instant, he swung ten feet in the air. It counted only two points on the scoreboard, but, for basketball thrills, it was a ten.

"That was a good trade Isiah made," Malone said afterwards, "a young Doug Christie for an older Willie Anderson. The kid'll produce for this team."

Sharone Wright brought three more tattoos to the Raptors. He wears his own name on his left arm, his daughter's name, London, on one leg, and, on his ample back, letters spell out the word "action." But a tragic story goes with the third tattoo.

It happened in 1991 in Macon, Georgia, where Wright grew up. He was in his last year at Southwest High at the time, just a big teenage kid who played good basketball. His father had a few drinks one night. Some policemen stopped him. There were words. Maybe there was more. Whatever happened, the policemen shot Sharone Wright's father dead. As a way of fighting off the horror of it all, young Sharone buried himself in his basketball. In basketball *action*. He went out and got the word tattooed on his back.

Wright grew huge, six-foot-eleven, 260 pounds, round, heavy-set, and possessed of terrific strength. He used all of this formidable bulk to make himself a star forward at Clemson University. He elected to leave school after his junior year, and was taken by the Philadelphia 76ers as the sixth pick overall in the 1994 draft. He produced pretty good basketball in his rookie season, six rebounds and ten points a game. But, in the middle of his second season, this season, the 76ers gave up on Wright.

Why? Why pass on an apparently promising twenty-three-year-old big guy? There weren't many of those around.

Impatience and money were part of the explanation. The 76ers had invested heavily in Wright, with a contract that still had five years and $15.2 million left to run, and they decided he wasn't *that* promising. They'd clear out the big contract for players who cost less – Pinckney and Massenburg filled the bill in that department – and use the money thus saved to sign a free-agent star in the summer of '96. At the same time, Philadelphia would be pleasing its fans, who had taken a vicious dislike to Sharone Wright.

Isiah Thomas figured Toronto could absorb Wright's contract, though it might take a bit of juggling under the salary cap. But the important factor was that Wright's low-post game, which could become vital to the Raptors' offensive, would prosper in the Toronto system. After all, Wright would have a clever point guard to get him the ball. He didn't have that luxury in Philadelphia. In Toronto, with Damon Stoudamire, Wright would automatically be worth a few more points.

And that was the way it seemed to be working out as Wright settled into the Raptors. In a game against Detroit on Tuesday night, March 5, Wright's first appearance at the SkyDome, Brendan Malone started him at centre, moving Oliver Miller to power forward, and Wright made himself right at home in the low post. Toronto fans had never seen anything like this guy, not on the Raptors, a restless, physical player who pounded his way to the basket from in close. There wasn't a lot of variety in his moves, not a lot of polish, either, but no Piston defensive player seemed thrilled about getting in Wright's path. He scored twenty-five points, and he had the wit, when Detroit double-teamed him under the basket, to kick the ball out to an open Raptor. Wright had three assists on the night, and it was a marvellous debut. Too bad it came on a night when Detroit's star, Grant Hill, was particularly starry and scored thrity-one points in the Pistons' 105–84 win.

The very next night, again at the SkyDome, Wright went up against the New York Knicks, a supremely tough defensive team that was adept at double-teaming an opposing centre. Wright saw double teams all night – from big tough guys like Anthony Mason, Patrick Ewing, even Herb Williams, the centre who passed so briefly through the Raptors' hands – and his shooting suffered, seven for twenty-one. But he scored eighteen points and never surrendered in the battle, which the Raptors eventually lost, 89–82.

In the next home game, Sunday, March 10, against the Dallas Mavericks, Wright looked as if he had the low-post game down pat. He was a hub in a Raptor offence that got everybody into the action. Toronto scored sixty-four points in the first half, their most ever in twenty-four minutes, and ended the game with a 128–112 win. All the players participated. Tracy Murray had twenty points, Stoudamire got twenty-five, sixteen for Alvin Robertson, fifteen for Oliver Miller. And Wright, a rambunctious performer, a primitive, intimidating force, but seeming to take on a little more guile with each game, scored twenty-one, and looked like the kind of man in the middle who gives other teams constant concern.

Wright was delighted with the way his life had changed since the trade from the 76ers. He wore a big smile in the locker room, at practices, with his teammates, with the media. He was a personable conversationalist, and, now and then, he produced a *bon mot* that got everybody within listening distance recording the quote. One of these came after the Dallas victory. Playing before the crowds in Philadelphia, Wright said, as opposed to playing before the SkyDome fans, was "like Godzilla compared to Snow White."

The 76ers crowds made for a tough house?

"It's a hard city to play any sport in. All the fans want to see is a winning team, because it's a hard-working town. They get off the steel mills, and they come to the game, and they want to see you win."

Whereas in Toronto?

"If you just play hard, they love you because you're theirs."

And then, five days later, in Charlotte, North Carolina, it all came tumbling down for Sharone Wright and the new Raptors' offence. In a game against the Hornets – which Charlotte eventually won, 113–101 – Matt Geiger's knees crashed into Wright's lower back. It was an accident. But Geiger, who resembled a larger, contemporary Genghis Khan, was a 240-pound seven-footer. His knees could do serious damage to an innocent back, even without intending it. Wright, who scored a glorious twenty points in the first half, couldn't play in the second half of the game, and afterwards, the official Raptor medical report listed him as suffering from "back spasms."

"That's a generic sort of term," says Dr. Hamilton Hall, famed back guru and the back doctor to the Raptors. "It just means the damage is mechanical and not to the nerves. It can be repaired with treatment and exercise."

In Wright's case, the treatment would take a few weeks. After eleven games with the Raptors, an average of 16.5 points per game, after demonstrating just how promising he really was, after giving new shape to the Raptors' offence, Sharone Wright was gone for the rest of the season.

15

THE SECOND SEASON

Brendan Malone figured that, for the Raptors, it was turning into a schizophrenic sort of year.

"It's like two different seasons in one," he said one day three weeks into March. "There was the one season before the trades, and there's an opposite season after the trades."

The February trades, masterminded by Isiah Thomas, had changed the team in age and experience. That was the first and most obvious difference in the Raptors' makeup. In the space of a few days, the team suddenly got younger by subtracting one player who was over thirty, Ed Pinckney, and another who was fast approaching that age, Willie Anderson, and adding two who were twenty-five or under, Doug Christie and Sharone Wright. Now the only elder left on the Raptors was thirty-three-year-old Alvin Robertson, who became captain in place of Pinckney; and now, at an average age of 25.2 years, the Raptors were the youngest team in the league, younger by more than half a year than the next-most-youthful outfit, the L.A. Clippers. The loss in depth of NBA experience gave the team a kind of basketball gaucherie in the games immediately after the trades. So many young guys on the floor, so many new guys in different positions – on some nights, the Raptors looked as if they were starting the season from scratch.

"Talk about young guys, about rookies," Malone said, "you could say that we have other players who've been in the league awhile but are really rookies. Tracy Murray is one. He's been in the NBA three years, but, until he came here, he never really played. That's almost the same as being a rookie. And Doug Christie is in close to the same category. The new team, after the trades, is more inexperienced than people think."

The second change that the trade brought about was to open up more playing time for one guy already on the roster, Carlos Rogers. With Pinckney, Anderson, and Tony Massenburg gone from the front line, there was room for Rogers. Since he, too, was twenty-five and in just his second NBA season, the youth movement was correspondingly accelerated.

The Raptors had a new look, and, at least for Malone, it also had a new emotional feel.

"My fondness is for the guys who were together at the beginning of the season," he said. "Ed, Willie, Alvin, Tony, Damon. When I'm long gone from here, those are the people, that particular team, who I'll have the good memories of."

Malone shrugged. "But you have to move people and improve the roster, and, no matter how fond I am of the people who've gone, that's what we've done. Improved the roster."

And that was the third change – ultimately the raising of the quality of the team – that the trades brought about.

In the same conversation, deep into March, Malone took stock of some of the players who spanned both Raptors seasons.

"Oliver Miller," he began. "This was a guy I worked with in Detroit, who I was not looking forward to coaching in Toronto. And I still wish he'd get in better shape, because, if he did, if he got in the best possible shape he's capable of, he'd be an NBA All-Star. His play has been that good this year. He can score. He's a very good passer in the low post. And on his long passes from under our basket, he can see people streaking down the floor and hit them with a pinpoint pass better than anybody I've ever seen in the game. He's got a very, very good feel for basketball. He's an intelligent player, and – I never thought I'd hear myself saying this – he'd make a great coach, because he knows the game."

Malone's face got its New York Irish gleam when he moved to Alvin

Robertson. "If everybody played as hard as him, we'd be goin' for the championship. He only knows how to play the game one way – to win. Okay, he turns the ball over too much and he's not a great shooter. But, you know, he gets that look in his eye. I wouldn't wanna compete against Alvin Robertson."

Malone wasn't quite so gleaming when he brought up the next name. "Carlos Rogers runs the floor, and he scores well in the open court. He isn't so good at scoring in the half court yet. We go to him, and he has trouble finishing the shot. But he can also block shots very well. I told him he should block more. I told him, as good as he is at blocking shots, he should block *every* shot. He's the same size as Bill Russell, one of the best shot-blockers that ever played. Carlos could be like Bill Russell. I told Carlos, 'Carlos, you're not as good a player as you think you are, but, if you work in the weight room, get stronger, and when you're not working on the weights, if you practise your shot, then one day you may be as good a player as you *think* you are right now.'"

Malone checked his mental list of players.

"Tabak. I haven't mentioned Tabak." Malone invariably referred to Zan Tabak by his last name alone. He seemed to like the cracking sound of the two syllables. "Ta-*bak*," Malone would say, and then, on this March day, he added a compliment. "He may have been the biggest surprise of the whole year."

On Zan Tabak's lap, as he sat in the Raptors' dressing room a couple of days after the Malone conversation, was a small map of what are still sometimes known as the Balkan countries. Yugoslavia. Romania. Albania. Bulgaria.

"This is my home town," he said, pointing to a speck on the Adriatic coast. "Very beautiful place. And very old. A Roman emperor started it. He built his summer home there, a palace, and that became my town, Split."

The Roman emperor in question was Diocletian, who ruled from A.D. 284 to 305. It was after he retired that he put up the palace near present-day Split, just at the point of the deepest harbour on the Adriatic. After the fall of the Roman Empire, Goths, Huns, Hungarians, French, Austrians, and Italians took turns ruling the area, which was mostly settled by Slavs who had drifted in from the northeast between the sixth and tenth centuries to get away from the murderous Goths, Huns, and Avars. The Slavs, who evolved into Croatians, were stolid, pastoral people, and their slice of the territory – Croatia – which was included in the country that became Yugoslavia in 1919, controlled Split, the Adriatic's major seaport.

"But by the time I was growing up, shipping wasn't so important any more," Tabak explained. "In Split, tourism was the biggest business. There are beautiful islands close by in the sea right here." Tabak's finger traced on the small map islands named Solta and Brac and Ivar. "The sea is very warm. Nobody in Canada seems to know about it, but this is just like the Caribbean. I go scuba diving here all the time, me and my father."

Tabak was born in Split on June 15, 1970. His father is a house painter, his mother, a tailor. Both parents are tall, the father six-foot-seven, the mother six feet, and Zan outgrew everyone in the family, all the way to seven feet. Basketball, to which young Zan naturally gravitated, wasn't a school sport in Split. It was, as a player moved up, a club sport, a town sport, a national sport. By the time he was sixteen, Tabak had already climbed to the national level, playing in the Yugoslavian league.

The quality of basketball, Tabak says, was high. There were plenty of players as good as any in the world; Toni Kukoc, now of the Bulls, is from Split, and so is Dino Radja of the Celtics. For that matter, the tall, blonde, elegant woman who became Tabak's wife, Gorana Turdic, was a first-division player for Croatia, and her father, Bruno, had been one of the finest players in all of Europe.

"I learned good fundamentals at home," Tabak says. "And when I turned professional there, I started to make money – not like in the NBA, but good money."

Tabak stepped up to the Italian A-1 league in 1992, playing for teams in Sivorno and Milano, and racking up great numbers in 1993-94 with Milano: 15.5 points per game and 10.3 rebounds. By then, he was already the property of the Houston Rockets, whose scouts had spotted him in the Yugoslavian league and made him a second-round draft choice in 1991. When Tabak's contract with Milano ran out in 1994, he decided to follow the trail that Kukoc and Radja had blazed a year earlier. He checked into the NBA, into the Rockets' training camp.

It was easy to spot Tabak in televised games of the 1995 NBA final between Houston and the Orlando Magic. He was one of the two pale seven-footers who sat at the very end of the Rockets bench, two guys who never got into the games. The other seven-footer was Pete Chilcutt, who had a few credentials – a degree for a major basketball school, North Carolina, four years in the NBA, a surprisingly nice outside touch for a tall man. He actually played some significant minutes for the Rockets during the year, though much less so in the playoffs. In contrast, Tabak, through the entire regular season and playoffs, saw action on the floor for a grand total of 213 minutes. It was a year confined to small satisfactions for him: ten points against the Clippers one night in February, eight rebounds against the Jazz in the last regular-season game. But Tabak enjoyed one major benefit.

"Every day in practice," he says, "I played against the best player in the world. I played against Hakeem Olajuwon. The rest of the time I was going a little crazy, because I wasn't part of the team that played in the games. But from Hakeem, I was at least learning something new about basketball every day."

On June 24, 1995, Tabak was walking through the Houston Airport on his way to Split and scuba diving. He glanced at a television screen in the airport, and, to his astonishment, he saw his own face. It was draft day for the two expansion teams, Toronto and Vancouver, and one of them, the Raptors, chose Zan Tabak. The Rockets had exposed him to the draft because they were certain neither of the expansion teams would have the wit to select him. After all, who had even seen him play? But Toronto fooled Houston.

"The truth is," Brendan Malone said later, "we didn't know anything about Ta-*bak*. All we knew was that he was another big man. We thought we might send him back to Europe to have more playing experience in the leagues over there. We didn't know what we were getting."

What the Raptors got, in personal terms, was a gracious, thoughtful man, who speaks in a deep voice with a soft Balkan accent. Tabak, the one man on the Toronto roster with no exposure to higher education, was in many ways its most sophisticated. Not that he read Joyce Carol Oates and watched "Masterpiece Theatre" – in fact, his favourite TV show was

"Fresh Prince of Bel-Air" – but he gave off an air of learned experience. Maybe it was a European thing. Maybe he seemed more worldly because he had seen more of the world than all of the other players, with the exception of the departed Tony Massenburg. Certainly Tabak's thoughts through his two seasons in North America were, often in sorrow, with his home and his country thousands of miles away.

"The fighting in the war never reached Split," he said. "But men from there went to fight further up in the mountains, over by Sarajevo. One thing" – Tabak smiled wryly – "not much tourism in Split right now."

What the Raptors also got in basketball terms was a guy who, even after he survived the pre-season cuts, was often tentative, sometimes flat-out nervous. "He has to learn to play with confidence," Malone said. Early in the year, on almost every trip down the floor, Tabak glanced over at Malone, his expression asking, Well, what did I do wrong this time? They say people from the Balkans have an infatuation with suffering, and Tabak seemed to be doing his share on the basketball court.

But Malone, the born teacher, had a willing pupil in Tabak, and, even if the lessons seemed basic, such as how Tabak should use his height to dunk more, he worked at them zealously. He learned. Malone started Tabak in four games early in the season, but Oliver Miller took over the centre spot, and Tabak served mainly as a backup. But he had fine moments: twenty points and fifteen rebounds against his old pal Olajuwon and the Rockets at the SkyDome on November 15; twenty-four points on deadly twelve-for-sixteen shooting against the Bulls in Chicago on December 22. Tabak kept absorbing new lessons, improving his game, developing into perhaps, as Malone described him, "the biggest surprise of the year." So, when Sharone Wright went out with his back injury, Malone didn't hesitate to use Tabak, frequently as a starter, along with Miller, Tracy Murray, and Carlos Rogers, in his front line.

On March 18, in the game against Denver at the SkyDome, Tabak had a lousy night. He missed all five of his shots and both of his free throws, committed two turnovers, and generally looked out of the loop. Malone played him for only seventeen minutes.

But, two nights later, when the Raptors took on the Charlotte Hornets at the SkyDome, Tabak was back in the starting lineup. Malone sent him onto the floor with some quiet words of advice. The words had nothing to do with technique or shot selection, no basketball wisdom. The advice had more to do with psychology.

"What I told him," Malone said later, "was to go out and have some fun."

Tabak complied. He looked positively coltish running up and down the court. For a tall man, he runs with good, fluid speed. That may have something to do with Tabak's build; he weighs only 240 pounds and has a willowy look. The fluidity is also obvious in his hook shots, which are high and graceful in the Kareem Abdul-Jabbar mode. He hit a couple of them in the Charlotte game. He hit almost everything he put up, nine baskets out of eleven attempts for eighteen points. And he pulled in eleven rebounds. He played superbly.

It helped that the entire Raptors team was in a running frame of mind. The players came out fast in the first quarter, pushing the ball up the floor, scoring in transition, taking the game away from the Hornets. Oliver Miller had fifteen rebounds and ten assists on the night. Damon Stoudamire scored twenty-four points and assisted on ten other baskets. Every guy had his moments. Carlos Rogers hit ten baskets in fifteen shots. But, in a redemptive sense, it was Tabak who, in a game that the Raptors won easily, 107–89 for their seventeenth victory of the season, provided the most satisfaction.

"What he did, Ta-*bak*," Brendan Malone said afterwards, "was go from his worst game of the year to one of his best."

16

MORE BULLS

A workman wielding a giant squeegee was washing down the blue tarpaulin that covered the side of the temporary stands. Two young women from the Raptors Dance Pack – Kim and Carla – rehearsed together at the end of the basketball floor, doing a number that looked as if it had been conceived by a t'ai-chi master on amphetamines. Doug Smith of Canadian Press sat at his laptop computer, the only occupant of the long row of press tables, writing an advance story. And a couple of ball boys came by wheeling a stand that carried two giant-sized Gatorade coolers. They parked it next to the visiting-team bench, then left to fetch another Gatorade setup for the home team.

This was the scene on the floor of the SkyDome at one o'clock on the afternoon of Sunday, March 24. The Chicago Bulls were coming in for their second Toronto visit of the season, and, in a couple of hours, in plenty of time for the 3:30 tipoff, the place would be filled with passionate fans. These were the Bulls, the team of Michael Jordan, the best team in the NBA this year, maybe the best team ever. And the prospects were that the SkyDome attendance record for a basketball game – the *Canadian* record – the record that had been set the first time the Bulls were in town on January 18, would be broken.

But the game was two and a half hours away, and, for now, the only people moving in the SkyDome belonged to various behind-the-scenes crews. Another workman began nailing down curtains of clean white plastic over the front of the press tables. "Looks better on TV this way," he said.

At 1:35, activity picked up on the floor. Oliver Miller arrived to shoot baskets. He wore a gold earring in his left ear. That would be gone by game time. NBA rules forbade any such decoration on the players, apart, of course, from tattoos. At the Bulls end of the floor, Scottie Pippen and Dickey Simpkins practised jump shots. For a few minutes, Simpkins did all the shooting, while Pippen fed him a steady supply of balls. Every time Simpkins put up a shot, Pippen's eyes followed it all the way through the air until it hit the rim or dropped into the basket. It seemed important to Pippen to know whether the shot went in. He'd probably watched a billion balls fall through hoops in his basketball life. But it still mattered to him whether these particular shots were good or not. And they weren't even his shots.

John Salley created a small stir. He walked behind the press tables, dressed in a snappy tan suit, single-breasted, all four buttons done up. Three weeks earlier, when the Bulls had lost several big men to injuries, Chicago's vice-president of basketball operations, Jerry Krause, had phoned Brendan Malone to ask his advice on signing Salley. "You won't have any trouble with John's ego," Malone told Krause, "because it'll be subordinated to all the egos you already got on the team, and John'll do a good job for you off the bench." Krause signed Salley on March 4 as a backup power forward, and, even though he had since played only a few minutes in a few games, he would be with the Bulls until the end of playoffs.

Now, coming through the SkyDome, Salley's head swivelled around as if he were looking for greetings to a returning hero. Two Raptors employees hurried over to embrace him, and someone far up in the otherwise-empty stands hollered his name. Salley waved extravagantly. He was on his way to tape a pre-game TV interview, and, a few minutes later, his smiling face appeared on the screens of the monitors placed at intervals along the press tables.

"I have a warrior's mentality," Salley told the interviewer. "I wasn't allowed to express that [with the Raptors]. I want to prove I'm a Bull and not a Raptor."

More players were shooting baskets. Doug Christie and Vincenzo Esposito at the Raptors' end. Steve Kerr and Jud Buechler at the Bulls' end. As Kerr found a groove, he was riveting to watch. He was, at this stage of the season, the league's leading three-point shooter, with an average of .515, and out on the floor, standing right at the three-point line, he was lofting shots that hung up there, hung and hung in the air, and finally dropped gracefully through the basket.

At the side of the court, Zan Tabak greeted Toni Kukoc, two Split homeboys. They yattered at one another in Croatian until Phil Jackson, the Chicago coach, got into the act. "How do you guys grow so tall over there?" Jackson asked, all smiles. Tabak repeated a line he'd used when he had been asked the question before. "It's something in the water." Jackson made the two of them, Tabak and Kukoc, stand side by side while he compared their heights. Tabak came out taller, an inch maybe. Jackson patted both men on the back. It's a fraternity, he seemed to be saying, different teams but all of us in it together, in the NBA.

The floor was busy with players, but Michael Jordan was nowhere in sight. Along the press section, which was beginning to fill, people chatted, but their eyes kept sneaking looks to the right, to the lane under the north end of the temporary stands where visiting teams made their entrance. No Michael Jordan.

Oh well, Johnny Kerr had arrived, and he was telling a funny story about Dennis Rodman's latest excess. Johnny Kerr – no relation to Steve – was one of the commentators for telecasts of the Bulls games, a tall man with an ample stomach, squinty eyes behind glasses, and enough pinkish shading in his hair to justify his lifetime nickname, "Red." Kerr had once been a fine basketball player, a centre for twelve years in the NBA, mostly with the old Syracuse team, from the mid-fifties to the mid-sixties. Not unexpectedly, he was knowledgeable about the game and generous in sharing a good story.

The Rodman tale needed a little background. In a Bulls game eight days earlier, on Saturday, March 16, against the New Jersey Nets at the Meadowlands, Rodman had been whistled for two technicals in the first quarter. The first T came when he pounded the ball on the floor in a display of anger at an official call, the second, after referee Paul Mihilak called him for a personal foul, and Rodman flashed an obscene gesture.

Mihilak didn't notice the gesture, but another ref, Ted Bernhardt, did, and he signalled the second technical, which meant Rodman was out of the game.

At that point, Rodman really lost it. Went ballistic. Over the top. He argued with Bernhardt, standing very close, getting in the referee's face in every sense of the phrase. He topped off his tirade by head-butting Bernhardt above the left eye. Rodman said later the butt was an accident. But in film clips of the incident, which were run over and over on television, the head butt looked as practised and intentional as a Three Stooges routine. In fact, it might be said that Rodman *had* rehearsed the butt; after all, he'd been suspended twice before for head-butting, both times when he was with the San Antonio Spurs – once in December 1993 for bonking Stacey King of Chicago and again in March 1994 for cracking Utah's John Stockton. When it came to butting skulls, Rodman was as expert as Larry, Curly, and Moe.

Anyway, to get to the funny part, as Johnny Kerr recounted the episode, it was Jayson Williams, New Jersey's power forward, who furnished the laugh line. It seemed that, the previous summer, Williams had tried out with the Bulls, and, as part of his Chicago audition, Williams was required to submit himself to a lengthy psychiatric assessment, partly because he was suspected of having a propensity for off-beat behaviour. The Bulls eventually turned Williams down, and he signed again with the Nets, the team he'd played for during the preceding three years. Now, at the Meadowlands, in the aftermath of the Dennis Rodman explosion – after Rodman had finally gone to the dressing room trailing swear words, leaving behind his jersey, which he had ripped off, and an overturned water cooler, which he had drop-kicked – Williams strolled over to the Bulls bench and leaned close enough for Phil Jackson and the players to hear him.

"And you guys thought *I* was crazy," Williams said.

Jackson laughed. It *was* a funny line. But a little later, with the game against New Jersey continuing, Jackson wasn't laughing. Neither was Michael Jordan. That was because, with Rodman banished, and with Scottie Pippen's injuries keeping him on the sidelines, who was going to handle Chicago's rebounding? By default, if nothing else, most of the job fell to Jordan. As well as scoring a team-high thirty-seven points, he pulled down a team-high sixteen rebounds. He carried the load in an unexpectedly tight 97–93 win, and he didn't care for the situation. Afterwards, Johnny Kerr said, Jordan told the media it was asking too much of him to take care of the scoring *and* the rebounding. Jordan was very miffed at Dennis Rodman for misbehaving and getting the Bulls into the predicament of having no frontline power forward.

Things got worse for Chicago the following Monday. That was the day when Rod Thorn, the NBA vice-president in charge of handing out player punishment, announced that Rodman was suspended for the next six games. This came at a crucial time for the Bulls. The team record, after the New Jersey game, stood at fifty-seven wins and seven losses. These were phenomenal figures, and they put Chicago right on course to become the first NBA team ever to record seventy wins in a regular season. In fact, the Bulls' chase for seventy was by far the biggest continuing story in the league. But without Rodman, with Pippen out for at least a couple more games – he had tendinitis in his right knee, two wobbly ankles, and a sore lower back – and with Luc Longley, the big centre, also on the injured list, Chicago looked weak on rebounding, and the chances of winning the big seventy could be seriously in jeopardy. What added to the difficulty was that the Bulls faced a busy week, playing Philadelphia on the road on Monday night, Sacramento and the New York Knicks at home Tuesday and Thursday, and the Raptors at the SkyDome on this Sunday afternoon.

Jordan rose heroically to the occasion. Against Philadelphia, in another squeaker of a game – which was inexplicable, since the 76ers held the league's second-worst won-lost record – Jordan had ten rebounds along with thirty-eight points. To put his rebound statistic in perspective, Jordan was averaging just under six rebounds per game on the season. Without Rodman and Pippen, he was stepping up that figure by half as many and more. The downside was, of course, that he was expending more energy than he wanted to so late in the season with the playoffs just ahead.

Against Sacramento, which didn't put up much effort, Jordan had it relatively easy, twenty points, nine rebounds in a blowout. But in the Knicks game, Jordan had to turn it up again. The last time the two teams met, in New York City two weeks earlier, the Knicks had embarrassed the Bulls by boffing them 104–72, Chicago's worst loss of the year. Now the Bulls were looking for revenge and a restoration of pride. They managed both, mainly on the strength of a 20–1 run to end the second quarter. Jordan was, naturally, the leader in this outburst, getting eight of the twenty points. Oddly enough, the second-highest contributor to the run was John Salley, with three layups and a free throw for seven points; the Bulls had signed him for rebounding and defensive purposes, but, in this one game, in this one quarter, he turned into a scoring fool. Jordan, however, still bore the heavy burden, playing thirty-seven minutes, scoring thirty-six points, grabbing eight rebounds, each a team high, in the 107–86 win.

All of this was by way of prelude to Chicago's visit to the SkyDome, giving the game an extra edge of anticipation. Was Jordan wearing himself out? Were the Bulls vulnerable in the rebounding department? Was Chicago beginning to feel the weight of its pursuit of the wins record? Could the Raptors, who had played the Bulls tough in the last Toronto game, pull out a surprise win over the best team in basketball?

Jordan didn't show up on the SkyDome floor until the whole Chicago team trotted out for the final warmup fifteen minutes before the start of the game. Brian Cooper's Events and Operations crew had a special greeting for him. It appeared on the Jumbotron, a clip from Jordan's stint a couple of years earlier as the guest host on "Saturday Night Live." In the sketch shown in the clip, Jordan sat facing the camera, while, behind him, an SNL character, Stuart Smalley, fed him lines, which Jordan repeated into the camera. The lines were meant to be uplifting confidence-boosters for Jordan, and the humour came in the slightly exaggerated way both men spoke the words.

"All I have to do," Smalley said, then Jordan repeated, "is be the *best* Michael I can be. And, doggone it, people *like* me."

It was silly-but-amusing stuff, and, down on the floor, the Bulls players paused in their practice shots to look up at the giant screen and watch their teammate. Jordan watched too. He watched and listened, and, at the end, he shook his head a little and giggled. Even Michael Jordan was sort of enchanted by Michael Jordan.

Jordan looked like he was playing closer to the basket than he normally did. Was that to put himself in better position to pick off rebounds? To compensate for Rodman's absence? Could be. He had four rebounds in the first half, the second-highest on the team. Offensively, he was relatively quiet. With Alvin Robertson guarding him, he took seven shots, hit on four of them, and went a perfect five-for-five from the free-throw line. A quiet thirteen points.

It was Steve Kerr who provided the dramatic points for the Bulls. At 9:29 of the second quarter, he took a pass from Scottie Pippen a foot beyond the three-point line. The pass came in at chest level, and, in one quick motion, Kerr squared his feet to face the basket, lowered the ball to below his waist, then raised it higher in front of his body, at the same time pushing himself into the air off both feet. When the ball reached a level over his head at eleven o'clock from his body, when his jump was at the highest point, he released the ball in the soaring arc that was familiar from his pre-game practice routine. The ball dropped from the air and swished through the centre of the hoop. Three points.

Exactly thirty seconds later, Kerr hit the same shot, another three-pointer, from the same distance, twenty-three feet out, and, towards the end of the quarter, he struck again with two more jumpers, one from thirteen feet and the other from twenty feet, both two-pointers. All the shots were made with the same swift, compact, rising motion.

The Bulls needed Kerr's points, because the Raptors were playing this game in an attack mode. Brendan Malone used only seven players in the first half: Murray, Rogers, Miller, Robertson, and Stoudamire as starters, Christie and Tabak off the bench. And everybody except Robertson, who had his hands full guarding Jordan, was firing at the Chicago basket.

In the first quarter, Miller threw down a dunk off a Rogers feed. Rogers came back twenty seconds later with a tip-in at the end of a Raptor fast break. Then a dunk for Murray. Stoudamire hit from eighteen feet out, from twenty-three feet, from eighteen feet again when he pulled up off a fast break, squared away, and fired over Michael Jordan. And Tabak, with less than a minute to go in the quarter, put up a gorgeous hook shot over none other than his childhood buddy, Toni Kukoc.

It was thrilling stuff, and the Raptors kept it up in the second quarter. Christie got hot, two three-pointers and another jumper, for eight points. Murray and Stoudamire kept putting the ball in the air, Stoudamire having his way with anybody who guarded him, Jordan or Kerr. He ended the half with fourteen points, Murray with eleven, and the Raptors took a two-point lead, 56–54, into the locker room.

Jordan had begun the second quarter sitting on the bench for a breather. His custom, on the bench, was to drape himself in two white towels. He didn't, as most players did, put on his warmup suit. Maybe he never expected to remain out of a game long enough to need a warmup suit.

At 8:05 of the quarter, Phil Jackson sent Jordan back into the game, replacing Scottie Pippen. Jordan walked to the scorer's table, still clutching the white towels. A ball boy stuck to Jordan's heels. His job was to take delivery of the towels. But Jordan ignored the ball boy. Instead, as he passed Scottie Pippen, Jordan tossed the towels to *him*. Pippen caught the towels, gave them a disgusted look, and threw them in the general direction of the ball boy.

Was this a Jordan ritual, the thing with the towels? A routine? Or just kidding around with Pippen?

The ball boy scrambled to the bench with the two towels, and play resumed.

At 11:13 of the third quarter, Toni Kukoc hit a basket from twenty-three feet. For a big man, Kukoc had a fine touch on his outside shot. His skills were sound in every area of the game: he could pass, run the floor, grab rebounds, drive the basket. His only drawback seemed to be in concentration. Now and then, he dozed off on the floor. Jackson and the other Bulls coaches had to yell at him, wake him up, get him moving.

Nobody yelled at Kukoc in the third quarter. He was on fire. After the first three-pointer, he scored on a fifteen-foot jumper and on a seven-foot hook shot. He set up Jordan for a driving dunk, and he passed to Bill Wennington, the centre playing in place of the injured Luc Longley, for a nice seventeen-foot jumper.

Before Kukoc joined the Bulls in 1993, he had been known overseas as "the Michael Jordan of Europe." In this quarter, he was living up to the old billing.

For the Raptors, the same two guys kept knocking down the baskets in the third period, Tracy Murray and Damon Stoudamire. Both hit two three-pointers. Murray's came in quick succession, within twenty-five seconds of one another towards the end of the quarter, each one a twenty-four-footer, and those six points tied the game.

With two and a half minutes to go in the quarter, a Murray shot rimmed out of the Chicago hoop. The ball bounced off a couple of pairs of hands reaching for the rebound. Oliver Miller wanted the ball. Bill Wennington wanted it. Hands poked and stabbed and grabbed. The ball stayed loose. One of Wennington's hands glanced off Miller's left eye. Miller danced away in pain, his hand wiping at the eye. The fray over the ball continued. Miller moved back into it. But this time, he was more intent on Wennington than the ball. The two men shoved one another. Miller said something directed at Wennington, a white guy. Even from across the court, it was easy to read Miller's lips.

"I'm gonna beat his white ass," Miller said.

Was this a racist crack?

Black players often refer to their own white teammates' "white asses" or "white honky asses," as in, "Hey, man, get your white honky ass over here." It's just kidding around. Or it seems to be kidding around. For that matter, black players say to other black teammates, "Get your black ass over here." But white players never refer to their black teammates' asses by shade. Never, "Get your black ass over here."

Suppose, in the short shoving match under the Chicago basket, Wennington had said to Miller, "I'm gonna whip your black ass." Would that have been considered racist?

Oliver Miller might have thought so.

Herbie Kuhn announced the attendance for the game. It was 36,131, thirteen seats more than had been sold for the first Chicago game in January, a SkyDome and Canadian attendance record. The people in the stands applauded themselves for setting the record.

With :48.9 to go in the third quarter, Toni Kukoc scored on a driving layup. Twenty-four seconds later, Michael Jordan dropped in a layup of his own. Those two baskets put the Bulls in front by four at the quarter's end.

Jordan began the fourth quarter catching a break on the bench, draped in the usual two white towels. At 8:18, Phil Jackson returned him to the game. Once again, Jordan was replacing Scottie Pippen, and once again, Jordan ignored the ball boy and tossed the two towels to Pippen, who caught them, gave his disgusted look, and flung the towels at the ball boy.

There must have been something in this towel business. Did it have superstitious meaning for Jordan? Pippen didn't give the impression, with his look of distaste, that he cared to be part of the ritual. But Jordan had done it twice, exactly the same procedure twice. What was the significance?

When Jordan went back into the game, the Bulls were up by one point. The action through the last part of the third quarter and the beginning of the fourth had been fast, anxious, spectacular, tense, edge-of-the-seat stuff. The crowd was in a steady uproar, and now, with Jordan on the floor, the tension kicked up a notch.

At the five-minute mark, with the Raptors ahead by two points, Stoudamire drove the Bulls' basket. Steve Kerr was sticking to him like glue and succeeded in making Stoudamire lose control of the ball. It fell into the hands of John Salley, who was lying on the floor at the time, knocked there by Oliver Miller in the jockeying under the basket. Salley passed the ball from his supine position, and the Bulls took off on a fast break. It ended when Kerr pulled to a sudden stop and nailed a twenty-four-foot three-pointer. His shooting form was impeccable. Bulls up by one.

From then on, the teams traded baskets and the lead. Christie and Miller hit jumpers. Toronto ahead by three. Jordan hit two consecutive jump shots, from thirteen feet and sixteen feet. Bulls in the lead by one. Murray sank two foul shots. Jordan knocked down a fourteen-footer. There was a pattern emerging in the quarter. Everybody was scoring for Toronto; only Michael Jordan, who didn't seem at all fatigued by the previous week's exertions, was scoring for Chicago. The pattern continued when, at 1:13, Jordan sank two free throws and put the Bulls up by three points.

Then came an exciting and furious episode under the Chicago basket, when the Bulls must have wished that Dennis Rodman had been on the scene. Jordan, Kukoc, and Pippen had been doing an okay job in rebounding, keeping Chicago just about even with the Raptors in that department. But in what was about to happen, the Bulls needed a guy like Rodman.

The sequence began with Stoudamire driving on the Chicago hoop.

Jordan fouled him. Stoudamire went to the free-throw line. He hit his first shot. Bulls lead cut to two. Stoudamire missed the second free throw. But Doug Christie leaped high to grab the rebound. Bill Wennington fouled Christie. He went to the line and missed both free throws. But again the Raptors got the rebound off the missed second free throw, and this time it was the smallest guy on the floor who pulled it in, Stoudamire. He dribbled away from the Chicago basket, turned, and shot from seventeen feet. He missed. The ball was loose, and Stoudamire retrieved the rebound off his own missed shot. He fed a pass to Oliver Miller, who was breaking towards the basket. Miller threw down an authoritative slam dunk. The game, after these thirteen seconds of passionate action, after the Raptors grabbed three rebounds under the Bulls' basket, was tied.

Jordan came back and nailed a nine-foot jumper. It was Jordan's thirteenth consecutive point. From 4:29 of the fourth quarter, he had scored all of the Bulls' points.

Jordan trotted past Brendan Malone after this last nine-footer.

"Don't you *ever* miss, Michael?" Malone asked.

"Not at this time of the game," Jordan answered. He was smiling.

Chicago was in front by two, and Malone called a timeout for Toronto.

The Raptors came back on the floor with a play designed in the huddle.

Oliver Miller inbounded the ball from a spot just inside the Chicago side of the centre line. In front of the Chicago basket, Tracy Murray darted to his right. Doug Christie set a pick that prevented Scottie Pippen from chasing Murray. Miller threw the inbounds pass to an open Murray, who scored on a layup. Tie game.

The crowd was screaming with joy, and Chicago called a timeout.

In the Chicago huddle at the side of the floor during the timeout, a couple of the players smiled and grinned. Who should worry? So the game was tied and there were only thirty seconds left in the fourth quarter. Old stuff. Michael'll score. Chicago'll win again. Worry? No need. John Salley was laughing.

In the Raptors' huddle, Brendan Malone made a defensive switch. He moved Doug Christie onto Michael Jordan in place of Alvin Robertson. This wasn't an insult to Robertson. He had done his usual tenacious job on Jordan, even if Jordan had scored thirty-six points. Malone just wanted to give Jordan a different look. When he saw Christie guarding him, he might be mildly, briefly discombobulated.

When play resumed, possession to the Bulls, Jordan got the ball at the top of the Raptors' paint and drove on the basket for a layup. Oliver Miller came out to meet him. Miller's hand brushed the ball, not much, maybe just enough to jar Jordan's sense of full control, but Jordan kept driving to the basket. He went up in the air to put in the layup. Doug Christie rose with him and swatted the ball with the back of his hand. The ball drifted away from Jordan, and Miller grabbed it. Miller cradled the ball and appeared to be on the verge of calling a timeout. But before he could say anything, Scottie Pippen fouled him.

Now the crowd was in an uproar. The Raptors had repulsed Michael Jordan, and Oliver Miller had a chance to put Toronto in the lead.

Miller hit the first free throw. Missed the second. Pippen grabbed the rebound and called time out. The Raptors were up by one.

In the Chicago huddle, nobody grinned. John Salley kept his laughs under wraps. This was serious. Twenty seconds left in the game and the Bulls a point down. Phil Jackson designed a play. There wasn't much question that it would be something that put the ball in Michael Jordan's hands.

Once again, Jordan had the ball at the top of the Toronto paint. Christie was on him. The Bulls were trying to set up a screen for Jordan, a couple of players who would seal off the Raptors and allow him to drive or to shoot from outside. He looked as if he was going to drive. Oliver Miller moved past the screen, which hadn't formed properly, to double-team Jordan. Jordan began to drive, but Miller had cut him off. Miller's hand hit the ball. It came out to Steve Kerr on the perimeter. Kerr passed to Pippen on the right wing. Pippen looked for a shot, couldn't see one, and passed the ball back to Kerr. The game clock showed 1.9 seconds left. No time for another pass. Kerr had to shoot.

If Michael Jordan couldn't take the final shot, Kerr was the next best bet for Chicago. He was the leading three-point shooter in the league. He'd already knocked down three three-pointers in this game and four other baskets. Who better than Kerr?

There was just one problem. Kerr wasn't standing in his favourite spot. He liked to shoot from just outside the three-point line, from twenty-three feet, no more than twenty-four. But, at this moment, he was standing twenty-six feet out from the basket. It might be too far.

Kerr went into his usual shooting drill. Lower the ball, raise it above his shoulders, body squared, feet rising, jumping into the shot, release the ball.

The shot soared high, very high, and when the ball came down, it hit the right side of the rim. It bounced away to the right, along the baseline. Kerr's shot had missed.

The Raptors began to celebrate. Four Bulls players sagged at the shoulders. Only Michael Jordan stayed hopeful and active. The buzzer hadn't sounded to end the game. There was a tenth of a second left on the clock. Jordan reached the ball in the corner, eighteen feet away from the basket. He spun and shot in a high arc. The ball looked as if it would hit the side of the backboard. It didn't. It brushed past and fell through the basket.

But, wait, the buzzer had sounded milliseconds before Jordan released the ball. The referees waved off the basket. It was an utterly magnificent shot, but it didn't count. The game was over. The Raptors had defeated the Bulls.

The cheers rolled down from the stands in one colossal, sustained sheet of noise. Maybe it had been louder in the SkyDome on the night in October 1993 when Joe Carter hit the home run that won the World Series for the Blue Jays. But maybe not. The building's floor seemed to shake, and the air over the court shivered in the tumult.

Brendan Malone, his face wearing a look of ecstasy, turned from the Raptors bench to face the stands. He stretched his arm high above his shoulders and pointed his finger. He was acknowledging the crowd, thanking them for their cheers, pointing all the way to the top of the SkyDome, to the fans up in the distant 500 level. The noise didn't let up, and Malone looked like a man sticking his finger right into the heart of the roar.

A few minutes later, in Malone's post-game press conference, his eyes moist, his voice hoarse, he got off a great line.

"Seattle, Orlando, Chicago," he said, referring to the three teams with the best records in the league, three teams that the Raptors had defeated. "We're ready for the playoffs!"

A reporter brought up the matter of Chicago playing without Dennis Rodman.

"Hey, c'mon," Malone answered. "We played without Sharone Wright. What's the matter? We beat the *Bulls*. That's Chicago, meat-packer to the world, all that, town of broad shoulders. We beat *them*."

(Malone liked to make literary and historical references. Once, in another post-game conference, he mentioned Franklin Roosevelt. He stopped, looked around, considered that his audience was made up mostly of Canadians in their twenties and thirties, and elaborated. "That's Franklin Delano Roosevelt, greatest president of the United States.")

For the Raptors, seven players had taken part in the victory. Tracy Murray played forty-seven minutes, forty-six for Damon Stoudamire, forty for Oliver Miller, thirty-four for Carlos Rogers, twenty-nine for Alvin Robertson, twenty-six for Doug Christie, then dropping away to eighteen for Zan Tabak (though, in that short time, he had scored an admirable twelve points and pulled in six rebounds). Five other players were dressed – Acie Earl, Vincenzo Esposito, Jimmy King, Martin Lewis, and Dwayne Whitfield – but none of them, essentially the kids of the team, had been summoned to play by Brendan Malone.

In the Bulls' dressing room, Michael Jordan was, as usual, accommodating. Hemmed in by dozens of media people, he answered all the questions. He thought Oliver Miller fouled him on his last attempt at a drive to the basket. And he thought Damon Stoudamire made the difference. He said the Bulls couldn't stop him.

Jordan was asked if he was shocked at losing to an expansion team.

"I'm shocked by all losses," he said, "not just this one."

Jordan wore an uncharacteristically grim expression. At that moment, generous with his insights as he was being, he didn't look as if he was in quite the frame of mind to reveal the secret behind the ritual of the tossing of the towels. Nobody had the nerve to bring the subject up, and Jordan eventually closed the press conference. He had a plane to catch.

17

BYE-BYE, BRENDAN?

On the Monday after the huge win over Chicago, Isiah Thomas thought about firing Brendan Malone that very day. His thinking was that no one could ever accuse him of letting Malone go as a result of a losing streak, which was the traditional reason that coaches got kicked out of their jobs. Thomas knew there was no *good* time to bounce Malone, but immediately after the Chicago game might be the least *bad* time. He fretted over the decision during the day, and finally backed away from it. He wouldn't fire Malone on that Monday.

But why get rid of Brendan Malone at all? What in the world was going on here?

Earlier in the season, in February, John Bitove had had a conversation with Malone. Malone was singing a blues that Bitove had heard from him before, a familiar tune.

"Three or four seasons," Malone said. "That's all I expect to be here. Maybe less."

"Brendan," Bitove said, a touch exasperated, "there's no reason why you can't be with us for many seasons, no reason why you can't be here as the head coach when we win the NBA championship."

Not long after that, Malone stopped using the small office he had at Raptors headquarters in the building at the foot of Bay Street. He cleared out the stuff he kept there and didn't return. People on the Raptors staff began to get the idea that maybe Malone himself didn't want his Raptors job to be a long-term commitment, that maybe he saw it as an entry on his résumé that would eventually propel him into an even better NBA coaching job. The Raptors people didn't know why Malone might feel this way. Nor did they have explicit evidence that it was the case. They simply began to think of it as a possibility. Malone, they figured, was acting in an odd way for a man who was supposed to be committed to the organization.

Isiah Thomas had a more specific beef with Malone. It concerned playing time, the number of game minutes that different Raptor players spent on the floor. Actually, it wasn't *different* players. It was the *same* players. And that was the problem.

All season, Malone had been relying on a core of six or seven players. The members of the core group shifted with trades and injuries, but essentially he played the guys whom he considered workers and winners. Except for Damon Stoudamire, this bunch tended to be veterans or, if not precisely veterans, then players who'd been around the league for three or four years. To Malone, they offered the best shot at wins, and that was why he was in the coaching business. To win.

Thomas didn't rate wins as a first priority. Not immediately, not in the first season. Thomas had a plan, and the plan didn't necessarily include a lot of victories right away. The plan was to reach the playoffs in the Raptors' third season, and, to accomplish that, Thomas needed to measure the team's strengths and weaknesses, to see for himself who could play and who couldn't, who, among the twelve players on the active roster and the three players on the injury list or in other temporarily non-active categories, was worth keeping and who made logical material for a trade. He needed to see all the players in at least some of the games, not some of the players in all of the games.

For example, as Thomas's thinking went, he had traded his first pick in the previous summer's expansion draft, B. J. Armstrong, to Golden State for five players. The five included two young guys, Martin Lewis and Dwayne Whitfield. But, as of the Chicago game on Sunday, Lewis had played only twenty-four minutes all season, and Whitfield had played sixteen. True, both had spent much time in various non-playing statuses. Still, they could have seen enough game action for Thomas to judge whether he had traded for gold or dreck.

Or, another example: earlier in the season, Thomas thought about working Carlos Rogers into a trade. But, at that point in the year, near the beginning, Malone wasn't giving Rogers much floor time, and, when Thomas talked to general managers around the league about a trade for Rogers, they would say, Why isn't Rogers playing for you guys? Is something wrong with him? Why would we take a chance on a player his own team isn't using?

For all of these various reasons, Thomas wanted the younger players – Lewis, Whitfield, Rogers among them – to share playing time with the veterans. He wanted Malone to use the entire bench, and Thomas thought, as the Raptors season began, that Malone agreed with this approach. He recalled Malone *expressing* his agreement.

But things changed in November and December. At least they seemed to change from the Malone perspective. The Raptors were winning games and coming very close to wins in other games. They played a better brand of basketball than the fans and other NBA teams expected of them, probably better than Malone himself expected. And he elected to keep playing the guys who were producing the exciting and the frequently winning basketball. He shortened his bench. He went with his favourites, with Stoudamire and the vets, and, for game after game, he allowed the young guys to chalk up opposite their names on the Raptors Official Scorer's Report the most discouraging notation in basketball: "DNP" – Did Not Play – "Coach's Decision."

This was the way Thomas saw things unfolding, and he didn't like it. Thomas said later that he spoke to Malone about the rigidity of the lineup that the coach was putting on the floor. He told Malone that he wanted – he *needed* – a good look at the rookies, the young guys, the players who might be the foundation for the team over the next half-dozen years. He especially asked that Jimmy King get some meaningful minutes at point guard. Was King skilled enough at the point to spell Damon Stoudamire? Thomas wanted to know the answer to the question. He talked to Malone about such things. That was how Thomas later remembered the development of his relationship with Malone. He said he made it clear to Malone that the future of the Raptors demanded playing time for the young guys in the present.

And now, in the wake of the win over Chicago, a great win, yes, but the same old story – the Malone regulars played and the kids sat – Thomas was fed up, and he went public for the first time with his distress. A couple of days after the Bulls game, he told Craig Daniels of the *Sun* and Mary Ormsby of the *Star* about his concerns. He talked of the need to play the young guys, to think of the future, that it was okay for the team to be competitive but that he wanted the competitive drive to be instilled in the younger players under game conditions.

Thomas talked of these matters, but he didn't mention that he had thought of firing Malone on Monday. He didn't mention that he was thinking of firing Malone at all. He hoped that he and Malone would work out their differences. Thomas said that. He said he would evaluate all personnel at the end of the season. The evaluation would include Malone. Not surprisingly, the reporters interpreted Thomas's words to mean something different. They figured Thomas probably intended to put the skids to Malone.

That was what they wrote in their newspapers, but, before the stories could appear, there was a game to be played at the SkyDome on Tuesday night, March 26, against the Atlanta Hawks.

Tracy Murray was mad.

This was at the beginning of the fourth quarter in the Atlanta game. The Raptors had played a terrific first half, scoring sixty-four points. That number equalled the team season high for points scored in a half, which the Raptors had set in the Dallas game on March 10. Toronto's baskets came on flashy fast breaks and on long outlet passes by Oliver Miller, passes he threw with the zip and accuracy of a John Elway, without the helmet and shoulder pads. Murray accounted for eighteen points and Damon Stoudamire for fifteen. Christian Laettner kept the Hawks in the game. Laettner, after years of whining about the losers on his former team, the Minnesota Timberwolves, had been traded to Atlanta in February, and seemed to be thriving with a winning team. He scored fifteen points in the first half. But that wasn't good enough to hold off the Raptors, who ended the half on top, 64–58.

Then Atlanta turned the tables in the third quarter, and Tracy Murray began to get perturbed. Atlanta became the team doing the running and scoring. It aided their cause that the Raptors' big guys were slow getting back on defence, giving the Hawks time to set up and bang in the shots.

The Raptors had their moments. Mostly they were Stoudamire's. At 5:01 of the quarter, as Laettner was getting ready under the Toronto basket to elevate for a dunk, Stoudamire slipped behind him and stole the ball. Stoudamire whipped around and took off down the floor, dribbling through the scrambling Atlanta players, changing directions a couple of times, ending his charge six seconds later with a driving layup. It qualified as one of the year's three or four most sensational plays, a few seconds on the basketball court that got the blood racing and the heart pumping.

But the rest of the quarter belonged to the Hawks, who outscored the Raptors by ten points and went ahead by four. Which was when Tracy Murray let his temper fly.

Murray has a wonderfully handsome face with the broad, slightly fleshy look of a young Robert Mitchum. It's also an expressive face, and, when he gets mad, he takes on the pained grimace of a man who has just slammed the car door on his fingers. That was the way Murray looked as he stood at the sidelines close to the press tables waiting with his teammates for the fourth quarter to start.

"C'mon, guys!" he barked. "Don't let this one get away!"

Carlos Rogers glanced at Murray and grinned, as if to say, Hey, what's with you? That cavalier attitude didn't make Murray any happier, nor did events in the fourth quarter. The Hawks went in front by as many as nine points, and, though the Raptors made it close at the end, though Murray and Stoudamire each scored thirty points for the game, Atlanta came out the winner, 114–111.

That – losing a game that the Raptors could have won – was Tracy Murray's problem, the source of his anger. Isiah Thomas's anger that night, the source of his distress, was something else, something familiar. To get their thirty points, Murray and Stoudamire had both played the entire game, all forty-eight minutes. Oliver Miller played forty-one minutes, and most of the rest of the time on the floor was divided among Doug Christie, Alvin Robertson, Carlos Rogers, and Zan Tabak. Acie Earl got in for thirteen minutes at power forward, and Vincenzo Esposito saw precisely one minute of play at guard. Jimmy King, Martin Lewis, and Dwayne Whitfield didn't leave the bench. For Thomas, this was more of the same old thing, more of Malone playing the regulars and not giving the kids a look.

Thomas thought the situation was getting ridiculous. What he didn't know was that, the very next day, it was about to get dangerous as well as ridiculous.

On the afternoon of Wednesday, March 27, in Philadelphia, where the Raptors were meeting the 76ers that night, Damon Stoudamire announced he wouldn't be playing in the game. His left knee hurt. It needed rest. The Raptors' doctors had told him he had tendinitis in the knee.

Tendinitis is a micro-tearing in the tendon that attaches the kneecap to the shin bone. The micro-tearing leads to inflammation and pain. The ailment is colloquially known as "jumper's knee," because it is often brought on during the landings after jumps. Damon Stoudamire did plenty of jumping and landing. And he had performed a lot more of both during the 1995-96 basketball season than he had during any other season in his short athletic life. At the University of Arizona, he played about thirty games per season. In his first year with the Raptors, he had already played more than double that number. And, in each Raptors game, he had put in forty-one minutes on the floor. Tendinitis in one knee? It seemed miraculous that he hadn't worn both legs down to stumps.

Without Stoudamire, Doug Christie and Jimmy King alternated at point guard in the game against the 76ers in Philadelphia, and though some Raptors played splendidly – notably Zan Tabak, who scored twenty-six points and pulled in eleven rebounds – Toronto lost to the pitiful 76ers, 103−94.

But as far as Isiah Thomas was concerned, the loss wasn't the bad news. It hardly qualified as any kind of news. Damon Stoudamire's knee was what mattered. Now Thomas was getting really upset. Not only was this cockamamie idea of Brendan Malone's to play the same guys night after night messing up Thomas's long-term plan for the Raptors, not only was it preventing Thomas from getting a look at the youngsters on the team, not only was it doing all of that – *now* it was making a cripple out of Thomas's star player!

"Damon would never complain," Thomas said to the press when he got the grim word from Philadelphia, "but we have to be smart enough to understand the big picture."

Which seemed to be calm and measured public corporatespeak for, Jesus, Brendan, are you *nuts*?

The only cure for tendinitis is a series of exercises that strengthen the area where the micro-tearing took place. Exercises and one other thing – rest. Stay off the knee. Give it time to heal.

Two days after he was diagnosed with tendinitis, but six days before he was scheduled for tests that would determine the extent of the injury to his tendon, Stoudamire decided the tendinitis wasn't painful enough to keep him out of the Raptors game at the SkyDome on Friday night, March 29, against the Orlando Magic. Maybe Stoudamire had fooled himself into believing the pain wasn't all that severe. Maybe he was simply so competitive that he couldn't bear missing a game against a major opponent like the Magic. He declared himself fit for the Orlando game, and nobody contradicted him.

The opening lineup that Malone put on the floor against the Magic was made up of the players he had lately been relying on as starters: Stoudamire and Alvin Robertson at the guard positions, Oliver Miller at centre, Tracy Murray and Carlos Rogers at the forwards. From the opening tip, the Magic – and especially Shaq O'Neal – rocked these five guys back on their heels. Just eight seconds of the game had gone by before O'Neal threw down a wham-bam slam dunk. O'Neal, seven-foot-one, three hundred pounds, just turned twenty-six, maybe the most powerful player in the game, a nineties sort of young guy, who recorded rap albums, made Hollywood movies, and shook the backboards with his jams – *broke* the backboards on a good night – this Shaq O'Neal was on his way to a monster first quarter against the Raptors. He threw down two more dunks, scored fifteen points altogether, and gave Oliver Miller fits. Trying to get in between Shaq and the Raptors' basket, poor Miller was whistled for three fouls. The third foul came with thirty-five seconds left in the quarter and the Magic up by seven points. That was when Brendan Malone began to make the substitutions that would later develop into a large controversy.

Malone might ordinarily have sent Zan Tabak into the game for Miller. But Tabak had pulled a groin muscle during his excellent effort against Philadelphia two nights earlier; the pull was so deep that Tabak, just hitting his stride as a player, was finished with basketball for the season. So Malone's choice to replace Miller was Acie Earl, and, at the same time, with the quarter almost over, he substituted Dwayne Whitfield for Carlos Rogers. Now there were two young guys from the end of the Raptors bench in the game.

Malone wasn't finished. At 10:31 of the second quarter, he sent in Jimmy King for Damon Stoudamire. Stoudamire returned to the game six minutes later. But King remained at point guard, and Stoudamire moved to shooting guard, though he put up only two shots and scored no points. For almost the entire quarter, the Raptors' lineup consisted of King, Whitfield, Earl, Doug Christie, some Stoudamire, some Murray, and a minute and a half of Vincenzo Esposito. The kids were on the floor, and the vastly superior Magic were killing them. At the half, Orlando led by twenty points, 60–40.

During the intermission, a group of dancers from the National Ballet of Canada, dressed in summery costumes, hit the floor and performed a pair of lively and charming numbers to two 1940s Andrews Sisters recordings, "Rum and Coca Cola" and "Oh Johnny." It was ballerina boogie, and, when the dancers finished, the basketball fans in the stands gave them polite and tepid applause.

"I guess it was an entertainment stretch," Brian Cooper said afterwards.

To open the second half, Malone went with the unit that had begun the game, the starters, the guys he relied on. And Orlando steamrollered them. Nick Anderson, the Magic's shooting guard, led off with a three-pointer. Horace Grant, the power forward, crushed a dunk and hit a fifteen-foot jumper. He stole the ball from Oliver Miller and fed Anderson for a fast-break layup. In no time at all, Orlando was up by thirty-two points.

Near the middle of the quarter, Stoudamire dribbled through the Orlando zone, looking frantically for an open Raptor to pass to. He couldn't spot anyone free. Nor could he get a clear view of the basket through the smothering Magic defence so he could make a shot of his own. Almost as an afterthought, Dennis Scott, Orlando's small forward, reached in and lightly fouled Stoudamire. It wasn't a shooting foul, and, as Stoudamire got set to resume play, his face a mask of misery, Penny

Hardaway, the Magic point guard, patted Stoudamire on the shoulder. It was a gesture that was telling Stoudamire, one point guard to another, "Mama always said there'd be nights like this."

At 5:22 of the third quarter, Orlando led by thirty-five points, and Malone sent in Christie for Tracy Murray and Esposito for Alvin Robertson. Five minutes later, with the Magic up by thirty-six points, Malone substituted Whitfield for Miller and King for Stoudamire. With the start of the fourth quarter, Malone made one final change – Martin Lewis for Christie. That ended the substitutions, and, for the entire fourth quarter, the Raptor lineup was made up of Lewis at small forward, Whitfield at power forward, Carlos Rogers at centre, King as point guard, and Esposito as shooting guard. All the kids were on the floor.

And the guys on the Orlando bench were giggling. They seemed to find the Raptors' performance hilarious, all those unknowns and beginners out there looking inept and disorganized. Shaq O'Neal was having fun on the bench, especially when he danced the pretend limbo. This was another piece of entertainment cooked up by the Events and Operations crew; during timeouts, a camera zoomed in on fans in the stands, who proceeded to dance the limbo under a line drawn on the Jumbotron screen. The camera focused on Shaq, and, big grin on his face, he obliged with a monster sitting-down limbo. He wouldn't have done *that* during a close game, during a game when the Magic were being pressed by the opposition, not during a game that hadn't turned into a laugh. This game was a laugh. Orlando won it by forty points, 126–86.

Brendan Malone's system of substitutions during the game might have been seen as an act of spite, intended to embarrass Isiah Thomas. Thomas wanted to see the young guys in action? Okay, they played, and look what happened. A disaster.

No way, Malone said after the game in answer to questions of such a motive on his part. The game was a blowout from the very first minute, he explained, and it was a natural opportunity to rest the regulars and give the other players a look.

"Oliver Miller got in foul trouble early, and I didn't have Ta-*bak*. So that meant I had to use the young big guys. And Dwayne Whitfield and Martin Lewis had been playing hard in practice, getting better, so they deserved a chance to play. Okay, they were playing in a situation where the game was over. They were playing loose. Vincenzo was playing very loose. That's a circumstance where it's hard to evaluate players. I admit that. But the younger guys were on the floor because a game where we're out of it anyway is a natural time to use the whole bench. And that's the only reason I had for putting them in."

And then, for the first time, Malone publicly addressed Isiah Thomas's comments in the newspapers about Malone's failure to go along with the plan that called for spreading the playing minutes around the entire roster. Malone hadn't seen Thomas all week, not since a brief chat right after the Chicago game. They hadn't talked face-to-face about Thomas's complaints, and now Malone would offer his side of the story.

"Isiah is a guy who wants to win, and I always got the impression we were supposed to go out there and do the best we could. The guys who got the playing minutes were the guys who deserved the minutes. We had a team that developed a style of competitiveness throughout the year, and the talk around the league was that, if you come into Toronto, you have to play hard. I'm proud of the team that worked to get that reputation."

Malone inhaled a deep breath.

"In that situation, up until the trades in February, there wasn't much room for guys like Carlos Rogers and Jimmy King to play. Carlos was behind Pinckney and Massenburg and Tracy Murray. Then, because of the trades, there were opportunities for Carlos to play, and he's had a good look. Martin Lewis and Esposito and Jimmy King have not had as good looks as Carlos. But, listen to this, we have an overload at the 2 guard. Alvin, Doug Christie, Esposito, Jimmy, and Martin Lewis are all 2s. It's very difficult to get playing time for five guys who play one position. The situation in general is there are only a certain number of minutes in a game when you can find time for all the people on your bench."

And Damon Stoudamire? All the minutes he played? His tendinitis?

"Damon plays forty minutes a game because, when he's not out there, we can't get anything going. I don't know why people make such a big thing of him playing forty minutes. Shaq O'Neal and Penny Hardaway play thirty-eight minutes a game, and nobody mentions it. Same with Grant Hill at Detroit and a lot of other great players. To keep us competitive and organized, we need to have Damon on the floor. Tendinitis? You ask Patrick Ewing about tendinitis. For eight years, he's been icing himself both before and after games and practices. It's an occupational hazard. If you play a lot of basketball, you develop tendinitis. You play through it. That's what you do."

A man was waiting in the wide, bleak corridor between the Raptors' dressing room and the lunchroom where Malone was holding his post-game press conference. The man was short, meticulously dressed, and had greying hair so beautifully coiffed that he appeared to have stepped from the "before" section of a Grecian Formula commercial. This was Brian Hill, the Orlando head coach.

Malone finished his press conference, and, when he stepped into the corridor, Hill took him by the arm. The two men walked alone down a narrow hall leading off the main corridor. Hill did all the talking. He looked very intent. So did Malone, who did all the listening.

The two emerged from the narrow hall after four or five minutes of intensity. Hill hurried away, back to the Orlando dressing room. One writer, waiting alone in the corridor, asked Malone what Hill had said.

Malone brightened. "He said I was doing a great job with the Raptors and I should keep up the good work."

Malone walked away, but didn't get far before he ran into someone else who wanted a word with him. It was Isiah Thomas. The two spoke briefly and in lowered voices. The word "embarrass" floated out of the conversation.

Malone headed down the corridor and around the corner to the press tables. The only people left in the area were print reporters. They were writing their stories for Saturday's newspapers.

"Don't make a big deal out of this thing," Malone said to the writers, referring to the differences he was having with Thomas. "It happens all the time between coaches and GMs. Don't exacerbate the problem."

Malone may have been closing the barn door. That was how the reporters saw things late that Friday night. But the horses were already out.

18

MAGIC

The moment that everybody had been waiting for, the principal reason why 36,046 people turned up at the SkyDome on the afternoon of the last Sunday in March, came at 11:07 of the first quarter. That was when the big guy with the marquee smile fed a sumptuous pass to his teammate Eddie Jones, who scored on a seven-foot jumper. Two points for the Los Angeles Lakers. Assist to Magic Johnson. The crowd – third largest of the season – delighted in it, even if the basket put the other guys, the visiting team, the Lakers, in front. It was the sight of Magic on the floor, doing the things that had made him a fabled player, that, for the moment, really mattered.

In the years after the day in June 1991 when Magic Johnson revealed that he had tested HIV-positive and was leaving the playing of basketball in the NBA, he got involved in many cool businesses. He opened Magic Theatres, an up-to-the-second theatre cineplex in South Central Los Angeles, which is Rodney King riot territory. He bought a 5 per cent interest in the Lakers (present value: $200 million). He peddled a new line of jazzy athletic shoes. And he delivered inspirational speeches to corporate audiences at as much as a whopping $100,000 per session.

So why, at age thirty-six, did he, on January 29, 1996, include himself back in the NBA, back on the Lakers roster?

At the press conference announcing his return, Johnson said he couldn't bear the thought that his three-year-old son, Earvin III, would never see him play in the Lakers uniform. But it seemed a bit thick to lay it off on the child. The truth might be more that Johnson himself missed basketball; perhaps, more to the point, he missed what went with the game – the noise, the drama, the adulation of the crowd, the feeling that he was once again in charge of events on the basketball floor, that he, the tallest point guard in captivity, controlled a team's destiny, and maybe part of the sport's destiny, too.

That was what attracted all the people to the SkyDome, to see for themselves if Johnson could still perform at the level that had brought him, in the past, five NBA championships with the Lakers, three MVP awards, three times the MVP in the championship final, election to nine straight All–NBA teams, and general recognition as the best point guard of all time (or, for older basketball fans with long memories, one of the three best, along with Bob Cousy and Oscar Robertson). Was Johnson still that good? Or even, for a guy approaching middle age and carrying a virus that was supposed to kill its bearer within fifteen years of contracting it, just any good at all?

On the afternoon of the Saturday before the game, Brendan Malone talked about Magic Johnson and the Lakers.

"I think this team has a very good chance at coming out of the west in the NBA finals," he said. "Earvin's made them into a contender. Look at their record coming into our building: they won against Orlando in Orlando, which ended the Magic's home unbeaten streak, and they beat Atlanta and Miami on the same trip. It's obvious why. They've got a good postup game in Vlade Divac and Elden Campbell. And Earvin, if he gets the ball down low, he can score and he can make their other people shoot well."

Malone paused in his assessment.

"But," he said, "they better not think we're gonna roll over for them. We're not."

Malone sounded in those words like a coach who wanted very much to catch a good team – the way the Raptors had caught Chicago a week earlier – and beat them. He sounded like a coach who absolutely burned to win next day, no matter what else might be going on in his coaching life.

Magic Johnson looked different. His hairline had retreated farther up his scalp. Chalk that up to advancing age. His biceps and shoulders swelled in thick layers of muscle; from all accounts, they were the result of a weight-lifting program he'd undertaken as part of his HIV therapy. And his stomach shimmied under his basketball jersey. That must have been too much home cooking.

He was also playing a different position from the old days, small forward rather than point guard. It would probably be putting an unnecessarily heavy load on Magic to have him take over the point responsibilities after four years away from the game, and besides, Nick Van Exel had performed well at the position over the previous couple of seasons. It was also true, however, that no matter where Johnson played on the floor, much of the Lakers' offence would go through him.

In another change of a different sort, Johnson came out in the starting lineup against the Raptors. At the beginning of his return, he'd played the sixth man, the first off the bench halfway through the first quarter. He liked it that way, said he was more effective as a reserve. But that arrangement had been thrown for a loop twelve days earlier, on March 17, when Cedric Ceballos had his hissy fit.

Ceballos was the Lakers' resident small forward, the leading scorer on the team, and co-captain. But when Magic Johnson began to eat into Ceballos's playing minutes, he vanished from the team in a huff for five days, most of which he spent, incommunicado, at the London Bridge Resort in Lake Havasu, Arizona. When he returned to the Lakers, apparently contrite, Los Angeles coach Del Harris took away his starting position. Nobody was pleased, not even Johnson. Or, perhaps, *especially* Johnson. "It's hard for me to deal with players doing things like this," he said. "Maybe I'm just old."

He occasionally looked old – or at least not like the Magic of yesterday – in the first seven minutes of the opening quarter at the SkyDome. In that span, he threw a long pass right at Doug Christie, who could hardly help making the steal. And later, Johnson went up for what appeared an easy layup, only to have it blocked by Oliver Miller; in past years, Magic would have put on a move to take the ball around a guy like Miller.

But in the same seven minutes, he laid another sweet pass on Eddie Jones for Jones's second basket. And, at 8:26, he took the ball at a point on the floor mid-way between the low post and the high post, his back to the basket, Carlos Rogers trying to force him away from the hoop, moved to his right, and, from nine feet out, he scored on a baby sky-hook, the shot he'd learned years earlier, with modifications, from his teammate Kareem Abdul-Jabbar. It was a gorgeous basketball moment, and with it and various other Magic contributions – his all-round smarts, which seemed to keep the Lakers alert to all possibilities on the floor, and his unignorable presence, which appeared to keep the Raptors in awe – Los Angeles had an eight-point lead at 4:21 of the first quarter, when Ceballos relieved Magic.

It was Tracy Murray who kept the Raptors reasonably close through the first quarter. He scored from every place on the floor, jumpers, a pair of spectacular dunks off fast breaks, all for a total of sixteen points. Still, the Raptors were down by eleven at the start of the second quarter, which was when they apparently lost their awe of Johnson and found their own sense of ball movement.

Suddenly the Raptors were wizards at passing. Alvin Robertson flashed a bounce pass to Rogers for a slam dunk. Damon Stoudamire, still playing despite the tendinitis, flashed down the floor on a fast break and capped it off with a crisp feed to Rogers for another dunk. And Stoudamire, again, zapped a pass that set up Oliver Miller for a fourteen-foot jumper. Toronto players racked up ten assists in the quarter, a statistic that showed just how active and accurate their passing game had become, and, when Stoudamire threw yet another exact pass to Alvin Robertson with less than two seconds on the game clock and Robertson jammed in a dunk, the Raptors ended the half with a one-point lead.

One sure giveaway of the fact that Brendan Malone longed to win the game showed in the players' minutes on the floor. Murray, Rogers, Miller, and Stoudamire played the entire half. Doug Christie and Robertson divided the time at shooting guard. Malone wasn't letting anyone he couldn't count on into this game.

At 2:31 of the third quarter, the Lakers' Nick Van Exel drove for a layup. Doug Christie leaped in the air and slapped the ball before it could fall through the hoop. Referee Jim Clark signalled goaltending on Christie. He'd struck the ball while it was on its downward path. The basket counted.

A few feet away, a man at the end of the Raptors bench jumped up. This was Acie Earl, the reserve centre. He waved his long arms in a show of angry protest at the call. He shouted something choice in Jim Clark's direction. Clark ignored him, and the game continued. Earl stood in the same spot, shouting as play moved away from him, a tall man crying in a void.

It was hard to miss Acie Earl at any time, even if he rarely got into games. His size caught the attention, six-foot-ten. So did his distinctive appearance: his hair style (straight up) and his body shape (slightly slouched) made him look like a taller version of Kramer from "Seinfeld." On the floor, in the short time that he played, averaging about eleven minutes per game, Earl had a disjointed way of moving, as if he hadn't quite got his body in sync. A February 1994 report by the Boston Celtics, the team that Earl played for in his first two NBA seasons, concluded, "He'll never make a dominant center in the league, but the skills are there for a decent one. He needs focus and maturity. One positive is that he doesn't appear to get discouraged."

Earl, on the floor or not, remained an enthusiast. He was a committed cheerleader from the bench, the first to congratulate players coming out of the game, the first to object, as he did on the Christie goaltending, when he thought a teammate had been done wrong. Earl was a team guy.

Acie Earl, twenty-five years old, was also a man with another calling that he kept more or less secret from the rest of the Raptor organization. He was writing a book, and it wasn't about basketball. In fact, he was annoyed during a conversation a few days before the Lakers game when he was asked if the sport was the subject of his book.

"Nothing to do with basketball, nothing to do with my autobiography," he said in his solemn voice. "It is a book about some principles I have formulated for the upliftment of black youth in America."

The ideas in the book, though they weren't personalized, came out of Earl's observations in the community in which he grew up. His home town was Moline, Illinois, a quiet city of about fifty thousand near the Iowa border.

"It didn't matter that Moline was predominantly white," Earl said.

"Anywhere there's a sizeable amount of black people, we have the things that black people in big cities succumb to on a regular basis. We have the gangs, we have the drugs, we have the black-on-black crime, we have the mothers in school who are trying to raise children at the same time. We have the negative situations that a black person should not fall into. That's the subject of my book: how to avoid these negatives."

It's a how-to book of a higher, more serious order?

"It is telling our youth about heading off the pitfalls. My book is aimed at people who are at the age when they know themselves and they know right from wrong. That is from age twelve up to college. They can read what I have to say about stereotypical negative situations for black people and say to themselves, Oh, maybe this is true, maybe I am going to check it out, maybe I am going to cut this situation out of my life."

Earl scribbled notes for his book on team flights, in spare moments, "times when basically my brain is storming over ideas." For polishing and structuring, the notes went to Earl's co-writer. This man was a member of the Canadian branch of the Nation of Islam, the American religious group headed by the controversial black nationalist Louis Farrakhan. If all proceeded according to plan, profits from the sales of the completed book would be split between the Nation of Islam and young black people who needed financial help in university. Earl intended to tour college campuses and speak to black youth in support of book sales. There was nothing in it financially for Acie. This was an altruistic endeavour, this book he called *Principles for Black Youth to Succeed in America*. He was optimistic about its sales. He was enthusiastic. Acie was *always* enthusiastic.

Out on the floor, as the game went on, Magic Johnson began to resemble somebody's dad who'd come out to play ball with the kids. He ran like somebody's dad, as if the bottoms of his feet hurt. And sometimes, up against the kids who were young, fast, and eager, he goofed and fumbled the ball in a dad's aging way. But his basketball moxie gave him the edge on the kids, the older guy who'd stored up a large repertoire of moves and still had enough of the physical stuff to pull them off.

And the Raptors didn't treat him like a dad. Oliver Miller and Carlos Rogers bumped him hard under the basket. But that worked to Johnson's advantage when the bumps sent him to the free-throw line. At 8:20 of the third quarter, Johnson took the ball in the low post and began to back in on Miller, looking for his shot. Miller shoved Johnson, and the referee signalled a foul. At the free-throw line, Johnson missed his first shot (it was his first miss after thirty-one successful free throws over four games) and hit the second. Two minutes later, Johnson posted up Doug Christie with the same result. This time, Magic sank both free throws. And at 3:08, after luring Rogers into yet another foul, Johnson hit two more from the free-throw line.

Five points on foul shots, and, at the end of the quarter, with the game tied and the time clock down to :00.9, Johnson slipped behind Rogers and was alone for a layup off a Lakers fast break. Magic's basket put Los Angeles in front, and, though the game stayed close and exciting through the last quarter, the Lakers never surrendered the lead that Johnson had given them.

In his dad-like way, Magic had controlled the game's outcome, a 111–106 win for his team.

Brendan Malone stuck with his game plan all afternoon, tried for the win, used only the same six players throughout the entire four quarters. Miller and Rogers played the whole game, Damon Stoudamire was in for forty-five minutes, Tracy Murray for forty-three, Alvin Robertson for thirty-two, and Doug Christie for twenty-four. None of the younger players – Jimmy King, Martin Lewis, Dwayne Whitfield, Acie Earl – got to move off the bench.

That was Malone's game plan, to go for the win at something close to all costs. But of course it wasn't Isiah Thomas's plan. He wanted to see the kids in action. Thomas wasn't at the Lakers game. He was scouting college players in the NCAA Final Four at the Meadowlands in New Jersey. But when word of Malone's strategy reached him, Thomas wouldn't be happy. Had Malone deliberately defied Thomas? Did Malone have a death wish?

At the press conference after the game, Malone explained himself. He seemed unusually testy and abrupt, but that might have been brought on by the reporters' insistent questions. They sniffed blood, and it was Malone's.

"I coach by feel," Malone said. "Every game is different. This game was different from the Orlando game. Today, I played it close to the vest because I thought the game would go down to the wire. It did. We were in it all the way, and I used the guys who wanted to win. I went with those guys. I *liked* the way they played. They played well. What more could I ask?"

Malone must have known he was in trouble. He had telephoned his wife in Birmingham earlier on the weekend. He didn't want to be alone in Toronto, not right then. Maureen came up for a few days. She was at the SkyDome for the Los Angeles game, and afterwards, after dinner, she and Malone went for a walk along Queen's Quay near the hotel to talk about things that might lie ahead.

Probably not good things.

19

DAMON

At nine o'clock on the night of Monday, April 1, while the rest of the Raptors players and coaches were settling in front of their television sets to watch Syracuse play Kentucky in the NCAA championship game, Damon Stoudamire was the guest on the CBC-Newsworld program "Pamela Wallin Live."

Stoudamire wore a natty single-breasted dark suit, white shirt, and patterned dark tie. He sat deep in the guest's chair, as if he were comfortable, not as if he were trapped in a place from which he wanted to escape. The appearance on the show was a breakthrough event for Stoudamire, exposure to a broad general audience, a step towards making himself a celebrity beyond the confines of the basketball world. And, though Pamela Wallin's questions were only a tad more challenging than the softballs that Leo Rautins lobbed up on the Raptors TV broadcasts, Stoudamire acquitted himself more than gamely. He hardly came on as a world-class charmer in the Michael Jordan manner, but he answered questions directly and often at length, and once he even allowed a small smile to unscrunch his usual tight expression.

At a moment mid-way through the program, in reply to one of the callers who phoned in, he said something utterly Stoudamirean. The caller praised Stoudamire's height, or lack of it, saying it was a small guy like Damon who made basketball accessible and possible for ordinary little kids. The point that the caller was getting at was that Stoudamire was a short man in a game that was almost exclusively given over to tall men. But Stoudamire immediately picked up on the word "ordinary." Yes, he hurried to answer, he was himself just an ordinary guy who liked to relax, lie on his couch, and watch a lot of TV. That was his favourite activity.

"I live an ordinary life," he went on. "Very private. I don't have a girl-friend, but that's private, anyway. I wouldn't talk about her. And how much money I make is private, too."

Of all the players on the Raptors team, Stoudamire, its unquestioned star, was the most guarded about his private life. In the media scrums around his locker after games, he sat on his stool and answered questions about the game, about his play, about the disappointment of yet another loss, in reasonably enlightening fashion. Early in the season, he took lessons in communication from a former broadcaster named Andrea Kirby, who specialized in coaching shy and uncommunicative young athletes on how to project some personality, how to help the reporters do stories and features that revealed the athletes as people the public and advertisers might warm up to. After Kirby's classes, she rated Stoudamire a seven on the scale of one to ten in communication skills, in speech, content, and body language. Seven wasn't bad for a twenty-two-year-old kid who was brand-new to the NBA and to big-time media. But that was Stoudamire on the subject of his professional life. His private life was another matter. On that, he was practically mute.

Now and again, minutiae about Stoudamire's existence away from the basketball court leaked out. He kept a diary. He didn't read books. He gobbled up chicken fettuccine by the plateful, heavy on the chicken. In his first weeks in Toronto, he enjoyed checking out new restaurants, but fans – too many autograph hounds, too many people who just stared – drove him back to his condo on Queen's Quay. He hung with the Oliver Miller–Carlos Rogers crowd. What colourful stuff did they get up to?

"Play some dominoes," Miller said.

That was Damon Stoudamire, ordinary guy.

One afternoon, earlier in the year, Stoudamire had been on the phone to the American west coast.

"No," he was saying, "I won't send you five hundred dollars. I know what you'd spend it on."

Pause while Stoudamire listened to the voice from the other end of the line.

"But I'll give you a thousand dollars," Stoudamire said.

Pause.

"I'll give you a thousand dollars if you use it to get yourself into a program."

Stoudamire was speaking to a friend who had a drug problem. The kid basketball player had taken himself a long way from the struggle and desperation of the world he knew as a child and a teenager, but the casualties of that world remained just a phone call away.

Portland is Stoudamire's home town. He grew up there, in the part of the city where respectability was something to be fought for. He was an only son in a family that became a single-parent household after his father, Willie, left and moved to Milwaukee when Damon was ten years old. The boy's mother, Liz Washington, and his grandmother, who had been left a widow with five children when she was a young woman, raised Damon. Liz Washington is strikingly attractive, and she seemed, on her visits to Toronto, to be a woman of strength and sophistication. She worked as an accountant with a Portland trucking firm, and she brought up her son, protected from the neighbourhood's gangs and drugs, in ways that left him with an unassailable sense of self-esteem.

And Willie Stoudamire stayed part of his son's life. Willie had played basketball at Portland State and been drafted by the Seattle SuperSonics, though he never stuck with the team. Willie's basketball career gave Damon something to shoot for and to eclipse. Later, Willie moved back to Portland and worked at running community programs at Mallory Avenue Christian Church. Damon, when he was in town, helped out at the church, and, after he entered the NBA, it was his dad to whom he turned for guidance in the business side of his basketball life.

From the time he was a little kid, Damon knew he'd be an NBA star. Not hoped. Knew. He led Woodrow Wilson High to two state championships and was named Naismith Oregon Player of the Year. At the University of Arizona, he emerged once again as a team leader. He didn't take Arizona all the way to the national championship, but the team reached the Final Four in 1994 and was twice the Pacific-10 Conference champ. In personal accomplishments, Stoudamire was co–Player of the Year in the Pac-10 in his senior year, sharing the honour with UCLA's Ed O'Bannon, and he became only the second player in conference history to rack up eighteen hundred points, six hundred assists, and four hundred rebounds.

When the Raptors drafted him in June of 1995, when the twenty-two thousand fans at the SkyDome, who wanted Toronto to pick Stoudamire's old rival, Ed O'Bannon, booed him, Stoudamire waved off the jeers. They didn't faze him, not the kid with the armour of self-confidence.

"I want to be Rookie of the Year," he said a little later. "I feel I'm probably in the best position to challenge for the award."

Stoudamire's faith in his own talent translated on the court into an aggressive, attacking style. It was also accompanied by a pair of complementary qualities. He had an insatiable desire to learn and a drive to win.

"Damon's a throwback," Brendan Malone says. "He's not of the generation that think they're all-stars before their time, that don't respect coaches and don't want to work hard. Damon listens to what coaches and his teammates have to say. He knows he'll find out things about the game he didn't know before. And he wants to win so bad. He gets frustrated and angry. I told him to stay angry, stay mad, don't change, stay the way he is right now. I think he will stay that way because his mother and father keep him straight. Damon's a champion in his heart."

But for Stoudamire, a rookie after all, it wasn't entirely smooth sailing in his introduction to the NBA. He needed help from his teammates in containing tall guards who liked to post up. Orlando's Penny Hardaway, six-foot-seven, was one of those. And John Stockton, the Utah Jazz's veteran all-star guard, who was closer to Stoudamire in height, took him to school in the Jazz game at the SkyDome back on November 13. Stockton and Utah's power forward Karl Malone were the league masters of the pick and roll, and they ran it on Stoudamire six or seven times in the second half. Stockton ended the game, a Utah win, with twenty-nine points and twelve assists to Stoudamire's seven and nine. For anyone except Damon Stoudamire, the experience might have been humbling. He learned from it and moved on.

And far more often, as the season progressed, the statistics ran in Stoudamire's favour. By the end of March, he was averaging nineteen points per game, nine assists, four rebounds, 1.4 steals. Of course, to rack up such splendid numbers, he was also playing forty-one minutes a game. That was a virtually unheard-of average for a rookie. In past NBA history, just six other top rookies had played more than forty-one minutes per game, and all of them were forwards or centres, except Oscar Robertson, who was a big guard. Stoudamire was the only little guy who'd played so much in his first year, and the minutes were having a dual impact on the Raptors. They were part of the reason for the friction between Isiah Thomas and Brendan Malone. And they were wearing down the little guy and possibly, given the tendinitis in his left knee, threatening Stoudamire's golden career.

A couple of hours before a game at the SkyDome in late March, Stoudamire sat in front of his locker looking like a man who wanted to be left alone. He had a sore knee. He'd played almost seventy basketball games that year – even more than seventy if the pre-season games were added in. He was tired, sad-eyed, and grumpy, and he didn't welcome a writer who had a few more questions about his views on life in and out of basketball.

His answers were models of brevity – not at all as expansive as he'd make his replies to some of the admittedly less-convoluted questions he was asked a few nights later on "Pamela Wallin Live" – but, on the subject of his tattoo, he got more voluble and self-revealing. Not the tattoo on his left biceps up near the shoulder, the one that read "DAMON" in Gothic script. The other one, the tattoo in the middle of his right biceps, the one of Mighty Mouse lifting a basketball in the air as if he were taking off for a miniature slam dunk.

"There's a comparison between Mighty Mouse and me. The way I see him, he wasn't a noisy character, more low-key, and he went flying in to the aid of people who needed rescuing. I kind of see myself that way. Mighty Mouse was little, but he was aggressive when he had to be. I don't really think of myself as little. If I go out there and play aggressively, it doesn't matter whether I'm short or not. The other people got to pay attention to me because I have the talent and the confidence. I come flying in to the rescue like Mighty Mouse."

At 6:59 of the first quarter in the game between the Raptors and the Los Angeles Clippers at the SkyDome on Tuesday night, April 2, the night after Damon Stoudamire's appearance on the Pamela Wallin program, Stoudamire brought the ball up court, drove to a point just outside the paint at the Clippers' end, threw in a little hop step that momentarily froze the man who was guarding him, Malik Sealy, and slipped a quick and surprising pass – at least surprising to all the Clippers in the area – to Carlos Rogers, who was streaking past Stoudamire's right side towards the L.A. basket. Rogers threw down a dunk.

At 6:30 of the second quarter, Stoudamire, directing play in the Clippers' zone, zipped a pass to Doug Christie, who barely touched the ball as he redirected it to Tracy Murray in the corner. Murray nailed a three-pointer.

At 4:55 of the third quarter, on a Raptor fast break, Murray whipped the ball to Stoudamire beyond the paint on the right side of the L.A. basket. Stoudamire got himself in the air, changed the ball from his right hand to his left to avoid Sealy, who was charging in on his right, and, as he floated upwards towards the hoop, Stoudamire reached forward and looped the ball softly through the basket.

At :00.5 of the third, as Murray broke to the L.A. basket, Stoudamire hit him with a sweetly timed bounce pass that Murray took at waist level. He continued on to the basket and dropped the ball in for a layup.

At 3:56 of the fourth quarter, Stoudamire dribbled close to the Clipper basket, no more than five feet out. Two very tall Clippers waved their arms in a way that appeared to surround Stoudamire with the human equivalent of a picket fence. Stoudamire stopped abruptly, squared his feet, leaped straight up, and popped a little jumper over the arms and into the middle of the basket.

With 2.1 seconds remaining in the game, Stoudamire had scored twenty-four points and assisted on twelve other Raptor baskets, but Toronto trailed Los Angeles by two points. The Raptors called a timeout and planned a last play.

Back on the floor, ready for the play, Doug Christie set himself to inbounds the ball on the right side of the L.A. zone near the centre line. Just before Christie threw the ball in, Stoudamire, Murray, and Rogers broke for the left side of the court. That left Oliver Miller isolated on the right side. Christie tossed the ball to Miller, who was eleven feet out with his back to the basket. He turned and put up a jumper. The clock showed :00.9, and the ball fell through the hoop. The shot tied the game.

In overtime, with the game tied 101–101, and 43.8 seconds left to play, Damon Stoudamire had the ball outside the L.A. three-point line. He was standing exactly mid-way between the two sidelines, dead opposite the L.A. basket, and he seemed to be alone on the floor. Isolated for just that instant, untouchable. He shot the ball. It arced up and dropped neatly into the basket. A three-pointer. This – Mighty Mouse to the rescue – turned out to be the winning shot in a thrilling game that ended 104–103 for the Raptors.

Altogether, on this night, Stoudamire scored twenty-nine points, had twelve assists, and turned the ball over only four times. He played forty-four minutes on a bum left knee.

Before the game, in the area outside the Raptors' dressing room, Isiah Thomas had been asked about Stoudamire's high number of minutes in playing time.

"Just because a player is willing to die for this organization," Thomas answered, "doesn't mean you have to kill him."

20

PLAYING OUT
THE STRING

Brendan Malone had Chris Whitney on his mind.

"That's the kid who would've saved us all this grief," Malone said. "Or a lot of it, anyway."

It was noon on the day after the win over the Clippers. Malone had just seen his wife off to the airport. Now he was sitting at a table in a familiar haunt, the lobby restaurant of the Harbour Castle Hotel. He had on a smart-looking warmup outfit, and he was holding an autographed copy of the Raptors magazine. It was a gift for his barber's son. The boy had Down syndrome. But, before Malone visited the barber, he had a few pointed words to say about what Chris Whitney might have meant to the Raptors.

Whitney was the point guard who had impressed Malone at training camp. He wanted to keep Whitney. Isiah Thomas didn't. Thomas said he couldn't fit Whitney under the salary cap, even though Whitney would be paid in the puny $250,000 neighbourhood. And besides, more to the point, Thomas preferred to see other young guys with large guaranteed contracts – Jimmy King, for one – get a shot at backup point guard. Three days before the season began, the Raptors waived Whitney.

"Last October, I was sitting right over there with Jim Lynam, Washington's coach," Malone said, pointing at a table across the room.

"The Bullets were in for a pre-season game. Jim and I got together, and I said to him, Listen, we're gonna be letting a point guard go. I hate doin' it, but this kid is better than any point guard you got on your team right now. You should keep him in mind, a kid by the name of Chris Whitney."

Lynam apparently stored away Malone's advice and brought it out several months later. In early March, after injuries had taken three of Washington's point guards out of commission, Lynam chased down Whitney, who was playing for the Florida Beach Dogs in the Continental Basketball Association, and signed him to a Bullets contract. In one of Whitney's first appearances for Washington, he came off the bench in the fourth quarter of a game against Atlanta, scored thirteen points, and sparked a Bullets win.

"If we'd have kept Chris Whitney," Malone said, "he would've given Damon ten, twelve minutes' rest every game, maybe more, and Damon would never have gotten his bad knee. In addition to that, with Damon being fresh, we probably would've won eight or nine more games this year. But Isiah didn't want Chris Whitney."

Talking about Thomas, the very mention of the name, seemed to get Malone's juices running. As he sat in the restaurant, slightly flushed, he appeared to take on a mood that was made up of two parts anger to one part bitterness and another part resignation.

"Notice the timing of what Isiah did last week," Malone said. "When he talked to the newspapers about Damon being hurt, about me not playing the kids, it was right after we beat Chicago. It was our biggest win of the year, and he talks to the writers at the *Star* and the *Sun*. And what did the newspapers say? Bye-bye, Brendan. They wrote about I'm not gonna be the head coach of the Raptors at the end of the year. Isiah *wanted* the shit to hit the fan. He's undermining me at every turn."

What was *this*? Was it paranoia on Malone's part? Or did he have a point worth pursuing?

"It's just the way Isiah is," Malone went on. "He reminds me of George Steinbrenner at the New York Yankees. Got to run the whole show himself. The thing that this is all about with me and the Raptors and Isiah is very simple: Isiah is like George Steinbrenner, which is that he's an absolute control freak. And that's the story."

The next night, Thursday, forty-five minutes before the tipoff in a game between the Raptors and the Cleveland Cavaliers at the SkyDome, the press was summoned from the buffet table for a conference outside the Raptors' dressing room. Damon Stoudamire conducted the conference. He said he wouldn't be playing that night. He said the team doctors had looked at his bad knee the night before and told Stoudamire he had acute tendinitis. The injury was more severe than Stoudamire had thought, and his knee needed a week's rest, maybe more. Stoudamire wouldn't play against Cleveland, and he would probably miss the next four additional games. He had to stay off the knee.

"The doctors weren't trying to scare me," Stoudamire said. "They just gave me the facts. It's time to take a break, because tendinitis can sometimes lead to some worse things that can end a career."

As Stoudamire talked, he looked his usual self, low-key, self-assured. But when he had finished with the press and turned away, an expression crossed his face that seemed, just for a moment, awfully sad and weary.

Later, out on the floor, no more than ninety seconds before the tipoff, Oliver Miller had an announcement for Brendan Malone. Oliver wasn't playing either, he told Malone; he had a bruised right calf. Miller went to the dressing room, donned a deluxe light brown suit, screwed the earring into his left ear, and returned to the bench. He seemed to enjoy watching the game unfold without him. But he enjoyed one piece of the entertainment even more, a new act cooked up by the people at Events and Operations.

It took place during a timeout in the second half. Two guys came onto the floor dressed in skin-coloured inflatable suits that made them look like sumo wrestlers. For ninety seconds, the two guys jumped and flopped on one another in a nutsy and very funny sendup of a sumo match. The crowd got into this wacky piece of vaudeville in a big way, and Oliver Miller got into it more than anybody. He laughed till he almost lost it. Oliver was having a good time at the game.

Isiah Thomas had developed a favourite place from which to watch the games. It was in the mouth of the tunnel that led out of the stands at the southwest corner of the court. Thomas stood in his accustomed spot for the Cleveland game, leaning against one of the railings. He had company on this night, Damon Stoudamire. Instead of sitting at the end of the Raptors bench with the other players who weren't dressed for the game, Stoudamire stood with Thomas.

Early in the third quarter, John Bitove walked down from his seat in the stands and crossed over to the media area, where he gave a short interview to a writer from *Canadian Business Magazine*. On the way back to his seat, Bitove paused at the southwest tunnel to chat with Thomas and Stoudamire. There was nothing sinister in any of this, just three guys, three significant guys, passing the time at the ball game.

But suppose Brendan Malone, busy coaching his team in the Cleveland game, happened to glance over at the scene in the southwest tunnel. His star player, his basketball boss, his boss of bosses, all clustered in a huddle across the court from the players' bench. If Brendan Malone was a man given to paranoia, at that instant he might have been ready for a restraining jacket.

Without Stoudamire and Miller, for that matter without Zan Tabak and Sharone Wright, Malone gave plenty of play in the Cleveland game to the guys who usually spent most of their time on the bench. Dwayne Whitfield, the twenty-three-year-old power forward, a shy young man with a guileless expression, played forty-two minutes (and showed some nice postup moves in scoring sixteen points). Jimmy King got in thirty minutes at point guard, and both Martin Lewis and Vincenzo Esposito played substantial time at the 2 guard. The kids were in over their heads against the extremely disciplined and defence-minded Cleveland players, who won the game, 98–77. Nevertheless, especially in the second half, the Raptors' youth movement – Whitfield, King, Lewis, Doug Christie – got some useful experience on the floor.

"I thought we did all right in the second half," Malone said after the game, smiling just a little, "considering it was a bunch of strangers playing together."

It was more of the same over the next seven games – many players out with injuries, lots of playing time for the younger contingent. One of the seven games was at home, and the other six were on the road. The Raptors lost all but one game. The exception was a win in Milwaukee, Toronto's twentieth victory on the season.

During this relatively down period for the Raptors, there emerged two small items of team history that were worth recording.

One was surprising and positive. With all the injuries to the centres and power forwards, Acie Earl got his chance to start at centre, and, in four games on the road, he scored twenty-six points against Washington, twenty-five against the New York Nets, twenty-eight against New Jersey, and a dazzling forty points against his former team, the Boston Celtics. The big, enthusiastic guy on the end of the bench had turned into a scoring machine.

And the other item was not so surprising, and negative. Damon Stoudamire announced that he was finished for the season. No more games. He was taking ultrasound treatment for the knee, and he was working on a program of exercises. He was following doctors' orders. He had also had a talk with Isiah Thomas about his knee. And it was everybody's view – the doctors', Thomas's, and Stoudamire's own – that he should wind up the season and save his knee for the seasons ahead.

In the meantime, Stoudamire flew home to Portland. His mother had tripped over a curb and fractured both of her arms. Damon, the dutiful son, looked after the shopping and vacuuming for the other patient in the family.

At the game in the SkyDome between the Raptors and the Washington Bullets on Friday night, April 19, the second-last game of the season, radio station Mix 99.9 put on the daffiest promotion of the year. At the northwest corner of the court, right on the floor, workmen installed a large hot tub. It came with all the usual hot-tub accoutrements – lounge chairs, cans of beer, people in bathing suits, plenty of towels. The towels weren't just for the bathers to dry off. They were also needed to mop up the water around the tub. The tub apparently leaked. One attractive woman submerged herself in the water, from the shoulders down, at the beginning of the game. When she climbed out two and a half hours later, she resembled a damp prune.

Chris Whitney played thirteen minutes of the game at backup point guard for Washington. He was a willowy young man, about six-foot-five, and for his first couple of trips down the floor on offence, he looked nervous. But, in his thirteen minutes, he also looked quick and smart. He had five points, three assists, and two rebounds. It was a nice night's work for a backup.

At 7:15 of the third quarter, Doug Christie drove the Washington basket. He was airborne, and while airborne, he put the ball behind his back to avoid a Washington defender, altered speed slightly, brought the ball around to his front, and slammed it through the hoop. The basket edged the Raptors in front of the Bullets by one point, and, through the rest of the exciting game, though it remained close for the most part, the Raptors kept the advantage and won, 107–103, the team's twenty-first victory. Christie played forty-two minutes of the game, scored thirty points, and played in the theatrical, thrilling fashion that seemed to promise NBA stardom.

By the end of Brendan Malone's press conference after the Washington game, there were only four reporters left in the room, three print people and a radio guy from The Fan.

Mary Ormsby of the *Star* stepped forward.

"Why do I feel like I'm gonna be hit by an atomic bomb?" Malone said.

Ormsby, her voice not above a hush, asked Malone what he thought about the "rumours" that he would be fired.

"It's been tough personally for the last month," Malone said, his face set in the expression of a man delivering a valedictory, resigned but not unduly unhappy. "I don't think I deserved some of the stuff that was in the papers. But I never wanted to get into a feud. That's not what basketball is about. And I always come back to the fans in Toronto. They're just great, the best. A lot of people have written to me, letters, cards, faxes, all in support. They made me feel good."

Another reporter served up a lightweight question about Malone's thoughts on his future.

"Right now, let's try to win number twenty-two. And then I'm going to get on my horse and ride into the sunset."

Where to?

"I think I'll go off and make a movie. Well, no, I think I'll go to Nepal."

The mood felt desultory in the Raptors' dressing room two hours before the start of the final game of the season, against the Philadelphia 76ers on Sunday afternoon, April 21. A tape of an earlier 76ers game was playing on the TV screen at one end of the room. Nobody watched it. Brendan Malone was drawing plays on the blackboard, but he seemed to welcome the interruption when a reporter from an out-of-town newspaper asked to interview him. Martin Lewis went silently and methodically down a line of encased basketballs on a table, signing his name on each; the balls, once they had been autographed by all the players, would be given as souvenirs to people in the Raptors offices. None of the players was doing much kidding around, no shouted jokes, not the usual banter. It wasn't end-of-term giddiness that marked the room. It seemed to be end-of-term gloom.

Alvin Robertson arrived and promptly deepened the gloom. Oliver Miller and Carlos Rogers, sitting at adjoining stalls, were talking in a half-hearted way about the next season and what it might hold. Robertson walked over from his stall on the opposite side of the room.

"This could be my last game today," he said. "My last game *ever*."

Miller and Rogers looked up at Robertson. They had nothing to say to that, and Robertson went back to his stall.

Did he mean the Raptors might drop him, that no other NBA team would pick him up, a thirty-three-year-old shooting guard? Or did he mean those court cases waiting to be heard might take him out of circulation? There was no reading Robertson's expression.

The cheerless mood refused to leave the dressing room.

At 5:12 of the fourth quarter in the game against Philadelphia, just after the 76ers called a timeout, Tracy Murray wound up and gave the scorers' table a hellacious kick. He had just made a bad pass that led to a 76ers' steal. He was frustrated. The entire Toronto team was frustrated. During the afternoon, the Raptors would make a disastrously high twenty-eight turnovers and lose to the team with the second-worst won-lost record in the NBA.

The game wasn't without its drama, though, particularly during the closing seconds of the fourth quarter. Philadelphia was up by three points with 42.9 seconds left in the game. Toronto brought the ball up court, needing a three-pointer to tie.

Murray put up a shot from twenty-three feet out on the right side. It hit the rim.

Murray rebounded his own shot and worked the ball to Doug Christie, twenty-four feet out in the left corner. Christie shot and got another rim.

Oliver Miller rebounded and fired the ball to Alvin Robertson. He was beyond the three-point line. He shot. Another rim job.

Acie Earl grabbed the rebound and whipped the ball to Murray, who dribbled backward until he was twenty-five feet from the basket. He shot. Hit the rim.

Christie got the rebound and backed into the corner, twenty-four feet out. By now the time clock showed 1.4 seconds left, and the crowd – an astonishingly high attendance of 27,118 – was practically hysterical over all the misses, all the rebounds, going the Raptors' way. Christie shot. The ball swished through the net. Tie game. Overtime coming up.

A clause in Oliver Miller's contract said that if, under a complicated system of computation, he achieved a certain total of points, rebounds, blocks, assists, and steals during the season, he would be entitled to a bonus of $500,000(U.S.). At the end of regulation time in the Philadelphia game, he was the equivalent of one basket or two points short of the required number.

At 4:03 of the overtime period, with Philadelphia in front by two points, Miller rebounded a missed Acie Earl jumper and tucked home a layup. He had his two points. He had his $500,000 (U.S.) bonus (he could use some of it to cover the $45,000 he had committed the night before at the players' windup dinner to the Raptors Foundation, the club's charitable wing). But Miller's basket was almost the only good news for the Raptors during overtime. The players took eight shots, missed six of them, including two horrendous air balls by Earl, and lost to Philadelphia, 109–105.

In the minutes after the game, with most of the crowd, at Herbie Kuhn's request, remaining in their seats, the floor filled with Raptors employees – the Dance Pack, the gang from the office, a couple of injured players in civvies. John Bitove spoke to the crowd on a hand-held microphone.

Thanks, he said, thanks for the support. Isiah Thomas said the same thing. And there was one other speaker, the only player in uniform who had remained on the floor. It was Oliver Miller. He thanked everyone too, but he singled out one person by name, one person for lavish praise.

"The man who put it all together!" Miller said in a raised voice. "Isiah 'Zeke' Thomas!"

Miller's short speech seemed to qualify as an instance of a guy knowing which side his bread was buttered on.

Miller hadn't mentioned Brendan Malone in his comments to the crowd, but later, in the dressing room, talking to the media, he made up for the oversight.

"He dug his own grave," Miller said, speaking of Malone. "I never want to see anybody lose their job. But the old saying is, 'You brought that shit on yourself.'"

Miller expounded on the theme, saying Malone had shown the Raptor players no respect, that he was confrontational with them, not a players' coach.

"I knew Brendan from Detroit," Miller went on. "I knew what he was like. Isiah kept saying to me, 'Give him a chance. Maybe he'll be different.' Well, he wasn't."

It was, Miller said, a personal thing, Malone vis-à-vis Miller.

"I knew Brendan didn't like me right from the start," he said. "Then about halfway through the season, he says, 'You were right. I didn't want you on the team, but keep up the good work.'"

Miller looked around at the reporters scribbling in their notebooks.

"How can I respect that?" he asked.

A few minutes earlier, across the hall in the converted employees' lunch-room, Brendan Malone had said to the media, "I talked to Isiah last night, and, if you can read between the lines, the change will be made soon. The decision has been made, and I'll soon be aware of it."

The part that Malone left out was that, at that very moment, his lawyer was preparing for a meeting in the evening with the Raptors' lawyers. The two sides would work out an agreement under which the Raptors would buy out the two years remaining on Malone's contract. The next morning, Malone would agree to the terms, resign as head coach, and the Raptors would name as his successor Darrell Walker, who had just finished his first season of coaching as one of Malone's assistants.

In the meantime, that Sunday evening, Malone went out to dinner with his wife, Maureen, and two of their daughters, Kelly and Shannon. The four Malones were celebrating. Not the loss of Malone's job, not that. They were celebrating a birthday.

Brendan Malone had turned fifty-four on April 21.

21

LOOKING AHEAD

John Bitove intended to act blasé about the NBA draft lottery. It was being shown live on NBC-TV at half-time of the game in the Eastern Conference finals between Chicago and Orlando on Sunday afternoon, May 19, and Bitove was thinking of passing it up. Not even watching the proceedings. But, in the end, he tuned in and found himself sucked into an irresistible basketball drama.

Thirteen teams took part in the lottery. They were the thirteen who failed to qualify for the playoffs. Each of these teams, which of course included the Raptors, was allowed into a lucky draw to determine the order in which they would be entitled to choose players in the all-important college draft on June 26. It was the lottery results that would be read on television by Russ Granik, the NBA's second-in-command. Granik would begin by announcing which team had drawn the thirteenth pick, then proceed resolutely up the line, as tension built, to the prized number-one pick. The conditions under which the Raptors entered the league a year earlier prevented them from holding the first pick, but it was number two that Bitove and the rest of the Raptor organization could, in their wildest dreams, hope for.

On this Sunday afternoon, Bitove and his family were at their cottage in Thornbury near Georgian Bay. As the Chicago–Orlando game broke for half time and the lottery announcement began, Randi

Bitove was blow-drying her hair, getting ready for the drive south to David Peterson's place in Caledon for a Victoria Day–weekend barbecue. Bitove, the blow dryer buzzing on his personal sound track, stood in front of the television set.

Russ Granik announced the thirteenth pick, the twelfth, the eleventh. None of them was Toronto. The Raptors stayed in the hunt. Tenth, ninth, eighth. No mention of Toronto.

"Russ got down to five, and still no Raptors," Bitove remembers. "My heart started to go flutter, flutter, flutter."

The fourth wasn't Toronto, either.

"He reached three. It was Vancouver, and I knew we were two, and I got a feeling like I'd never had before in my life except on the day in September 1993 when Russ phoned and said we'd won the franchise."

The number-two pick – the Philadelphia 76ers ended up with number one – meant that, of all the promising young players coming out of American college basketball in the spring of 1996, the seniors who were graduating, the twenty-one underclassmen who were opting to leave school early, even the two high-school boys who had declared for the draft – the Raptors could choose from all of these kids except one, the one whom the 76ers took. And it meant much, much more.

"We can trade our number-two pick down to another team for an established NBA player plus their lower pick," Bitove says. "It means so much. It means that other teams have to talk to us. It means we can do a job of balancing our team. We're set at point guard with Damon. But what about small forward? Can Carlos Rogers handle it? Or should we look at the kid from the University of Massachusetts, Marcus Camby? What it means, getting the number-two pick, it means we, the Raptors, just in our second year, we're in the driver's seat."

On Tuesday morning, two days after the draft lottery, John Bitove picked up a message on his office voice mail.

"We're number two, baby! We're number two!"

The jubilant voice belonged to Darrell Walker, the new Raptors head coach. He'd been Toronto's representative in the TV studio during the lottery ceremonies, sitting in front of the cameras with reps from the other twelve teams. He looked composed on television, a tall, slim man with a toothy smile and a thin moustache trimmed in the style of a 1930s

Hollywood actor. He kept the look of composure to the end, in control, even though, as he later said, he felt as if he were bursting inside.

Through the basketball season, Walker had seemed that sort of guy, friendly but projecting a sense of cool under fire. Brendan Malone wasn't a head coach who did much delegating to his assistants – or perhaps he just wouldn't delegate to Walker and John Shumate, who were essentially Isiah Thomas's choices as assistants – but Walker, calm, handled everything that came his way. He broke down film of Raptors' opponents, worked on the practice floor with players who needed help with their shooting. And he honed his sense of basketball's xs and os; it was Walker who designed the play ending in Oliver Miller's crucial basket in the last second of regulation time in the win over the Los Angeles Clippers late in the season.

The play came from the old Detroit Pistons book, a play that Walker remembered from his season with the Pistons in the early 1990s. That season, one of ten with five teams that Walker spent as a guard in the NBA, made him an Isiah Thomas teammate. But his friendship with Thomas reached further back, all the way to their youth together in Chicago.

Walker grew up as another kid in a single-family household, raised by his mother and grandmother on Chicago's south side. Walker and Thomas played teenage basketball against one another, and, years later, after their brief reunion on the Pistons, after Walker retired from basketball in 1993, the two connected again. Thomas was president of the NBA Players' Association, and Walker was one of the association's paid employees. He was in charge of caution, teaching the players how to avoid HIV infection, how to stay clean of drugs, how to sock their giant paycheques into savings plans. Walker was the perfect man for the job, a retired player who looked after his health, hung on to his money, and had a wife, Lisa, three sons, and a home in Little Rock, Arkansas, where he and Lisa had gone to university.

It was the Isiah Thomas connection that got Walker to the Raptors, that eventually got him appointed head coach. Thomas liked Walker's clean style. So did John Bitove.

"Darrell communicates," Bitove says, leaving hanging in the air the thought that maybe Brendan Malone didn't. "I mean by that, that Darrell communicates with everybody. Not long after he was named head coach, we had a wrap-up affair for the team's sponsors, Air Canada, Ford, all the biggies, and Darrell came to it. He stayed right till the end. That's important, to have a coach who's affable and gets along at every level. Darrell's perfect for what we need right now. And he buys into the long-term plan, which is to develop the young players and not to worry about whether we win or lose right away, because the winning will come."

All of which, the last part of Bitove's commendation, raised the issue of Walker's independence. Would he operate as a head coach with his own ideas? Brendan Malone tried that, and it didn't work. Or would Walker function as a mere conduit for the Raptor front office's notions of the way the team should be run? Isiah Thomas's notions?

The question had come up at the press conference on April 22 that introduced Walker as the new head coach, and Walker worked nimbly through it, then offered his own bottom line.

"I wouldn't say I'm a puppet," he said, looking very cool.

When Macedonian immigrants began arriving in Toronto in the years after the First World War, they settled in the lower Cabbagetown area of the city. The Irish were there before them, in a neighbourhood of narrow two-storey houses and of men who took jobs that began at five in the morning. The Caribbeans would come long after them. The Macedonian kids of those years, the 1920s, went to Park School on Shuter Street, and, on Sundays, the families attended St. George's Macedono Bulgarian Eastern Orthodox Church south of the community on Trinity Street.

The parents of John Bitove, Sr., reached Toronto in the mid-twenties, a couple of years before John senior was born. They took up residence east of the Macedonian core, on the other side of the Don River. John senior's father operated a butcher store at Queen and Broadview, and John went to Bruce Public School and Danforth Tech. But he dropped out of school early. The kid always had a money-making deal on the go. The year he turned twenty-one, he got married and opened the Java Shoppe on north Avenue Road.

"I worked from six in the morning till midnight in the restaurant," Bitove senior says. "Customers used to say to me, 'I saw your brother in here last night.' It wasn't my brother. It was me. I was *always* in the place."

Through the years when he was moving up in the food business, making his fortune, Bitove continued to attend St. George's Church. He contributed much money to the church's upkeep and refurbishment. And, on Easter Sunday 1996, he was worshipping at St. George's – which had moved to Regent Street in the heart of Cabbagetown, where it sat alone among the acres of public housing – when another church member, another wealthy contributor to its well-being, slipped up to him.

"We should talk," Steve Stavro said.

Stavro had accumulated his millions with Knob Hill Farms, a chain of supermarkets, and had extended his reach in the 1990s when he bought Maple Leaf Gardens and the Maple Leaf hockey team. Stavro's mother and Bitove's mother were sisters, which made the two men first cousins. There had been persistent rumours that the Stavros and the Bitoves didn't see eye-to-eye. "That's just stuff that sells newspapers," John Bitove, Jr., says. "There's no family feud." There didn't appear to be hard feelings on the Easter Sunday when Stavro approached Bitove senior at St. George's.

The two men took themselves off to an empty side room in the church. They didn't progress far in their confidential conversation, because other men of St. George's, elders, insisted on interrupting to bring greetings and Easter wishes. But the point of the talk was clear, the reason why Stavro wanted a word with Bitove.

Stavro was debating the pros and cons of throwing in his lot with the Raptors in building a basketball-hockey stadium, the one the Raptors already had on the drawing board, the one they planned to erect on the site of the old Post Office Building, the one for which they needed a hockey team as a partner or tenant. Should Stavro go in on the deal? He was making a first tentative approach to the patriarch of the Bitove family.

Around this time, Stavro put together a committee, which included himself, to check out the merits of a two-sport facility. The committee would visit the new stadiums in Chicago, Boston, and Vancouver and draw some conclusions. Stavro had much to weigh. On the one hand, he had already accomplished a lot of what he sought in Toronto hockey. He was the proprietor of perhaps the most-storied building in Canada, the "House That Conn Smythe Built." Why would he want to involve himself in a new stadium? He was a man nearing seventy, and new stadiums didn't begin to yield profits until their fifth or sixth year of operation. On the other hand, the Gardens lacked – and, given space limitations, always would lack – the corporate boxes that were an absolute necessity to a money-making contemporary stadium. Stavro had plenty to ponder.

"I hope common sense prevails on both sides, hockey and basketball," John Bitove, Sr., said one late-May morning in his office over Wayne Gretzky's restaurant. "Maple Leaf Gardens, as much as everybody loves it, has had its day. So doesn't it make more sense, if there's going to be a new basketball arena and a new hockey arena, that each party spends $100 million on one joint arena than both parties spend $200 million on two arenas?"

The stadium appeared to be the one cloud that hung over the Raptors' future. What combination of groups was going to build it? And when? These issues had been kicking around for almost three years and still hadn't been resolved. The fans would undoubtedly stick with the Raptors at the SkyDome through another couple of seasons, but they'd grow impatient for a stadium more suited to basketball. It was a problem, heading into the second year of the Raptors, that the Bitoves would have to answer in a hurry.

John Bitove, Jr., was talking slower than a tobacco auctioneer, slower than Don Cherry on a rant, slower than Hamilton Berger summing up a case against Perry Mason's client. For Bitove, this came as close as he gets to normal conversational speed. It was the end of the basketball season, and he had begun to unwind. When he sat in his small retreat at the back of the Raptors offices, he *sat*, as in leaning his back against the sofa and stretching his legs in front of him. John Bitove was relaxed and content and, if not precisely slow-talking, then going at a speed that a stenographer trained in Pitman shorthand could handle.

"The truth is," Bitove said, "at the beginning of the season, I thought that by our third or fourth year, we'd have people going gaga over basketball. But this year? Not this year. I couldn't have imagined twenty-seven thousand people turning out to our last game against Philadelphia. One of the worst teams in the league, probably *the* worst, and the SkyDome was electric. I could never have imagined that. I could never have imagined that, at the end of our first season, we would have the numbers we have."

The numbers were on a sheet of paper in Bitove's waving hand. He ticked off the statistics, mostly from memory. Third in the league in attendance, with 23,179 per game. First in group sales. Fifth in season-ticket sales. Fifth in worldwide merchandise sales. And a point guard, Damon Stoudamire, who was named, in a landslide vote by reporters and broadcasters around the league, Rookie of the Year.

"Coming from an expansion year, a team's first year," Bitove went on, "one of the big things you do in getting ready for the second year, you ask, Can we play with the big boys, with the best teams in the league? Well, c'mon, we've *already* shown we can do that. We've beaten the big boys. We beat three of the four semi-finalists that are playing right now for the NBA championship. We beat Chicago, Seattle, and Orlando. So our players know that, if they continue to play hard, communicate with one another, respect each other, they can beat the best teams."

John Bitove smiled.

"Now, for next season, all we have to do is organize ourselves to beat everybody else."

EPILOGUE

The Chicago Bulls beat the NBA record for most wins in a season, the record they had been chasing all year. They won seventy-two games, and went on to take the league championship by beating the Seattle Super-Sonics in the final, four games to two. Michael Jordan swept the boards in personal accomplishments – the league MVP, the All-Star Game MVP, the playoffs MVP. But one other player improved his reputation in the final series. He was Shawn Kemp, the Seattle power forward who, early in the season during the SuperSonics game at the SkyDome, had seemed to be a one-dimensional slam-dunk artist and a rather vulgar performer. In the playoffs, he showed himself to be newly mature and a gifted all-round player.

A familiar face showed up in the crowd of coaches and advisors at the end of the Seattle bench throughout the finals. The face belonged to Brendan Malone. The SuperSonics had hired him as an advance playoff scout. Malone was also shortlisted for the newly vacant job as head coach of the Milwaukee Bucks. But in the end, when the contest came down to two men, Malone and Chris Ford, Ford got the nod. Malone later settled for a consolation prize when he was hired on as a New York Knicks assistant coach.

As for the Raptors, at the draft of college players on June 26, they picked Marcus Camby. He was six-foot-eleven, capable of playing all three front-court positions, full of promise, a youngster who had been chosen U.S. College Player of the Year in 1995-96.

"We got the guy we wanted," Isiah Thomas said.